NEXT GENERATION DEMOCRACY

For Steve & Kelly,
With thanks for
your friendship &
commitment.
Your Cous,

NEXT GENERATION DEMOCRACY

WHAT THE OPEN-SOURCE REVOLUTION MEANS FOR POWER, POLITICS, AND CHANGE

JARED DUVAL

BLOOMSBURY

NEW YORK · BERLIN · LONDON

Published by Bloomsbury USA, New York

All papers used by Bloomsbury USA are natural, recyclable products made
from wood grown in well-managed forests. The manufacturing processes
conform to the environmental regulations of the country of origin.

LIBRARY OF CONGRESS CATALOGING-IN-PUBLICATION DATA HAS BEEN APPLIED FOR.

ISBN 978-1-60819-066-9

First U.S. edition 2010

1 3 5 7 9 10 8 6 4 2

Typeset by Westchester Book Group
Printed in the United States of America by Worldcolor Fairfield

To Eloise McGlaflin Dutton,
a teacher who imparted a love of books and learning to her
children, grandchildren, and great-grandchildren

and Mary Daubenspeck
light keeper, writer, and friend

CONTENTS

FOREWORD

The use of technology to connect government with the governed is not a new idea. The printing press was the Internet of the seventeenth and eighteenth centuries; news and opinion were circulated by myriad homegrown newspapers eagerly read and discussed in coffeehouses and cafés. Benjamin Franklin pioneered the idea of a "publick printer" in Pennsylvania and other colonies before the American Revolution (though the U.S. Government Printing Office was not established as a federal function until 1860).

Governments quickly adopted radio and television as well. In the United Kingdom, the BBC was established in the 1920s to harness the new power of radio to advance the mission of the government. In the United States, government funding of radio and TV came later, with Voice of America established in 1944, PBS in 1970, and C-SPAN in 1979. Starting with the activism of Carl Malamud, which led to the Securities and Exchange Commission going online in 1993 (www.public.resource.org/sec.gov/index.html), the first federal government Web sites appeared only a few years after the introduction of the World Wide Web.

Open government is also not a new idea. The conviction that transparency is a check on the power of governments is a crucial element of modern democracies. When it was forbidden to provide transcriptions or reports of debates in the British Parliament, Samuel Johnson, among others, was hired by the *Gentleman's Magazine* to imaginatively re-create the debates as if they'd happened in some other, fictional kingdom. Freedom of the press is enshrined in the First Amendment to the U.S. Constitution. Napoléon reportedly said, "I fear the newspapers more than a hundred thousand bayonets."

Organizations like MySociety in the United Kingdom and the Sunlight Foundation in the United States, which apply the latest technology to provide greater government transparency, are the direct heirs to the newspapers of the eighteenth, nineteenth, and twentieth centuries, which played so important a role in shaping the expectations of modern democracy.

Next generation democracy means more than just reporting on the activities of those in power. Society today is much larger, more complex, more impenetrable than in former eras. The entire U.S. Constitution can be read and understood by a layman; today, a single bill may run to thousands of pages, full of loopholes and language that even trained lawyers might disagree over. What's more, the "information economy" is inseparable from the industrial economy of nations. Vast databases collect information about every aspect of society, but while the complexity of society and the amount of information necessary to make decisions have increased by orders of magnitude, most government decision-making still relies on processes designed decades, or even centuries, ago.

There is a greater and greater gap between the systems used to manage complexity in the private sector and the same systems in the public sector. An average citizen carrying an iPhone has access to real-time "situational awareness" that outstrips that of military systems costing millions of dollars. From Walmart to Wall Street, from Google to the next generation of personal robotics, intelligent algorithms process massive amounts of data in real time, and respond automatically in close to real time. Meanwhile, government regulators too often rely on paper-based processes and reports that trail events by months, if not years.

The enormous explosion of innovation in the private sector has resulted from a confluence of several factors. The personal computer started a process of commoditization for computer hardware that has continued unabated for nearly thirty years; every eighteen months, you can get twice the performance for the same or a lower cost. The open-source-software movement and the open protocols of the Internet have brought the same commoditization—and the same competitive acceleration—to software and even to information products.

One remarkable discovery made by open-source pioneers was that providing complete software source code (for free) to a community of volunteers not only sped up development but also improved quality. Even more important, it sped up innovation, as developers could easily build on the work of others. But it wasn't just access to source code: Systems like Linux, the Internet, and the World Wide Web have "architectures of participation." They are designed as loosely coupled systems that allow a wide range of independent actors to build a collaborative product.

Collaborative content creation is also possible, as demonstrated most convincingly by Wikipedia. A system of structured entries that anyone can edit (though with a management layer of active volunteers policing activity) turns out, however improbably, to work remarkably well. Other kinds of content aggregations, from Flickr and YouTube to Facebook and Twitter, don't allow collaborative editing of content, but they do rely heavily on user contribution to drive the most valuable content to the top and to find content that is relevant to individual users.

The next generation of applications, often referred to as "Web 2.0," are based on massive databases that harness the collective intelligence of all their users. This collective intelligence goes far beyond just "crowdsourcing" or "the wisdom of crowds." It relies on algorithms that detect patterns and hidden meanings in everyday user activity. Google's PageRank, which improves search results by using citation analysis of links to find the most authoritative pages, was the marquee demonstration of the strength of this concept, but today it powers everything from search engine advertising to online games. Systems respond to their users; they have become adaptive.

The result has been the emergence of a new worldwide computing platform: connected, data-rich, and increasingly intelligent. Cloud-computing back ends drive data applications delivered on mobile devices.

Now government is getting into the act.

The Obama administration's Open Government Initiative is about far more than transparency. It is about making government a first-class player in the emerging Internet data-operating system. When government data is made available as a set of Web services rather than a set of documents, computer applications can process that data, draw meaning from it, and make it relevant to the daily lives of citizens. You can see Data.gov as the "software-development kit" for government as a platform.

The same process is happening at state and local levels.

And now, the applications are starting to arrive. In this time of budget deficits, there is a unique teachable moment unfolding with the success of the iPhone app store. Apple produced a phone with unique new features. But it wasn't just those new features that electrified and transformed the mobile-phone market; it was that Apple offered an open platform for developers. Now there are hundreds of thousands of specialized applications for the iPhone and tens of thousands more for other smartphones that have followed Apple's lead.

The idea of building a platform, rather than building all of the end user applications yourself, turns out to be surprisingly relevant for government, allowing the private sector to build applications that the government might never have imagined, or been able to budget for if it had. As governments open their data and services to developers, we're seeing an explosion of innovation, and the development of new citizen services by the citizens themselves.

Some of the early applications might almost seem trivial if they weren't so useful. SeeClickFix, for example, allows citizens to report potholes, graffiti, burned-out streetlights, and other similar problems to their city officials. When citizens carrying mobile phones can act as data collectors, a city will eventually be able to devote resources that once were occupied by inspection to responding more quickly to problems.

Thankfully, the lessons of the Internet—open standards, open-source software, and data-driven applications—are all being followed, albeit with greater or lesser focus in one project or another. (That's true in the private sector as well.) Open APIs are being developed that will allow applications to work across the country (and eventually, internationally), rather than being bound to the systems of any one city. Projects like Code for America are working to build mechanisms for sharing code, expertise, and best practices between cities. We're seeing new alliances between governments at the federal, state, and local levels to increase citizen services, eliminate redundancy, and reduce costs.

Next Generation Democracy is perfectly timed to tell these stories of success and failure, of thinking differently, of connecting communities to strengthen bonds, of sharing and coming together to solve problems, and of working on stuff that matters. It connects the dots from humanitarian relief in disaster situations such as Katrina to the open-source movement (which continues to evolve in exciting ways), to changing the way government works by engaging citizens via simple apps and Web 2.0 tools, and, most importantly, to the challenges of our connected lives. These are all big problems, but by working together we can build a better world and government.

There's a clear vision from the top, not only in the United States and the United Kingdom but in many other countries, that now is the time for government to reinvent itself, to take the old idea of government "for the people, by the people, and of the people" to a new level.

—*Tim O'Reilly, CEO and founder of O'Reilly Media*

INTRODUCTION

To look always for an answer, a solution to the ever-puzzling riddles that confront us: that is our responsibility, our curse, and our blessing.

—STUART M. HESS

Don't ask yourself what the world needs; ask yourself what makes you come alive. And then go and do that. Because what the world needs is people who have come alive.

—HOWARD THURMAN

IT STARTED with a book that I found in the late winter of 1999, when I was sixteen years old. My mom was wise in her placement, leaving it seemingly at random atop a pile of things on the stairs leading up to my room. It didn't look like any of the other books I had seen her bring home from the small publishing company where she worked. Instead of a hardcover with a high-resolution, glossy jacket design, this had a thin, pale blue paper cover and a spine that looked as though it were held together with some faded electrical tape.

On the front, in rough ink, was a Greek column with a guitar leaning against it, with the mysterious title *Believing Cassandra* written above. As I turned the book over, I found a stamp declaring that this was an "uncorrected proof," the format in which a book goes out for review before it's been published. Intrigued, perhaps, by the guitar on the cover, I walked across my room, sat down on my bed, and opened it up. It began with a Greek myth.

Cassandra, as the story went, was the last daughter of the King of Troy and happened to catch the eye of the god Apollo. When she did not return his interest in her, Apollo devised a scheme to win her over. He offered her the gift of prophecy in return for her love, which she readily accepted. Not long after, though, she realized too late that love is not a thing to be sold—not even in exchange for something as grand as the gift of prophecy.

When Cassandra decided to leave Apollo, he begged her for one last kiss. As she gave him this, he breathed into her mouth and cursed her: Although she would still be able to tell the future, no one would ever believe the words that came out of her mouth. A string of tragic events followed her to the end of her life. She was captured when the Greeks invaded Troy, just after she had warned the Trojans, in vain, not to let a huge horse figure inside the city gates.

From there, the book took off. Alan AtKisson, the author, went on to characterize our modern-day scientists—who have warned us about everything from the collapse of the world's fisheries, topsoil, and water tables to the destabilization of the world's climate—as modern-day Cassandras: Their words are true but are tragically ignored by a majority in our society, especially political leaders, as we rush heedlessly onward.

Fascinated, I read on, unable to put the book down until I finished it. After turning the final page, I looked at my clock. It was three in the morning, and I had been reading for about ten hours straight. Nevertheless, I couldn't go to sleep. Instead, I wrote up a plan to start a group at my high school, which I originally wanted to name Students Believing Cassandra but which, as it formed, friends wisely suggested we call Students for a Sustainable Future.

And so it was that at the age of sixteen I became a student organizer. At the time, there was a proposal in front of the city council for a huge (larger than an NFL football field) construction project on wetlands between our combined elementary-high school and an elder-care facility. This was in Lebanon, New Hampshire, a city with a population of thirteen thousand residents that was the commercial hub of the Upper Connecticut River Valley, quadrupling in size during the day, when nearly forty thousand commuters showed up for work.

The problem was that growth in our city was both relentless and seemingly random. The construction on the wetlands was not going to be along the existing shopping corridor, but rather would set a precedent for sprawling development in a residential neighborhood where kids walked to school and elderly people spent their final years enjoying the scenery out the window. Even leaving aside the shortsightedness of plowing over wetlands (which, in addition to supporting the most diverse ecosystems around, happen to be irreplaceable when it comes to water filtration and flood control), eighteen-wheeler delivery trucks were not something either of those groups should be encountering on a day-to-day basis. We weren't going to sit for it.

So we transformed our once-sleepy city hall meetings into large public events attended by groups of students, as many as fifty per meeting. We testified alongside our allies in the community, including the local dentist (whose office was adjacent to the property) and old women from the elder-care facility, who would tear up at the thought of looking out their window to see and hear not the birds in the trees that they had become accustomed to but rather a concrete loading dock.

It was an epic campaign. There was TV coverage and dueling

letters to the editor. The developer of the project even summoned me, along with the faculty adviser for our group, to a meeting with him and our school's principal. Afterward, the developer, an imposing man with Just for Men hair and an outfit from the pages of *Esquire*, cornered me in the hallway and inquired about my first choice among the colleges I was then applying to.

I told him, and he said in a hushed, serious tone, "Oh, I happen to know the head of the admissions committee there." He went on to imply, not subtly, that this hubbub at city hall was probably all just one big misunderstanding and that if I would only realize the error of my organizing ways, he would be willing to put in a generous call on my behalf. I didn't, he didn't, and I didn't get in to that school (not because of him, I'm sure, but rather because my grades started slipping once I began spending more time preparing for meetings in city hall than doing my physics homework).

In the end, after a year and a half of city meetings, we won a nail-biting victory when the Planning Board voted 4-3 to deny the permit to build; it was the only major construction project the board vetoed that entire year. The developer would later appeal the decision all the way to the state supreme court, but there it was upheld.

After the excitement of our victory, I felt more empowered than I ever had before. Who knew that a group of students could help preserve a part of their city and reshape local politics? I went off to college, Wheaton, in Massachusetts, with the organizing bug.

A People-Powered Run for the Presidency

Throughout the winter of 2002 and 2003, I followed the fledgling presidential primary campaign of Vermont's former governor Howard Dean with increasing interest. Though he was garnering only 1 percent support in polls of Democratic voters, he was my home-state governor, and I was well aware of his accomplishments (near-universal health coverage for children and pregnant women, and becoming the first governor to sign civil unions into law, to name but two).

I was also drawn to the fact that Dean challenged the traditional liberal and conservative stereotypes that bogg down our politics. Here was a Democratic governor from a rural state who managed to pass balanced budgets every year he was in office and consistently earned the endorsement of the National Rifle Association. Howard Dean, in other words, was certainly not your run-of-the-mill liberal. I decided I would devote my summer to his bid, no matter how improbable.

After classes ended for the spring semester of 2003, I loaded up my 1986 clunker of a car with some clothes, my laptop, a sleeping bag, and an air mattress and set off for Burlington, Vermont. I was prepared to spend the next three months volunteering at the headquarters of Dean's presidential campaign, even if that meant doing little but licking envelopes and making copies day after day. I had no idea what I was getting into.

Soon after arriving at the campaign headquarters, I happened to introduce myself to some members of the finance team. As I mentioned that I was from Vermont, one of them quickly interrupted and, with wonder and relief, said, "You're from Vermont?!" It seemed that most of the arriving volunteers were coming from out of state and were still trying to orient themselves in this strange new place. "Do you happen to know where Banknorth is?" he asked. I said that I did and was promptly handed a pile of folders oozing checks and receipts, with instructions to go and deposit the checks.

Now, in case this does not sound alarmingly odd to you, let

me offer a quick recap: Random, unknown college kid shows up at presidential-campaign headquarters and, within minutes of starting his first day (with no background check, I might add), is entrusted with depositing the hundreds of thousands of dollars keeping the whole thing afloat. Clearly this was not your typical presidential campaign.

Instead, Howard, as we all called the governor, was a long shot running an insurgent campaign against the Democratic Party establishment, and was developing a campaign model to match. With most of the party operatives and professionals on other campaigns, this had the wonderful effect of putting me and assorted other young upstarts in positions of some responsibility as the campaign took off over the next few months.

Michael Silberman, for instance, was a recently graduated Middlebury College alumnus who was managing the campaign's efforts on Meetup, a Web site that had only recently started up when the Dean campaign was getting off the ground. Meetup enables groups of people to identify pretty much any common interest and then helps individuals find each other locally. Today it has over six million members and hosts about two thousand meet-ups daily. The fastest-growing groups on the day I write this include Interracial Couples & Families, Frugal Living, Women over 40, and Skydiving. In that sense, the site serves as a kind of mirror to some of the demographic, economic, and cultural trends happening in our country. Back in the summer of 2003, the Dean campaign was fast becoming the phenomenon of Meetup, soon boasting the most groups on the site. By the end of the campaign, Michael had helped Dean meetups happen in twelve hundred cities worldwide, which accounted for much of the campaign's fundraising and volunteer recruitment.

In this open and collaborative atmosphere, it soon became

clear that, with a little initiative, I could probably do whatever work I wanted and avoid having to lick envelopes. Confident from a congressional internship the year before, I wandered over to the policy team and asked if they could use some help drafting policy briefs on energy and environmental issues. They could, and I proceeded to spend the rest of the summer in their office drafting press releases and speeches and filling out candidate questionnaires as the youngest member of their team.

My desk was about ten feet away from the door of the legendary Joe Trippi, the brilliant campaign manager, who would intermittently emerge from his office, eyes red and hair scraggly, looking for a refueling of Diet Coke. It was rumored that he often slept in there, and indeed it looked like it was set up for the purpose, with a big couch along one wall. He also had a book titled, I believe, *What It Takes: The Way to the White House*, perched high on a shelf and secured behind a barrier of crossed pieces of masking tape, presumably only to be taken down once he had reached his ultimate goal.

Once, as the campaign was taking off (thanks in large part to the Web strategy that Trippi had invested so much time and hope in), he suddenly burst out of his office to exclaim to everyone within earshot the pithiest summation of our Web-based campaign strategy: "We're standing on top of this fifteen-story building. Now, what we have to do is jump . . . and just hope that the American people are there to catch us!" There was stunned silence at first, followed shortly thereafter by a loud round of applause and cheering.

It was in these surroundings that I spent most of the summer, both because of the amount of work and because the three-bedroom apartment that nine of us shared was so littered with air mattresses and ramen-noodle wrappers that it became like an obstacle course.

We affectionately dubbed it "the flophouse," as we pretty much only went back there to do just that: flop down and sleep.

It seemed as if everyone I met that summer had a story about being inspired by the campaign and abruptly leaving home or work—an acting gig, a high-powered law firm in New York, etc.—to endure such conditions, receiving little or no pay in a quest to help the former governor of the second-smallest state in the country achieve the highest office in the land.

What was it that attracted all of us so? The campaign's most important contribution—indeed, the reason most of us came to Burlington—was perhaps as much the revolutionary approach Dean helped bring to campaigning as it was the candidate himself. By using the Internet to pool vast numbers of small contributions, monetary and otherwise, a small-state governor with no national name recognition was able to take on the centralized power of Democratic party politics, becoming the front-runner and favorite for the nomination for nearly six months (that is, until the Iowa caucuses).

What the Dean campaign challenged most of all was the top-down, centralized way campaigns had always been run. The DeanforAmerica blog and Meetups, for example, served as open platforms that allowed volunteers to share ideas and self-organize events, innovations that would live on and be adopted by nearly every campaign during the 2008 election cycle.

With the success of Barack Obama's fundraising and information-sharing campaigns, it is easy to underappreciate now how big of a shift our politics has gone through in just six short years. Back in 2002, for instance, I volunteered to organize a student voter-registration effort for a Senate campaign in New Hampshire. I drafted a flyer encouraging students who were home for the summer, but who would soon return to school out of state, to sign up for their absentee ballot at city hall before heading back to college. Before I could mail this flyer, I had to fax it down to the campaign headquarters in Manchester. When it finally came back, approved and with no real changes, two weeks later, most of the students in question were already headed out of town, and we had missed our chance.

With the "flatter," more empowered Dean campaign model, such centralized-coordination problems largely became a relic of the past as we empowered the network. Dean's e-mail list of supporters was even asked to vote on campaign-strategy decisions, like whether or not we should opt out of public financing for the rest of the campaign and rely on our network of small donors to pull us through (we did).

I was intrigued by the possibilities this new approach held for our politics, with the potential for people to become active participants at all levels of our democracy, rather than being confined to the role of "passive observer of thirty-second television ads every two years." Raised in both Vermont, the New England state where the tradition of town meetings and direct, real democracy is perhaps strongest of all, and New Hampshire, which holds the nation's first presidential primary of the season, I was fascinated to see the best of these two states' political traditions starting to come together.

From the Valley to Dar es Salaam, Tanzania

With the organizing structure of the Dean campaign still on my mind, the following summer I departed for Dar es Salaam, Tanzania. I had managed to get an internship through the Foundation for

Sustainable Development, which had set me up teaching at a high school for ten weeks and staying with a host family nearby. Wheaton had provided the money I needed for the round-trip plane ticket, and I was on my way.[1]

My host parents, Baba and Mama Mhina, truly treated me like a son, while the rest of my wonderful host family treated me like a brother. They were all incredibly patient with my struggle to grasp the names of things; the students on the basketball team I coached would come to call me Mr. Polepole, which means "Mr. Slow" (though that may have also had something to do with how I played basketball under the oppressive east African sun). We lived in the Mwenge neighborhood, not far from St. Mary's International High School, where I was assigned to teach.

I taught economics, one of my undergraduate majors-in-progress. My classes, Pre-form 5 and 6, were mostly made up of students my age or older, and in the days and weeks that followed, we quickly became friends, especially after classes on the basketball court. But as I listened to the informal banter before and after our practices, it soon became clear to me that the topic of greatest interest for my students was not their economics classes. It seemed that every student either knew someone infected with HIV or had known someone who had died of AIDS.

How could they not? Almost 5 percent of the country was HIV-positive, and in some urban neighborhoods, the figure was closer to 20 percent. After a couple weeks of hearing misinformation about the virus shared in shy, muttered breaths—the rigid religious atmosphere did not help—I realized that the school's taboo on this subject was part of the problem.

With the Meetup model from the Dean campaign fresh in my

memory, I and some fellow teachers, most notably the basketball coach and my fellow economics teacher, Mr. Michael (known by his first name, as we all were when not being teased for slowness), started Straight Talk St. Mary's. The group began meeting after school, simply to provide a safe and comfortable space in which to share stories and explore rumors about the virus (e.g., "no, having sex with a virgin is *not* a cure"). After our first few conversations, we started exploring what students thought could be done to improve the situation, letting them lead the group in the empowered, open tradition of the Dean effort.

The students decided to organize an HIV/AIDS education day that would forgo the usual lectures in favor of freestyle rap, spoken word, and other performance pieces. If HIV/AIDS wasn't something to hide behind closed doors, then why not make awareness of and education about it fun? We planned the event over the course of about five weeks, tracking down sound systems and tents all over the city. When the day finally came, over five hundred students packed the stands around our basketball court. Nearly the entire student body was there, on a *weekend*.

A Swahili phrase later emerged among the students to express the empowerment we all felt during and after the event. "Gumu kachizi kama ugali" became our unofficial motto. Translated, it means "crazy strong like *ugali*" (you can think of *ugali* as akin to really thick grits).

Though my time at the school would soon come to an end, the St. Mary's students were just getting started. From educational materials produced by international public health nonprofits, they learned that one of the most important ways to stop the spread of HIV is simply to know whether or not you are infected. Reading this, the group had a conversation about why students were failing to find out.

It immediately became clear that what was stopping them was not so much a fear of what the results might reveal as a fear of going to a distant, unfamiliar testing center by themselves. Once they voiced this, the Straight Talk students began organizing trips to go to the testing center in groups, after school. They rode in *daladalas*, very large minibuses that get packed so full there are always people leaning out windows or sitting on your lap. *Daladalas*, interestingly, also seem to all have revealing names on the signs across their tops, from the honest (Mambo Slow Slow) to the redemptive (One More Chance; Jesus Power) to the frankly disconcerting (Hearse).

Despite their transportation challenges, I later learned that in the year after Straight Talk St. Mary's was formed, 370 students went and got tested for HIV, something only a handful had done previously. And those for whom education and testing were not enough—those who wanted to *do* something for people already affected—began visiting orphanages for children whose parents had died of AIDS, playing with the kids and bringing them toys and needed supplies. All this flowed from the first simple act of creating a space for open dialogue, in a way that demystified a politically and culturally charged health issue, and then letting the students lead themselves.

As my summer there wound down, I thought we'd figured out a pretty good way of combating HIV. Indeed, other schools in the country would later adopt the "straight talk" model. But here's the thing: Throughout that summer of organizing around HIV and AIDS (and teaching some economics), there was disturbing news in the country's papers. As I prepared to leave Dar, I read reports about drought and climate change that brought back to mind the scientific warnings I had first read in *Believing Cassandra*.

An Ujamaa Carving

Mount Kilimanjaro is not just any mountain. Its majestic snow-capped dome has long been the pride of Tanzania. As Africa's tallest peak and the tallest freestanding mountain in the world (Everest is part of a larger range and so "begins" at a higher elevation), it is climbed by tens of thousands each year. That summer, soon before I was to leave, I read that "Kili" was given ten years before it would lose all of its snow due to climate destabilization.[2]

How could this be? Situated in the southern hemisphere, Tanzania has a warm "winter" from March to June, which overlapped with the time I was there. Coming from Vermont, a state whose winter temperatures can hit thirty below zero, I knew that Tanzania's winter would be quite a bit warmer than I was used to. But I wasn't expecting the hottest weather I'd ever experienced.

As it turned out, Tanzania was in the midst of a prolonged major drought that had begun a year earlier. The lack of water, a by-product of warmer temperatures due to fossil-fuel-induced climate destabilization, was forcing the country to abandon its hydro-power stations in favor of constructing . . . new fossil-fuel-based generation.[3] Talk about tragic irony.

In 2003, Tanzania's Ministry of Agriculture and Food Security had identified fifty-two districts in the country with acute food shortages due to decreased rainfall. The result was that by February of the next year, the government's own statistics had identified over *four million* people—one tenth of the country's citizens—in need of food aid, including over a million in the three most drought-affected regions alone.[4]

So, right about now you might be wondering what all this has to do with HIV and AIDS? Quite simply, we realized that when people outside of our school didn't have enough food to eat, buying condoms wasn't going to be their top priority. Even if the government were to design the best HIV-education-and-awareness programs possible, success would still be dependent on reducing hunger and poverty in the country, a prospect in turn imperiled by climate destabilization. We realized that any attempt to address the challenges of HIV, poverty, or hunger in isolation was likely to miss underlying factors driving the overall situation, such as climate destabilization.

I and some others in the Straight Talk group soon began to see the issues of HIV and climate destabilization as though they were part of a kind of carving known as Ujamaa. Showing dozens of people connected to one another in a tall, elaborate family tree, these carvings are formed from a single unbroken piece of wood.

With these images in our minds and reflecting on what was happening with Kili and the HIV/AIDS challenge, it became vividly clear to us that the great global problems of the twenty-first century are all inextricably connected. After all, how is a country going to be able to devote the necessary resources to combating HIV if twice as many people might not even have food to eat?

I was overwhelmed by the enormity of this realization. Not one of the issues I cared about, from poverty to AIDS, could be addressed as a distinct challenge—certainly not in any lasting way—unless the response also got to the root of the other, exacerbating challenges.

Climate of Negligence

On my next-to-last day in Tanzania, I was walking home from school and stopped at a dusty tent—four sticks with a sheet over them—where a friendly guy I'd passed a few times before was polishing shoes. I sat down and took my shoes off, more so I had an excuse to stop and talk than because I thought I should get my shoes touched up (they were pretty much beyond repair at that point). Anticipating my return home, I asked him, "What message would you want Americans to hear, and what would you want me to say about Tanzania when I go back?"

Without missing a beat, the guy, who had already started shining my shoes, said, "Americans don't understand how much of an impact you have on the world. The things we want in Tanzania depend on your leadership. Like if you don't sign Kyoto, the rest of the world won't act on global warming."

By the time I returned for my senior year of college, I had become convinced, by my HIV/AIDS organizing experience as well as by my conversation with the shoe shiner, that climate destabilization was not an "environmental issue" but rather one of the root-level global challenges blocking long-term progress on almost every social issue I cared about. So figuring out the answer to the shoe shiner's implicit question—how do we get the United States to lead on climate—became the focus of my senior thesis.

Indeed, why wasn't the United States, the country responsible for a quarter of the world's climate pollution, doing much of anything meaningful to combat it? I had learned from my experience on the Dean campaign that politicians were increasingly using their Web sites to communicate their priorities to constituents. So in my thesis, "Climate of Negligence: Climate Destabilization and the US Political Agenda," I reported that of the thirty-one U.S. senators on committees directly responsible for dealing with climate destabilization, only *four* even mentioned global warming (or related terms like greenhouse gases or climate change) in the issue sections of their Web sites.

Take Nevada's Harry Reid, the Democratic leader in the Senate. The front page of his Web site's environment-issues section at one point had a big headline declaring that he was committed to fighting "the scourge of Mormon crickets," which is, apparently, a threat to agriculture out west. I suppose Nevadans are lucky that they have a senator so concerned with local infestation issues. But I have to ask: If the Senate leader of one of the two major political parties in our country is so focused on bugs, then who is going to focus on—and do something about—the much larger problem of our deteriorating atmosphere?

After nearly a year spent researching the science and the politics of the issue, my conclusion read in part,

> If we are to heed the predictions of the best climate science currently available, we must act quickly to prevent the worst impacts of climate destabilization from occurring . . . A serious response requires near immediate and total transformation of our energy infrastructure.[5]

As for what to do about the political problem, I mused,

> While this thesis focuses much attention on the potential role of individual political leaders, the truth is that leaders of social movements (usually inspired religiously and sparked by youth)

have almost always been the ones to initiate mass social change throughout history, with politicians in power at the time just lucky enough to take credit for victory after acquiescing to the movement's demands.[6]

Soon after, in 2005, I received one of the greatest opportunities a graduating student can dream of when I was offered the position of national director of the Sierra Student Coalition (SSC). Launched in 1991, the SSC came into being nearly one hundred years after its parent organization, the Sierra Club, was founded by John Muir. As the national student chapter of the Sierra Club, the SSC organizes with student and youth groups on over three hundred high school and college campuses that have decided to affiliate with America's oldest and largest grassroots environmental-advocacy organization. Ready to put my thesis to the test, I eagerly accepted the offer and headed for Washington, D.C.

A New Movement

For two and a half years, my driving goal was to help build a movement to create the political will for the transition to a clean-energy economy. As I began, with no professional organizing experience, I fell back on examples from the past for guidance. During 2005's Group of Eight (G8) meeting, attended by representatives of the world's largest national economies, I and a group of about twenty others fasted for three days in front of the White House, calling for solutions to the interconnected challenges of climate destabilization and world hunger.

That same summer and the following fall, I joined members

of youth environmental organizations across the United States and Canada in starting a campaign called the Campus Climate Challenge. We knew that none of our organizations, in isolation, had the ability to spark a nationwide campus movement, but we thought that if we shared the successes of individual campuses that were becoming models of sustainability, the effort could spread.

In less than two years, we managed to collectively raise millions of dollars for our collaborative campaign, which has come to be run on over seven hundred U.S. and Canadian campuses. Many student groups worked successfully with their administration, convincing their school's president to sign the U.S. Presidents Climate Commitment, a pledge to reduce, over time, participating schools' climate pollution down to zero.

Beginning to think beyond our campuses, some of us studied the civil rights movement and became inspired by the Freedom Summer campaign that students a couple of generations before us had led, all descending on one state to try to change the course of a nation. While our predecessors had to risk life and limb for their beliefs—a choice we were lucky enough never to have to make—we believed in our cause with a similar conviction. During the summer of 2007, students from across the country engaged citizens in two politically influential states—Iowa and New Hampshire—in an attempt to bring "a clean energy economy for real global warming solutions" to the top of the national political agenda.

That summer saw over thirty students working full-time across both states, where they engaged over ten thousand citizens. The effort culminated in five-day marches of hundreds of people to each state's capital, where luminaries such as author Bill McKibben and NASA scientist Dr. James Hansen addressed the assembled crowds.

At the end of the summer, and after two and a half years of

leading the SSC and co-chairing the Energy Action Coalition, I was beat. The truth was, the longed-for tipping point in our national conscience concerning the imperative for clean energy was still far away. Indeed, the effort we had just poured ourselves into for over a year had ended up getting some great statewide media coverage but had otherwise pretty much been ignored nationally.

Intensely worried about the increasingly dire predictions of scientists, I racked my brain trying to come up with tactics to "spark the movement." I had trouble sleeping and became increasingly anxious and frustrated. "The scientists say we have three years to begin reversing course!" was the constant echo in my head, which refused to tune out Cassandra's message.

Then I remembered the lesson I had learned in Tanzania: There are often larger, systemic forces blocking progress on narrower issues. I started to wonder whether the social-change models taught in history classes were even that effective anymore, whether our decision-making and problem-solving institutions were even up to the tasks now before us.

I concluded that sometimes it doesn't help to just keep banging your head against a wall. Instead, sometimes it makes more sense to stop, step back, and then, just maybe, with time and space, figure out a better way to take down the wall. Architects, not surprisingly, seem to grasp this better than most. Buckminster Fuller, designer of the geodesic dome, once famously wrote, "You never change things by fighting the existing reality. To change something, build a new model that makes the existing model obsolete."

It is possible that this wisdom has never been needed more than with regard to the climate challenge. Indeed, the gap between what climate scientists say we need and what politicians say we can do seems impossibly large. Take, for instance, this simple statistic.

Leading climate scientists report that in order to stabilize our climate at a safe level, we need to have a CO_2 concentration of no more than 350 parts per million (ppm) in our atmosphere. Not only have we already passed this figure—we're now at about 390—but most political organizations, in the United States and internationally, can't even work up the will to set 450 ppm as a long-term target.

Surveying this situation, I couldn't help thinking that there is something terribly and tragically wrong and ineffectual about the approach we organizers and political folk have been taking with regard to the climate crisis. If we can't come up with solutions that allow us to have a habitable planet, then what is the point of politics?

Our great global challenges combine to create an interconnected web in which it becomes impossible to solve any of them to a meaningful degree or for any meaningful length of time without a more systemic approach that addresses their underlying factors simultaneously—what the great writer Wendell Berry has called "solving for pattern." I believe that figuring out how to "solve for pattern" for challenges like HIV/AIDS, climate destabilization, and poverty is the great calling of our time, most of all because the consequences in years and lives of however we respond will be measured not in generations and millions, as with past generational challenges, but rather in *millennia and billions.*

Yet it is as if our political system is designed to fail, dividing as it does complex challenges into narrow and discrete policy issues, the "solutions" to which always seem to be focused on symptoms rather than getting to the interconnected roots of the problems. Rather than collaborative innovation, we get small political "victories," driven by factions and interest groups. Even minor policy progress assumes an attention span that no longer exists in our politics, with the rise of hyper-money-driven, special-interest-hounded "permanent campaigning" allowing less and less time for actual governing and rewarding more and more money for smaller and smaller wins.

What opportunities for truly transformational human progress are being missed because our existing decision-making processes rarely allow for comprehensive problem solving—say, combating HIV/AIDS and the climate crisis in coordination? Perhaps more important, what contributions of wisdom and will are we losing out on because these money-driven processes so often shut out the meaningful voices and participation of citizens increasingly capable of and interested in playing a part?

I have come to believe that the way so many of us are organizing and organized around "issues" and "interests," the very way we conduct our politics right now, is simply not up to the tasks that will define our generation (and by generation, I mean all of us blessed enough to be alive at this moment in our planet's history). Of all the billions of people on the planet, how many are truly able to contribute to the extent of their ability and desire?

As I thought about this and looked around at the youth organizing I was part of and other youth efforts I was aware of, I began to notice something interesting. All of the hopeful, innovative things emerging from our work seemed to have something in common with the Internet: the so-called Web 2.0 approach of transparency, open participation, and diverse collaboration.

Fortuitously, that same summer I also happened across both James Surowiecki's *The Wisdom of Crowds* and Ori Brafman and Rod A. Beckstrom's *The Starfish and the Spider*. Their profiles of decentralized problem solving and open, collaborative leadership resonated instantly. From my travels around the country and the world, speaking, recruiting, and organizing students on climate and clean-energy issues, I had already come to realize that young people see the climate crisis not as some sub-issue of environmental interest groups, but rather as a broad societal challenge that demands far greater collaboration and participation, such as is increasingly happening online.

Thus at the end of the summer of 2007, I was left with the following questions: Can online innovations that come from Web 2.0 technology, things like open-source software and wikis (which I will explore in chapter 2), be effectively taken beyond the Internet to improve age-old approaches to social-change organizing and governance (chapters 4, 5, and 6)? Further, what can we learn and expect from the rising generation of so-called digital natives, or Millennials? How are we different, if at all, from previous generations, and what skills, ethics, and approaches will inform our work as we rise to positions of influence in our society (chapter 3)? Lastly, does the fact that the great global challenges of our day—climate, poverty, and genocide, to name but three—are all dynamic, complex, and interconnected necessitate new models of problem solving and leadership in our society (chapters 4, 5, and 6)?

I am not going to use the following pages to suggest that there is some magical technological fix, some digital panacea that will eliminate our most pressing global challenges. Nor will I claim that the Millennial generation is going to overcome the failures of our political system simply because it happens to know how to text message and tweet.

Rather, I will show that there is *far* greater potential than we have yet realized for applying lessons from the world of Web 2.0 to the global challenges that now demand solving. Further, I will argue that the rising Millennial generation is unique in numerous and important ways that make us well poised to lead many of these efforts.

Likewise, I won't try to convince you that my experiences as a student organizer—in small-town New Hampshire, on the Dean campaign, or in Tanzania—hold all or even a majority of the answers we are looking for. While each of these experiences has served as an invaluable seed of curiosity, learning, and hope for me, I have written this book seeking answers far beyond my own short past.

Beyond this introduction, then, the stories I share are less mine than they are of people whose innovation and leadership go well beyond my own limited experience to give us glimpses of what "next generation democracy" could look and feel like.

ONE

KATRINA REVISITED

Upon this gifted age, in its dark hour,
Falls from the sky a meteoric shower
Of facts . . . they lie unquestioned, uncombined.

Wisdom enough to leech us of our ill
Is daily spun; but there exists no loom
To weave it into fabric

—EDNA ST. VINCENT MILLAY

It really all boils down to this.
That all life is interrelated.
We are caught in an inescapable network of mutuality,
tied to a single garment of destiny.
Whatever affects one directly affects all.

—REV. DR. MARTIN LUTHER KING JR.

DR. VERA TRIPLETT is a quintessential New Orleanian. A lifelong resident, she is part of the third generation of her family to call the historic city home. An African American woman now in her late thirties, she looks as though she might be a decade younger and speaks with an energy and purpose difficult to keep up with.

Vera grew up in the working-class Seventh Ward during the 1970s and describes her mother, Dianne, as a "taker-inner," someone who would always care for family and friends in times of need. Within the city health department, Dianne worked at child-care and well-baby clinics, where kids would get immunized if their parents couldn't afford a doctor. In her spare time, Dianne also served as the secretary of the church where her then husband and Vera's father was minister. Service and activism were a part of Vera's life from the very beginning.

The center of activity in those days was the neighborhood. Vera remembers how in the summertime one family would buy an aboveground pool that everyone else in the neighborhood would use, and how all the kids played stickball together, with their parents taking turns watching them. More than anything, that sense of neighborliness is what Vera recalls from her childhood. She can sound like a nostalgic grandmother remembering how everyone, just by default, walked to school and how all the parents of her friends were involved in the school.

Several decades later, when Hurricane Katrina roared ashore in 2005, it dispersed the city's families and communities, threatening to replace a culture of neighborliness with one of loneliness. Throughout New Orleans, what Vera calls the "neighborly infused culture" was, she says, both the thing most at risk from the ensuing floodwaters and, ultimately, the factor that most helped the city to persevere.

In the days after the storm hit, the most important thing was knowing if loved ones were OK. For Vera, that meant finding her godson, Elie, the baby she had christened and the child who had lived with her from the age of six to fifteen, while his mother, Vera's cousin, was getting her life back on track. He was living with his birth mother again, and Vera knew that they did not have a vehicle or many resources at their disposal. Unable to reach him when almost all phones with New Orleans's 504 area code were out of service, she had no way of trying to find out if Elie was safe other than using some hastily set-up online missing-persons boards.

Using the sites daily, Vera was able to find a universal phone number set up by the Red Cross, which she used to reach Elie. When she reached him from Houston about six days after the storm, her first words were "Oh my God, thank God you are OK!" Elie replied in disbelief, "How did you find me?" Overjoyed by the chance to hear her voice, Elie went on to tell his godmother the story of what happened to him, from taking a small boat to the Superdome to eventually finding a bus headed out of the city to rural Mississippi. Exactly how Vera was able to contact Elie is a story in itself, with roots in another tragic event four years earlier.

Finding the Missing

What Michael Tippett remembers most from the days that followed the attacks of September 11, 2001, are the missing-persons posters taped up across New York City, in any public area people could find.[1] Knowing no other way to track down their loved ones, friends and relatives covered the city with thousands of these sheets of paper, the pictures cut, cropped, or scanned from wedding albums and graduation celebrations.

Tippett had moved to New York a few years earlier to work for an early social-networking Web site called theglobe.com, which helped pioneer blogging, or what was referred to then as simply "personal publishing." Tippett spent five years with the company and likens the experience to getting a Ph.D. in "user-generated content," a technical way of describing the stuff *you* create on a Web site that is not your own—the heart of what has come to be known as Web 2.0. This trend of online creation forms the common link between blogs, wikis such as Wikipedia, and open-source projects such as the Linux operating system or the Mozilla Firefox Web browser.

Two years after 9/11, Tippett decided to leave New York and head home to Vancouver. He continued tinkering with blogs, all the while also posting pictures to a new Web photo-sharing start-up also based in Vancouver, called Flickr. Over the next few years, Flickr would become so widely used, along with YouTube, MySpace, and similar sites, that *Time* magazine would decide to name "YOU" its Person of the Year in 2006. In prophetic words, the accompanying article explained the choice:

> It's a story about community and collaboration on a scale never seen before . . . It's about the many wresting power from the few and helping one another for nothing and how that will not only change the world, but also *change the way the world changes*.[2]

In 2003, though, that insight was still a long way from popular acceptance. Nevertheless, Tippett decided he wanted to contribute to the then still-emerging world of Web 2.0 with his own start-up company, a site he called NowPublic. Allowing the general public to post news reports for anyone to read, the site is, in Tippett's words, "like a newspaper except all the news comes from the readers."[3] As of February 2010, NowPublic claimed to be the largest "participatory media"[4] site on the Web, with over 190,000 contributors and seven million to ten million page views a month.

Some of the early users of the site included a few "citizen meteorologists" who had previously worked for oil companies. In late

August of 2005, they began posting warning after warning to the NowPublic forums, predicting that a tropical storm named Katrina was about to turn into a "monster Hurricane." As the storm's track bore down on New Orleans, Tippett decided to take these warnings to heart.

Thinking back to the days following September 11, he realized the potential need for a search-and-rescue effort and wondered if NowPublic might be able to provide the tools to help. An open forum that included photo sharing, he figured, might at the very least help prevent a repeat of the scattershot missing-persons-poster scene in New York. And so, before the storm hit, NowPublic got ready, just in case, with a Katrina missing-persons board that anyone could post to, or simply use to search for names and pictures.[5] With a common place where anyone could post online, people could search for loved ones more easily, bypassing the hassle of photocopying flyers and the worry of wondering whether they'd posted them in the right spots or if they would get taken down.

On the morning of August 28, Katrina hit southeast Louisiana as a Category 3 hurricane. Later that day, when the levees broke, forecasters' worst predictions of a city engulfed by rising floodwaters came true. NowPublic, ready with its missing-persons board, began receiving hundreds of pleas for help.

For a sense of how the forum was used in those desperate days, I include a few of the direct posts. For the privacy of the families, I've omitted names and contact details; otherwise, these are unedited, with the time-and-date stamp included.

at 09:31 on August 31, 2005
I have a son [incarcerated]@ 3000 Perdido Street New Orleans L.A. 70119 I have not heard [anything] about the ones that are

jailed. I called a radio station here in Arkansas and the [spokes-person] said he heard that the prisoners were put on an overpass to be picked up, then he said some of the overpasses where down. I am really concerned about my son . . . I have not heard Anything please help if you can.[6]

at 19:25 on August 31, 2005
Our family is heartsicken trying to locate and hear from the family of . . . The last word our family had was around 11 pm Sunday night as they were moving up to the second floor— running from rising waters. Please help.[7]

at 11:20 on September 2, 2005
I am looking for . . . a New Orleans resident. She is black and in her 70s, wears glasses and is of medium weight . . . She is a kind, self-educated woman. She collects teacups and saucers. Please, if anyone knows her whereabouts, just tell me she is safe and well.[8]

at 11:20 on September 2, 2005
We have located them.
Thank you so much for your web site.
Our family called us today and informed
us, they were safe and sound. Thank God![9]

In addition to the written postings with their accompanying pictures, NowPublic also had a voice report system that people could use to leave a message to be transcribed and posted directly to the site.[10] Even so, Tippett says that the site, like the city's levees, was "only designed for a Category 3 storm," not the ensuing Category 5 storm surge that flooded New Orleans. NowPublic did what it could for the first forty-eight hours and then started directing people to the Red Cross site that had soon after been created.

NOLA.com, the Web site for the *Times-Picayune*, New Orleans's daily newspaper, was another of the innovative sites that developed a searchable, user-generated missing-persons board for the storm. In the days leading up to landfall, NOLA.com editor Jon Donley had the same foresight as Tippett and contacted the Web-services company hosting the publication's site to ask it to prepare a page to handle missing-persons reports. The site was ready in just two days, right as Katrina hit and the levees broke.

As the storm came ashore, a group of *Times-Picayune* and NOLA.com staffers bravely decided not to evacuate so they could continue reporting from the city. This allowed the missing-persons board that had just been set up to have constant monitoring.

The NOLA.com staff held out amid sleeping bags and air mattresses in a makeshift "Hurricane Bunker," housed in a building just blocks from the Superdome. In addition to hosting the missing-persons page on NOLA.com, Donley decided he would also turn his own NOLA View blog over to readers so they could post real-time calls for help. For three days, Donley and others managed to keep the blog updated and also—amazingly—publish the newspaper online while physical printing and distribution were impossible. As with the NowPublic site, many of the posts that appeared on the blog were relayed via voice mails or text messages sent from mobile phones. In an interview with Mark Glaser for the Online Journalism Review, Donley explained,

It was weird because we couldn't figure out where these pleas were coming from . . . We'd get e-mails from Idaho, there's a guy at this address and he's in the upstairs bedroom of his place in New Orleans. And then we figured out that even in the poorest part of town, people have a cell phone. And it's a text-enabled cell phone. And they were sending out text messages to friends or family, and they were putting it in our forums or sending it in e-mails to us.[11]

The pleas weren't falling on deaf ears. Tracking the NOLA.com blog was a team led by Lieutenant General Russel Honoré, the commander of the military's Joint Task Force Katrina. As soon as new information was posted to the NOLA.com forum, rescue crews were deployed to the address. The joint task force was so dependent on the site for information that at one point, when the server for NOLA.com was having problems, the aide coordinating the tracking effort for Honoré frantically contacted Donley, pleading with him to "get this up as soon as you can, peoples lives depend on it. We've already saved a number of lives because of it."[12]

With everything that was to go wrong during the aftermath of Katrina, the availability of Web sites like NowPublic and NOLA .com was one of the few things that actually went right. Without these open sites, the death toll would certainly have been higher. But aside from lives saved, they also made it easier for Vera Triplett to find out that her godson was OK. By allowing for such peace of mind, the sites lessoned the need for dangerous and time-consuming searching. Instead, Vera and others like her who otherwise would have been frantically searching for loved ones, were able to stay put, at less personal risk, or spend the time helping neighbors or other family members.

Using the online missing-persons boards, though, was just the beginning of Vera's post-Katrina struggle to reclaim connection and make it home. Gathered with her family in Houston, she crammed into a hastily rented house with thirteen relatives, including her husband, her pregnant younger sister Aisha and her three children, their older sister and her three children, and their mother, father, and grandmother.

Not with the family was Marlin, Aisha's husband, who was a researcher at Louisiana State's Health Sciences Center. With animals under his department's care, he had to stay and watch over them. But the facility soon flooded, and Marlin then escaped by boat, eventually finding his way north via bus.

In Houston, Aisha and the rest of the family had no way of knowing this. For three or four days, the fourteen of them could only wonder where Marlin was and if he was OK. One afternoon after some of the longest days of their lives had passed watching their hometown come apart on live TV, a phone rang in the kitchen. When Aisha picked up, Vera heard her sister yell out in relief. It was Marlin on the line, calling from a borrowed out-of-state cell phone. He had made it aboard a bus headed to Houston and would arrive in the middle of that very night, tired but safe.

Meanwhile, back in New Orleans, Vera's brother-in-law, Lamar, and his wife, Lashunder, were out of touch for nearly five days. They had decided to stay in their home, determined to ride the storm out with a stocked refrigerator and freezer. But as the floodwaters rose above their six-foot-high windows, they were forced to retreat into their attic with a backpack full of food, water, and photo albums. There they spent a sleepless night.

The next morning, Lamar was able to cut a hole wide enough for him to see outside. The view was nothing but water. "It looked like the house was in the middle of a lake," he tells me. "If I didn't know better, I would've thought someone had dropped us there."[13] Cutting the hole bigger, Lamar was able to crawl out onto the roof, where he and Lashunder spent the day on scorching black roof shingles yelling out to neighbors and waving at passing helicopters.

As evening approached, a helicopter headed for them and slowed down to hover over their house. With blades whirring and the smell of jet fuel in the air, the helicopter lowered one man down in a harness. After some quick instructions, Lashunder was soon wrapped around him and lifted up and away. A half hour later, the same helicopter was back for Lamar. How this Coast Guard rescue happened—along with tens of thousands of others like it—is another story of collaboration, small decisions, and commitment to a cause.

The Rescues: The U.S. Coast Guard

In Katrina's aftermath, it was the U.S. Coast Guard, the oft-overlooked fifth service of the U.S. military, that deserved the most thanks for saving lives. At a time when news headlines were blaring, WHY FEMA FAILED,[14] the Coast Guard was being hailed as "the silver lining in the storm"[15] and praised for "get[ting] it right."[16]

And while the mayor of New Orleans, the governor of Louisiana, and the president of the United States were pointing fingers at each other, it was the Coast Guard that was relentlessly picking up people like Vera's brother-in-law from rooftops and pulling them from floodwaters. With rates as high as fifty rescues per chopper over the four days following the storm's landfall, the Coast Guard's nonstop heroics provided some of the only inspiring footage to come out of New Orleans in an otherwise tragic string of negligence broadcast 24/7 on cable news networks.[17]

What most separated the Coast Guard from the roundly criti-cized Federal Emergency Management Agency (FEMA) and other more-inflexible authorities during the response to Katrina was its approach to leadership and decision making. Similar to the open Web sites that hosted the missing-persons boards, the Coast Guard's unique role requires amazing levels of open information sharing, which in turn has created an organizational culture that values de-centralized leadership and individual initiative.

At different times in its history, the Coast Guard has been part of the Treasury, the Department of Transportation, Homeland Se-curity, and, under certain circumstances, the Navy.[18] Beyond what it is most famous for—search-and-rescue missions—the service also oversees the cleanup of oil spills in U.S. waters, secures interna-tional waterways and U.S. ports, intercepts illegal drug shipments, enforces laws against overfishing, and regulates all commercial shipping in the United States, among yet more responsibilities.

This multi-mission charge makes the Coast Guard seem like the marine version of the Environmental Protection Agency (oil spills), Customs and Border Protection (port security), the Federal Aviation Administration (commercial-shipping regulation), and more, all rolled into one small agency. And yet, for all that it does, the ser-vice costs American taxpayers less than a single new aircraft carrier annually.[19] Just what is it that makes the Coast Guard so incredibly adaptive and cost-effective?

For starters, to a far greater extent than the other branches of the military, it practices the antithesis of the assembly-line, centralized, hierarchical way of doing things. In his book *Character in Action: The U.S. Coast Guard on Leadership*, former Coast Guard commandant James Loy speaks of the service as being "uncorrupted by the 'busi-ness management' thinking of the industrial age." He explains,

We work in small teams where there is more rapport, more communication, and less bureaucracy. We have more than two hundred stations throughout the United States and, as such, we are a decentralized organization that serves the public where the rubber meets the road. The level of day-to-day oversight from a centralized headquarters unit is minimal.

While members of the Coast Guard get specialized training for certain skills and jobs, of greater importance is "cross-training" for multiple tasks and learning to take initiative as part of an adaptive leadership structure. As the *Washington Post*'s Stephen Barr wrote of the service following Hurricane Katrina, "while the employees often specialize in certain types of operations, they all train to a standard so that they can form up as teams . . . with each person knowing what each job entails and how it fits into overall operations."[20]

Partly, this sharing of roles across the Coast Guard stems from necessity. With a slew of missions and relatively few personnel, the service does not have the luxury of specialization. "When I was in the academy, people used to joke that we were smaller than the New York City Police Department," Coastie Brian Thomas tells me. "I don't know if that's true, but our size certainly leads to people having to wear many hats."[21] Indeed, with only 42,000 active-duty personnel, the Coast Guard is dwarfed by the U.S. Army (approximately 550,000 active-duty members), the Air Force and the Navy (both around 330,000), and the Marines (just over 200,000).[22]

Given the Coast Guard's fundamentally humanitarian missions, its culture is also more directly people-focused than those of the other military branches. In an illuminating 2005 cover story about the service for *Time*, Amanda Ripley interviewed Wil Milam, a rescue swimmer from Alaska who had previously served in the Navy. Comparing the two branches, he said, "In the Navy, it was all about the mission. Practicing for war, training for war. In the Coast Guard, it was, take care of our people and the mission will take care of itself."

Interestingly, the people whom the Coast Guard trusts to perform under these terribly complex circumstances are some of the government's youngest employees; the average age of Coasties below the rank of admiral is in the twenties.[23] With such a steep learning curve, it is not surprising that leadership and initiative are instilled from day one. In former Coast Guard rescue swimmer Gerald R. Hoover's book, *Brotherhood of the Fin,* he tells the story of a particularly dangerous search-and-rescue mission in which, prior to takeoff, the aircraft commander stresses the importance of the open leadership structure by giving his fresh young crew the following order: "You are required to speak up if something is not going as you think it should."

Think about that: Rather than have his crew unquestioningly follow his orders (which he knew, if based on faulty assumptions or a lack of information, could get someone killed), the commander demanded that his new crew question his authority if necessary. Hoover believes that such an approach allowed the commander to "reach a level of expertise" that he wouldn't have attained following the more traditional follow-orders-don't-ask-questions model.[24]

The Coast Guard is replete with stories that embody this approach. One of the most famous in the service's history is that of the 1952 *Pendleton* rescue. In that rescue, twenty-three-year-old Coxswain Bernard Webber and his three crewmen steered a thirty-two-foot motorboat under the stern of a sinking ship while a nor'easter storm churned up sixty-foot seas around them. After managing to pull thirty-three men from the freezing water and into their life-boat, Webber and his team heard their onshore ranking officers arguing over their radios—presumably about whether the rescuers should wait for the storm to die down or head back to shore regardless of the conditions. They just turned the radio off and made their own decision to head for shore, saving all aboard.

As Hurricane Katrina came ashore, this approach was on full display. Early on in the rescue-response operations, a junior-level pilot on a planned environmental-inspection overflight decided to shift missions in midair in order to provide a badly needed communications platform for other aircraft. Her quick thinking enabled search-and-rescue helicopters to communicate with hospitals and safe-landing areas, ensuring safer skies, both over the city and around landing strips.[25]

With an official motto of "Semper paratus" (Latin for "always ready"), it should come as no surprise that the Coast Guard was the first federal agency to make any rescues in New Orleans. In fact, over the first seventeen days, approximately fifty-six hundred Coasties were involved in rescue efforts across New Orleans—half of whom had themselves lost homes and were now separated from their evacuated families.

All told, out of the 60,000 rescues made by local, state, and federal officials, more than half—33,500—were made by the Coast Guard.[26] This number is even more impressive when you consider that the service was carrying out other missions simultaneously, such as taking water samples while making boat rescues.

Yes, water samples. With everything involved in pulling people to safety, you might wonder how it could possibly make sense to take time to reach out and collect a water sample. But as curious as they may seem, those samples were vitally important, allowing officials to prioritize cleanup efforts in what was not only a humanitarian crisis but also an enormous environmental and public health disaster. Consider that an estimated *eight million gallons* of oil spilled across the region during the storm.[27] And with its multimission training, performing multiple duties at once came naturally for the Coast Guard.

Throughout all of this, the service did not experience a single accident or casualty. This is simply astounding when you consider the extreme conditions it was operating in: making rescues a mere nine hours after the storm first made landfall amid flying debris, poisonous snakes, and downed power lines. There was even something of an unruly, Wild West scene for aircraft in the skies over New Orleans, with shots fired at helicopters from one hospital rooftop.[28]

Central to the Coast Guard's success in this situation was its ability to work closely and collaboratively with other local, state, and federal agencies during the rescue mission. In addition, it brought in twenty-eight hundred active-duty and civilian Coast Guard personnel from other parts of the country. Beyond reserve forces, this included the Coast Guard Auxiliary, a group of volunteers, most over the age of fifty, who provide their boats, aircraft, and communications resources to assist Coast Guard missions that do not involve military or law enforcement operations.[29]

The auxiliary—which provides more than two million man-hours and one billion dollars in service to the country each year, free of charge—can be deployed at the drop of a hat, immediately doubling the Coast Guard's numbers, as was the case on September 11, 2001, and, to a lesser extent, during Hurricane Katrina.[30] If this volunteer mobilization sounds vaguely familiar, consider that it is the exact same approach as that utilized by NowPublic and NOLA .com: Empower a diverse, disparate group of citizens who have the tools to contribute to a larger effort.

These open, decentralized, and collaborative approaches stand in stark contrast to the example of FEMA, which turned down significant resources offered by corporations, nonprofit groups, and state and local governments. The city of Chicago, for instance, offered up nearly five hundred personnel, including police, firefighters, and medics, but their path to New Orleans was blocked by FEMA.[31]

While part of the reason for FEMA's poor response was the budget cuts the agency had sustained throughout the Bush administration—which made it difficult to coordinate such resources—much of the responsibility lay with the failings of Michael Brown, the former Arabian horse commissioner who had no experience in disaster management before being appointed to direct FEMA by President George W. Bush.[32]

When Katrina was named an "Incident of National Significance" three days after the storm hit, it was Brown whom the administration selected to be the "principal federal official" in charge of post-Katrina rescue-and-recovery operations. But rather than mobilizing and coordinating the federal response, Brown was sending e-mails to his press secretary requesting wardrobe advice and asking, "Can I quit now?"

The man who had gotten his position for his fundraising and loyalty to Bush was in way over his head. His press secretary responded by advising him to just roll up his sleeves—not figuratively but literally. "Please roll up the sleeves of your shirt, all shirts. Even the president rolled his sleeves to just below the elbow. In this [crisis] and on TV you just need to *look* more hard-working."[33]

Finally, after nine days of Brown's fumbling and disastrous re-sponse, the secretary of Homeland Security, Michael Chertoff, named a Coast Guard leader, then–vice admiral Thad Allen, to re-place him as the principal federal official in charge.[34] Allen's first step was to bring Coast Guard principles to bear on the situation.

In a revealing interview with James Kitfield just days after his appointment, Allen asserted his belief that "transparency breeds self-correcting behavior" and, in a clear break with his predecessor, signaled his intent to "open the process up, shine the light of media scrutiny on the entire recovery project, and let the American people judge their efforts."[35]

As rescue efforts wound down, thoughts began turning to re-building. For that, the model of transparency and openness would prove useful again, employed by Dr. Vera Triplett as she took on a unique role in the city's rebuilding. But before that could happen, she needed to get home from Houston.

The Rebuilding: The Unified New Orleans Plan

Before Hurricane Katrina, New Orleans was a city of nearly half a million people. Five months later, only *a third*—less than two hun-dred thousand—of those residents had returned.[36] Considering that 80 percent of New Orleans was flooded, destroying most prop-erty, it's amazing that even that many returned.[37] For historical context, Katrina was twice as costly as the next most destructive hurricane in U.S. history, with the bulk of the more than eighty bil-lion dollars in total property damage centered in New Orleans.[38]

If, like me, you did not go through the experience of returning to New Orleans under such circumstances, just try to imagine what it would have been like. Maybe you would be mourning the loss of friends or relatives who were among the more than thirteen hundred people who died. Even if you could salvage your home or find another place to live—and if you did, you would likely have four or so friends and relatives who had lost theirs living with you—there would be a severe shortage of job options. The schools for your children might be gone. Four months after the storm, the bus routes that had once provided a quarter of the population with transit were only running at 10 percent, so a car would now be necessary to get around, a huge cost if you were part of the nearly 40 percent of New Orleanians who had been making less than twenty thousand dollars a year before Katrina struck.[39] And always in the back of your mind would be the question of whether the levees that were supposed to protect the city in the first place would ever be rebuilt, and to what strength. This was the atmosphere pervading the city when Vera moved her family back to New Orleans that November.

With their house severely damaged by thirteen feet of floodwater, Vera and her husband, John, had to sublet a friend's place on the edge of the city and then stay with Vera's mom until their house could be gutted and repaired enough to be livable. By July 2006, just ahead of the one-year anniversary of Katrina, their house was ready. But even then, Vera and John were the first to return in a twelve-block radius. "It was just desolate," Vera says. "There was no electricity in the neighborhood. There were no streetlights. I relied on a corner store out near my mother's house for bottled water, then drove out to Metairie for groceries. On my way back home, I would go pick up the mail at a central distribution center since there were not enough people back yet to justify delivery, not that there were any mailboxes left anyway."

Initially, Vera and her family powered their house with a generator. With the electricity out for blocks around, the darkness of the city made the night sky show more stars above than she had ever seen. The *Times-Picayune* ran an arresting picture illustrating this, a nighttime aerial shot of Louisiana with a dark spot where New Orleans once was.

Despite all this, for Vera moving back to New Orleans was never a question of if, only of when. That they moved back so early says much about her personality. Vera is the kind of person who, when you tell her she can't do something, will do it just to prove you wrong. Asked what she was trying to prove, she pauses for a second and says very clearly, "I needed my daughter to see that you can lose everything and get it all back, that she didn't have to give up. She was born in that house, and I was pregnant with her when we bought it. So when people were saying we couldn't move back, something in me said, 'You just watch.'"

Indeed, the fact that Vera and John owned the house at all was a testament to that very same spirit. They had gotten married in 1997, a year after Vera had graduated from college. Later that year, she was pregnant, and they were living in an apartment with John's child from a previous relationship and Vera's godson, Elie. As her pregnancy progressed, Vera realized that they simply would not be able to have three children living in an apartment: They needed to get a house of their own.

At the time, John was making $5.25 an hour, and Vera, as a schoolteacher, was clearing maybe $500 a week. To help save up the money they would need to buy a place, John decided to leave his job for one at a casino, where he increased his salary to $10 an hour. During this time, they lived off canned foods and Hamburger Helper to save on groceries and even sold their computer, whatever they could do to come up with the down payment. Making a gamble—the lease for their apartment ended on the very day that they were supposed to close on the house—Vera and John, with two kids in tow, showed up at the closing in a U-Haul with all their stuff. It was the first "big thing" they had done on their own as adults. Two months later, Vera's first daughter was born into the nice Gentilly neighborhood that Vera had wanted for her—just like the one she herself had grown up in.

So when they moved back into that house in 2006, it wasn't enough that it was livable for them; Vera wanted their neighbors and neighborhood back too. She joined a local listserv for Gentilly and helped organize some neighborhood cleanups out of a local church that was one of the few places that had not flooded. But it soon became clear that with twenty-five or twenty-six different neighborhood commissions—some representing smaller Gentilly neighborhoods with five people back, or ten—the area wasn't really set up in a way that would allow everyone to come together with one voice and get more done.

That's when Vera decided to convene everyone across the twenty-five or so sub-neighborhoods in a group they named the Gentilly Civic Improvement Association. The first step for the association was simply letting people know that Gentilly as a whole still existed. "We would call up different authorities and say, 'Here's where we are: People want to come back, but we need resources and infrastructure,'" Vera says. "When it became clear that these were not coming and we'd have to do it ourselves, we knew it was up to us to come up with a plan for rebuilding the community."

With that mission, the members of the Gentilly Civic Improvement Association next took it upon themselves to contact business owners—of gas stations, grocery stores, shopping chains, and so on—and ask them if they were planning to return to the neighborhood. After all, if they were going to move forward, people needed to know what services they would be able to rely on. After meeting with Vera and other members of the association, some business owners agreed to come back, convinced that they would still be able to make a living. Vera credits their local city councilwoman, Cynthia Hedge-Morrell, with really stepping up during this time (and ever since).

Indeed, as work in Gentilly began, planning for the future of the entire city was simultaneously taking place across town in the city council chamber and the mayor's office. Beyond Gentilly, the *entire* city needed a comprehensive redevelopment plan to chart a strategy for rebuilding. In fact, it was stipulated that until a plan of this sort was completed, New Orleans could not receive the federal funding it so badly needed.

The city had embarked on not one but *two* rebuilding planning initiatives—put together separately by the mayor's office and the city council. Mayor Ray Nagin's initiative, begun just a month after Katrina, was called "Bring New Orleans Back." To the presiding commission, he appointed an elite group, including some of the city's wealthiest businessmen. In attempting to meet the mayor's December 2005 deadline for a plan, the commission bypassed local neighborhoods, taking a top-down approach that alienated many in the city.[40]

The mayor's commission brought in a group of outside planning experts, who proposed converting the lowest-lying, hardest-hit neighborhoods—which also happened to be predominantly African American—into green space. Whatever the theoretical merits of such an idea, it was the kiss of death in a city with a tense history of racial and class divisions. When a map of the group's proposal showed up on the front page of the *Times-Picayune*—with green dots indicating where existing neighborhoods would be replaced—public outcry stopped the mayor's planning effort in its tracks. Ahead of his reelection campaign, Nagin distanced himself from the commission's recommendations, thereby effectively ending Bring New Orleans Back.[41]

Meanwhile, the city council, trying to overcome flaws in the mayor's effort, had begun its own planning process. But it overcompensated: This time, it was only the needs of neighborhoods that had seen more than two feet of flooding that were to be addressed, thus excluding some of the wealthier, predominantly white and "dry" neighborhoods.[42] The city council ended up with a set of nearly useless plans, or "wish lists," that could not possibly get funded because they didn't cover the whole city, or even follow the federal requirements for getting funding.

As the mayor and the city council pushed forward with their divergent planning efforts, little was accomplished. The one-year anniversary of Katrina approached, and each had failed to give New Orleans what it really needed: a serious, comprehensive plan for the entire city that would get recovery funding flowing from the federal government.

Finally, on the day before the one-year anniversary of the storm, the city government took a turn in a more promising direction. With the help of the Louisiana Recovery Authority (a state oversight body established to coordinate requests for federal recovery funding), the city launched a sort of "direct democracy" comprehensive planning process called the Unified New Orleans Plan. The new plan was the city's best hope for taking the positive pieces of the previous two efforts—professional planning expertise and neighborhood engagement, respectively—while leaving the old efforts and their baggage behind.

For all the hope that surrounded it, the Unified New Orleans Plan did not get off to a promising start. At the first Community Congress, in October of 2006—an event set up to engage residents in developing the plan—the participants were largely the same elite folks from the earlier Bring New Orleans Back effort. Just a quarter of those attending had incomes under forty thousand dollars, compared to the over 60 percent of New Orleanians with incomes below that level pre-Katrina. And over 40 percent of the participants represented the very wealthiest in the city. Adding further insult to injury, in a city that was two-thirds African American, over three quarters of the attendees at this meeting were white.

It was clear this wasn't a truly open and representative group to be planning the future of the whole city. Moreover, worries that such a group might again seek to raze neighborhoods for the sake of "green space," as was the case with the mayor's initial planning effort, put the African American community back on guard.

Tasked with overseeing Unified Plan to make sure that the whole community was heard and represented in the process was the Community Support Organization (CSO). Needless to say, the CSO was not pleased with the results thus far. The person chairing the CSO was none other than Dr. Vera Triplett, and in the wake of the first, failed Community Congress, she communicated the following message to the leaders of the Unified Planning Plan:

> If this is a process that is really, truly supposed to engage the public and get their opinions and find out what they need . . . you need to do it not in a traditional marketing way because a lot of these people don't have access to that. People don't have televisions and radios. They're living in tents; they're living in trailers; they're living in shelters. So you have to find another way.[43]

With the city facing yet another credibility and momentum collapse, the organizers of the Unified New Orleans planning process needed to step up big time. If they didn't, they would only keep getting the same wealthy white people who didn't represent the full diversity of the city. It was at this point that a woman named Carey Shea made a suggestion that Vera says she "will believe was the turning point until the day [she dies]." Shea proposed they start working with America*Speaks*, an organization whose express mission is "engaging citizens in governance."

For nearly fifteen years, America*Speaks* has been integrating technology into small-group, face-to-face dialogue to bring thousands of people together to deliberate simultaneously on important public issues and come to shared priorities. The goal is to create smarter, more comprehensive solutions that draw on the public's diverse experience and expertise. In an America*Speaks* 21st Century Town Meeting, members of the public, government leaders, and issue experts together create viable paths forward in complex situations. Because large-scale and diverse participation results in strong citizen support, the recommendations that emerge from a 21st Century Town Meeting "have legs."

Brought on board to plan and run the second Community Congress of the Unified New Orleans Plan, America*Speaks* faced a monumental task in making the meeting substantially more politically credible than the previous planning efforts. To achieve this, staff and volunteers spent two months going door-to-door with Vera and the other members of the CSO to convince people to come to the congress and participate in the planning process. They covered every neighborhood in New Orleans, from Broadmoor to Mid-City to Uptown, offering residents travel assistance and child care if they otherwise would not be able to attend. It was an all-out effort.

As Vera says, "we knew if we didn't get this one right, we might as well just hang it up."[44]

Saturday, December 2, 2006, was the date of the second Community Congress. There was to be a Saints football game the next day—their first game back in the Superdome since Katrina—so the attendees were a sea of black and gold as they entered the hall of the New Orleans convention center, many having used the transportation that had been set up by America*Speaks*. As citizens arrived, many dropped their kids off for the child care that had also been organized. Red beans and rice were laid out, and a brass band played second line jazz. The whole scene was like a big New Orleans neighborhood festival.

Vera, clad in her Saints T-shirt, went onstage to begin the congress. She called out to the crowd, "Where are all the Saints fans?" The response was immediate and explosive, cheering that channeled all the pride they felt about the perseverance of the city. But Vera felt a nervous anticipation as things were about to really get under way. This gathering wasn't about a football game or a parade, after all; it was to discuss complex and contentious issues that would ultimately decide the future of their city.

The big question on the organizers' minds as the meeting began was who was there and who was not. After all, it was a lack of diverse representation—and the resulting illegitimacy of the process in the public's mind—that had doomed efforts up until now. At the door, every participant was given a keypad-polling device, like a television remote control. The keypads would allow each of them to anonymously and instantaneously share anything from their demographic information to their opinion on an issue, pretty much anything that could be put up on the screen in multiple-choice format.

As the demographic profile of the congress streamed in, capturing participants' race, neighborhood, income, etc., organizers and participants breathed a collective sigh of relief: 64 percent of the group was African American, and 28 percent was white, *almost exactly* the same as the pre-Katrina demographics of the city. Just as important, nearly half of the participants reported an income of less than forty thousand dollars, while only 20 percent were in the wealthiest category—much closer to a representative sample of the city's residents than at the previous Community Congress.

In total, twenty-five hundred people were there, from *all* of New Orleans's neighborhoods. Additionally, residents who had not yet been able to move back but wanted to participate were able to join the conversation via a telecast set up by America*Speaks*. New Orleanians waiting to come home from Baton Rouge, Atlanta, Houston, Dallas, and *sixteen* other cities participated, via either telecast or the Internet. In Vera's words, opening the meeting up like this was like saying to members of the diaspora that "as human beings and as New Orleanians, we still care about you, and we know this is still your city too."[45] As a result of such diverse participation, from this point onward people were able to see the meeting—and the overall Unified New Orleans process—as a fair and legitimate way to make decisions about the future of their city.

With the assistance of several hundred volunteer, trained facilitators, participants sat at roundtables of ten and talked to one another about the city's future, and, with the help of balanced informational material, considered a range of specific planning issues and options. After having an opportunity to discuss a certain topic or question with the others seated at their table, participants across the convention center floor were polled on their keypads about their views. An instantaneous accounting of the community's thoughts and desires was then projected back to the room on large screens.

As the facilitators of the meeting went through the group discussions table by table and had everyone vote on each planning
issue via keypad, an interesting thing happened. Not only did the
participants want to vote on the questions and options that had
been prepared for them in advance (such as where and how to locate government service facilities), but they also wanted to add in
their own ideas. In other words, not all of what the community
ended up voting on were pre-developed ideas. The process allowed
for innovative suggestions to be taken up and considered in real time,
no matter where they came from.

Vera told me that one of the topics that came up in this way
was what kind of rights a home owner should have if her neighbors
did not move back to the property next door. Should the home
owner get the right of first refusal to buy the property? The question was put to a vote by the whole assembly, and 100 percent of the
participants said yes: If a lot next door was abandoned, the neighbor should have the right to buy it before anyone else did. This innovative suggestion made it all the way to the final Unified New
Orleans Plan and is now known as the "lot next door" program.

Participants in the Community Congress also considered and
weighed in on a wide range of other planning issues, such as how to
ensure safety from future flooding, empower residents to rebuild
safe and stable neighborhoods, provide incentives and housing so
that people could return, and establish sustainable, equitable public
services. The success of this second Community Congress resulted
in America*Speaks* doing a third session seven weeks later—in which
nearly thirteen hundred citizens continued to refine plans for the
rebuilding of New Orleans.

The overall effect of this experiment in deliberative democracy
was profound. Abigail Williamson, at the time a Ph.D. student at

Harvard University, conducted a set of interviews of the congress participants for her report "Citizen Participation in the Unified New Orleans Plan." Tarence Davis, an African American charter-school teacher she spoke with, described that second Community Congress as "an unprecedented democratic process."

With the Unified New Orleans Plan back on track, it was only a matter of months before it was agreed upon by the mayor and the city council and then approved by the City Planning Commission. In June of 2007, the Louisiana Recovery Authority accepted the Unified New Orleans Plan as the official recovery blueprint for the city, allowing federal funds to begin flowing and, most important, to be spent according to a common vision that had been developed by New Orleans's own residents.

For Vera, the whole experience has done nothing less than transform her view of what democracy is all about. "At the end of the day, it's about letting people who are impacted by something be a part of the decision-making process," she says. "I mean, if you try to do something for me but without me, it's really not about me. For a long time, our city elected people who thought of us as too stupid to make our own decisions. But now I've begun deciding who to vote for based on whether they are willing to have us actually be a part of the problem-solving process. Before, we would give them votes or money. Now we want to give them evidence and case studies, and we want them to make decisions on the ground with us, not from some isolated and untouchable ivory tower."

In the end, ten thousand people had been involved in the making of the Unified New Orleans Plan. Out of this participation emerged common principles and priorities, such as that elevating homes in flood zones was better than abandoning existing neighborhoods. This exercise in direct democracy also resulted in specific changes to governance strategies in New Orleans: for example, clustering services around neighborhood nexus points (usually schools) to allow communities to rebuild around a common, accessible core, rather than at random and separated from one another.

While the city still, even five years later, has a long road to recovery, the Unified New Orleans Plan was what finally allowed New Orleans to begin moving in the right direction. The plan's approval led to the Louisiana Recovery Authority's making its first disbursement of $117 million in federal Community Development Block Grant money it had received.[46] Since then, the first phase of funding for the city's schools has begun to flow to the parish as well, totaling $700 million.[47]

A New Dawn

I open with these stories about New Orleans after Katrina because what happened there represented a turning point in our society. In the aftermath of the storm, it was almost as if every social challenge of our time—lack of economic opportunity, racial disparities, the destruction of our natural world, and political inaction—came to a head, signaling our society's need for a new, more comprehensive and participatory model of problem solving.

It would be a shame if stories of hope were lost alongside everything that was devastated by Katrina. Whether through the decentralized missing-persons boards of NowPublic.com and NOLA.com or the Community Congresses that America*Speaks* hosted, New Orleans has given us powerful new examples of effective social change and responsible citizenship. From them, we can see that the scale of our challenges—and the inability of our existing institutions to solve them—demands not continued blind reliance on a failed "invisible hand" but rather "all hands on deck."

We have seen this type of open, collaborative problem solving work in the face of other crises too. In his pathbreaking book, *The Wisdom of Crowds*, James Surowiecki details how the global health community responded to the SARS outbreak of 2003. In a bid to ascertain the source of the SARS virus, the World Health Organization asked eleven research laboratories around the world to form a "collaborative multicenter research project." By sharing research openly, the teams were free to pursue promising new leads. With the benefit of having fully current information from their colleagues, they had a better sense of what was working and what was a dead end. As Surowiecki tells it,

> Working on their own, any one of those labs might very well have taken months or years to isolate the virus. Together it took them just a matter of weeks . . . This cobbled together multinational alliance found an answer to its problem as quickly and efficiently as any top-down organization could have.[48]

In many ways, what New Orleans faced during the recovery and rebuilding following Katrina is simply a domestic example of the kinds of dynamic global challenges that we will increasingly face as the twenty-first century unfolds.

Channeling the lessons of the SARS response, *New York Times* columnist David Brooks recently wrote of the 2009 swine flu (H1N1 virus),

The correct response to these dynamic, decentralized, emergent problems is to create dynamic, decentralized, emergent authorities: chains of local officials, state agencies, national governments and international bodies that are as flexible as the problem itself.[49]

But the idea that a decentralized group, working without strict hierarchy, could overcome such problems runs up against powerfully ingrained cultural beliefs about efficiency and leadership. As you know, the familiar narrative for effective action goes something like this: institute a top-down, centralized hierarchy, closely oversee specially trained experts, and then demand quick and measurable results.

In the twentieth century, many of our great challenges were certainly solved this way. Take, for example, the Manhattan and *Apollo* projects. Both of these efforts—building the first nuclear bomb and putting the first man on the moon, respectively—were models of mind-boggling efficiency under pressure in a high-stakes race against other countries. When it comes to issues like these, where the primary asset is technical expertise, a top-down, centralized approach often does make sense.

But the dominant challenges of our time don't fit in quite the same box. Exploring outer space is no longer the pressing need it once was. Now we have our own planet to worry about, with the emergent threat of the climate crisis requiring more cross-disciplinary problem solving than chemists and engineers alone can provide. As for nuclear weapons, we don't really need to build any more; the greater challenge is working in concert with other countries to stop their spread.

The authors of *Getting to Maybe: How the World Is Changed* provide a helpful way to distinguish between the types of challenges we may face. Using the examples of sending a rocket to the moon and raising a child, they illustrate the different nature of problems that are simple, complicated, or complex.[50]

I prefer using the example of putting out a fire to make the distinctions. With a campfire, all you need is a single person to smother it with some dirt or pour some water over it. Pretty simple, right? A house fire, though, is more complicated. Usually, the best role for the people in the house is just to get out safely, letting trained experts—firefighters—put it out, without interference. But things get a little more complex when a whole city block, or a whole city, is on fire (or underwater, for that matter). In that case, expertise and rigid protocol can only get you so far. To respond effectively, you really need to adapt and engage citizens to help in the effort—a combination of the individual action used for the campfire and the professional expertise needed for the house fire.

While broad strokes inevitably oversimplify, I believe that we are moving into an age in which complex, dynamic challenges define our existence more than complicated ones. For the complex challenges of our time, centralized industrial management, with its closed-off nature, rigid hierarchies, and separate areas of specialization, is poorly suited. Therefore, collective will is just as important as individual expertise.

To be sure, not all of our challenges lend themselves to a participatory, "wisdom of crowds" approach. Combating terrorism and nuclear proliferation, for instance, clearly require secret investigative work not well suited for decentralized, open groups. However, aspects of the open approach are still beneficial here: for collecting tips from the public about threats or, in turn, for sharing and acting upon such information with relevant agencies. On balance, however, I believe that the majority of the global challenges that define our time—especially climate, hunger, health, genocide, and poverty—call for more of a participatory and collaborative approach to social-change organizing and public problem-solving.

The bottom line is that the primary obstacle to solving these complex problems is not a lack of technical expertise or policy innovation. Rather, the biggest problem is that with these interconnected challenges, we fail to use comprehensive problem-solving methods that can fully engage a public with amazing degrees of untapped knowledge, ability, and power.

Perhaps Steven Bingler, one of the coordinators of the Unified New Orleans Plan, best sums up what he, Vera, and the rest of New Orleans have learned throughout the aftermath of Katrina:

> The most important element in rebuilding a city—because of a disaster, in spite of a disaster, or even in preparation for a disaster—is the act of coming together and working collaboratively. The community has said that they will not tolerate the school system not working with the city government. They will not tolerate the city government not working with the housing authority. And they will not tolerate the housing authority not working with our city institutions. *The community sees all of this as one challenge as opposed to silos of challenges addressed by separate governing systems.*[51]

As daunting as they may seem, one thing that all of these complex challenges have in common is that they were created by us and can therefore be solved by us. Even Katrina, a supposed "natural disaster" or "act of God," cannot rightly be termed so. For years, New Orleans's levees have been underfunded and deteriorating in quality, despite repeated warnings of what would happen if a storm like Katrina hit. The greatest damage was caused not by wind or rain but by flooding because man-made—and man-neglected—levees failed.

For all the good they did, the models of NOLA.com, the Coast Guard, and the Unified New Orleans Plan alone are not enough, then. Merely applying them earlier and better, with more resources, is not the lesson to take away. In the end, the challenges of Katrina expose a question more fundamental and systemic: Are we, as a society, set up with the governing and decision-making processes to effectively meet the emergent, complex challenges of our time? If not, what is the alternative?

In the early part of the last century, poet Edna St. Vincent Millay wrote of how, even for all our strands of wisdom, we lacked a loom that could connect and act on them.

What is amazing about this moment in history is that we now have the tools and the imperative to build such a loom—a new way to bring people together, improve how our governments make decisions and solve problems, and turn our daily activities into something lasting. But before we tackle that issue head-on, we need to take a tour of the open-source-software movement to understand the unmet potential it holds for us beyond the Internet.

TWO

THE RISE OF THE OPEN-SOURCE MOVEMENT

Every man takes the limits of his own field of vision for the limits of the world.

—ARTHUR SCHOPENHAUER

Given enough eyeballs, all bugs are shallow.

—ERIC RAYMOND

IF NECESSITY is the mother of invention, the most important failure in the history of computers may have been a jammed printer. In 1979, Xerox sent the Massachusetts Institute of Technology a brand-new laser printer. Like many first generation pieces of technology, the machine had its problems, namely paper jams. Unlike most of us, however, the folks at MIT had the know-how to do far more than bang the side of the thing while cursing at it.

One of the leading researchers there, Richard Stallman, got so sick of the paper jams that he decided he would try to fix the problem. Stallman figured he could write a simple program to alert the researchers in the lab whenever the printer jammed. Then someone could go and clear the paper to make sure that print job after print job wouldn't pile up behind it. Simple, right?

But this wasn't just any laser printer. In fact, it was the first to leave Xerox corporate headquarters. Wary of sharing the secret to its technology, Xerox decided not to include the source code—

basically a set of electronic instructions—for the software that ran the printer. Without the source code, MIT couldn't go in and add a fix.

Then one day, Stallman heard that a colleague at Carnegie Mellon had gotten the printer source code he needed. On a visit to the school, he decided to stop in and ask for it. As Stallman retells it, he walked to his colleague's office, and this exchange took place:

> "Hi, I'm from MIT. Could I have a copy of the printer source code?" And he said, "No, I promised not to give you a copy." I was stunned . . . All I could think of was to turn around on my heel and walk out of his room. Maybe I slammed the door. And I thought about it later on, because I realized that I was seeing not just an isolated jerk, but a social phenomenon that was important and affected a lot of people . . . See, he had promised to refuse to cooperate with us—his colleagues at MIT. He had betrayed us.[1]

To understand the tone of Stallman's reaction, some history is in order. While protecting the information that gives a company a competitive advantage has long been standard practice in the corporate world, the same is not true in academia, especially in computer science and artificial intelligence labs, where research results have long been freely shared for peer review.

In fact, one of the first computer operating systems, Unix, was improved and more fully developed at UC Berkeley after AT&T, for a minimal fee, gave the university full access to its source code. Going beyond computer science departments, the world of academia has long been built on the idea, in Isaac Newton's words, of "standing on the shoulders of giants." The assumption is that when information is freely shared, anyone will have the opportunity to build on it and, in turn, contribute new discoveries to the world of human knowledge. In return, all that's asked for is a simple citation.

In 1969, the Defense Department's Advanced Research Projects Agency (DARPA) began linking universities with other research centers and defense contractors via the ARPANET, the precursor to today's Internet, to facilitate just this type of sharing and collaboration. Gradually, a unique "hacker culture" emerged thanks to the new network, allowing information sharing to flourish.[2]

According to Stallman, the hacker ethic at MIT meant that anyone was free to ask for and get a copy of any software developed there. "There were no copyright notices on these programs," he says. "Cooperation was our way of life."[3] Stallman's view of science and technology is positively Newtonian: We make discoveries and share information to improve the human condition, not to make a profit. Blocking people—anyone—from being able to participate in that endeavor is a betrayal of the mission of his field.

So when Xerox's laser printer signaled that a twenty-year tradition of sharing software in a close academic community was under threat, Stallman couldn't stand for it. For him, proprietary, or "nonfree," software was (and is) a moral outrage. "Free," let's be clear, here refers not to price but rather to access to information. As he puts it, "think free speech, not free beer." Or, if you prefer a little alliteration, you might say "free" as in liberty, not lunch.

To Stallman's dismay, the Xerox incident was the beginning of the end of MIT's academic hacker community. As the 1980s unfolded, most of his colleagues were hired away by private firms, signing non-disclosure agreements that forbade them from sharing their work with anyone outside the company. But instead of caving in and going to find a nice paycheck for himself, Stallman decided to stand up for the principle that had drawn him to MIT and computer science in the first place: freedom. The decision that he made next would end up changing the course of the software industry forever.

While free operating systems had already been written (including at MIT), they started becoming obsolete in the 1980s when a new generation of computers came on the scene. These were designed to run only on a certain kind of operating system—the kind being produced by the very companies that Stallman's former colleagues had left to work for—and the world was soon left without a single fully free alternative. It was up to Stallman to keep the dream of free software alive.

The starting point for his revolutionary project was obvious, if daunting. An operating system is, after all, the most important and basic piece of software that runs a computer.

In 1984, Stallman left MIT to devote his life to developing the new free operating system, "or die trying . . . of old age."[4] In keeping with the hacker tradition of adopting recursive acronyms, he named the fledgling effort GNU (pronounced guh-NEW), for "GNU's Not Unix" (Unix being the operating system he and his team based the initial design on).[5] He supported himself during this time by selling tapes of the code he wrote for $150 a pop (remember, "free" as in speech, not beer). In this way, he was able to work on the project full-time.

Soon after, Stallman founded the Free Software Foundation (FSF) to act as a tax-exempt charity promoting "the freedom to share and change software." Among other things, the FSF began supporting programmers who wrote code for the GNU operating system. By 1991, the FSF had, in the words of famed hacker-historian Eric Raymond, "produced a fairly complete set of Unix tools as free software." Fairly complete, that is, except for the piece of code known as the kernel.

This wasn't a small problem. The kernel, or what computer scientists once called the "nucleus," is a foundational piece for an operating system, facilitating all communication between each utility or application and the computer (the hardware) itself. An operating system without a kernel is essentially unusable, a bit like a restaurant without a kitchen.

Stallman and the GNU team had saved the most complex and challenging piece for last, hoping someone else would develop a free kernel they could use. Once (or if) it came along, they figured, they would just add it in and find some way to make it work alongside all of the other applications, thus making a complete system. Little did they know that the kernel they were looking for would not be the research project of a famed professor at some other research university in the United States, but was waiting to be written by a twenty-one-year-old student across the Atlantic Ocean.

By this time, Stallman had received a MacArthur "genius grant," a multi-year, multi-hundred-thousand-dollar fellowship given by the John D. and Catherine T. MacArthur Foundation for "exceptional merit and promise for continued and enhanced creative work."[6] No longer having to worry about money, he was free to do public speaking around the world, spreading the free-software gospel. In 1991, one of the invitations he accepted was to speak at a university in Helsinki, Finland. Aside from talking about the GNU operating system project, Stallman used that particular appearance to explain the innovative license that the FSF had developed to ensure that any work he and his team did on GNU would remain free for anyone to use, share, and improve upon, forever.

The idea, called the General Public License (GPL), turns the concept of copyright on its head. Instead of using copyright law to exclude others from using someone's work, the GPL invites anyone to share the work—so long as they promise to do likewise for any work they add to it. The FSF's "copyleft" means that instead of "all rights reserved" (as with copyright), all rights are *reversed*.[7] More specifically, it guarantees four freedoms that distinguish copylefted work from copyrighted, proprietary software: the freedoms to access and/or copy the source code; the freedom to improve that source code; and the freedom to share those improvements far and wide with a community of other developers.

Actually, as Stallman explained to the Finnish audience that day, the last freedom isn't so much a choice as it is a requirement, built in to cement and perpetuate the other freedoms. Known as the "viral clause," it ensures that all work done by free-software coders can and will always remain in their community.

Stallman explains the decision to include the viral clause—the heart of the copyleft license—as the only way to "give the community a feeling that it was not a doormat," adding,

> If you don't use copyleft, you are essentially saying, "Take my code. Do what you want. I don't say no." So, anybody can come along and say, "Ah, I want to make a non-free version of this. I'll just take it." And then, of course, they probably make some improvements, those non-free versions might appeal to users, and [they] replace the free versions. And then what have you accomplished? You've only made a donation to some proprietary software project.[8]

In essence, then, the GPL is about creating a form of copyright that prevents further Xerox incidents. By requiring anyone who wants to use GPL-protected software to respect the community ideals that the code emerged from, the GPL copyleft establishes freedom, inclusion, and cooperation as principles to be protected in perpetuity. As Steven Weber, author of *The Success of Open Source*, writes, the GPL "shifts the fundamental optic of intellectual property rights away from protecting the prerogatives of an author and toward protecting the prerogatives of generations of users."[9]

One of the audience members who heard Stallman explain all this on that day in Helsinki was a young Finnish programmer of the next generation named Linus Torvalds. Neither of them knew then that Torvalds would soon write the code for GNU's missing kernel, use Stallman's GPL license to release it, and then help take the idea of free and open-source software across the planet.

The Birth of Linux

Linus Torvalds was born in Finland three days before the dawn of the 1970s. His parents, active campus radicals at the University of Helsinki, brought him into the world, as Torvalds writes in his autobiography *Just for Fun*, "between campus protests, probably with something like Joni Mitchell playing in the background." His first crib was a laundry basket in his grandparents' apartment.

When Torvalds was about five years old, his father left for a year of study in Moscow, where he ended up serving as a minor official in the Communist Party. Torvalds, teased by other kids for this, was so embarrassed by his father's radicalism that he developed a healthy disdain toward politics and ideology, a sentiment that continues to this day.[10]

His preferred role model was his bookish grandfather, a statistics professor at the University of Helsinki. When Torvalds was about ten years old, his *morfar* (Swedish for "mother's father") purchased an early computer in order to do some of the calculations he wanted to run. Sitting on his lap, Torvalds would help type in the programs and read the manuals.

A few years later, when his *morfar* died, Torvalds, by this time an avid user, inherited the computer and became the only fifteen-year-old around town to own one.[11] Now that he could play on the computer whenever he wanted, his obsession became more intense. In *Just for Fun*, he recalls pretending to sleep just long enough for his mother, Mikke, to leave his room and then getting back in front of the screen and staying there throughout the night. Mikke describes her son as so focused and low-maintenance as a child that all he needed was "a spare closet with a good computer" and an occasional feeding of dry pasta.[12]

It was with this kind of single-minded focus that Torvalds would begin writing a kernel for a computer operating system in the spring of 1991. Aware that Stallman's GNU project had yet to produce one that was workable, he spent six months holed up in his mother's apartment, writing the code for his kernel.[13] He would roll out of bed, still in his bathrobe, and begin working on the computer. To minimize distraction (and glare on the computer screen), he put up thick black shades to block the sun from coming into his room.

Mikke describes him this way:

When you see a person whose eyes glaze over when a problem presents itself or continues to bug him or her, who then does not hear you talking, who fails to answer any simple question, who becomes totally engrossed in the activity at hand, who is willing to forego [sic] food and sleep in the process of working out a solution, and who does not give up . . . Then you know.[14]

Her description calls to mind the work of Professor Mihaly Csikszentmihalyi, a former chair of the University of Chicago's psychology department, who introduced to the discipline the concept of a "state of flow," in which worry and time fall away as one devotes one's full energy to the task at hand.

It is important to note here that Torvalds was only able to devote himself to writing his operating system kernel—able to enter that state of flow—because Finland's government happens to provide its students with free tuition and subsidies for living expenses while they're at university. With no deadline for graduating, Torvalds decided to take his time, earning his degree over eight years. During this period, he spent far more time writing code than writing papers—and the result speaks for itself.

On September 17, 1991, Torvalds released version 0.01 of his operating system kernel. It was originally dubbed Freax, but the person who posted the kernel to the university's public site for Torvalds so disliked that moniker that he unilaterally changed the file name to Linux.[15] More important than the name were the notes that accompanied the file posting, in which Torvalds included a fateful request:

> Anyone with questions or suggestions (even bug-reports if you
> decide to get it working on your system) is encouraged to
> mail me.[16]

Responses, ranging from comments of encouragement to bug fixes, trickled in from maybe five or ten curious users. A month later, version 0.02 was released with some of their suggested bug fixes and additional programs. As more and more improvements were added, Torvalds released more updated versions. Before the year was out, eleven new versions of the code had been posted for anyone to use and improve.

As the project progressed, Torvalds gave more thought to what form of copyright to protect it with. Early in 1992, remembering the talk Stallman had given the previous year, he decided to release version 0.12 under the copyleft terms of the General Public License. With that decision, users now knew with certainty that any labor they contributed to the project would be not for Torvalds's enrichment but rather for the growing community of fellow Linux contributors. By the end of that month, hundreds more had downloaded, used, and improved the now-GPL'ed Linux.

Torvalds went to such lengths to keep money from corrupting the growing community that instead of following the standard practice of accepting donations from users who downloaded a copy of Linux (as Stallman had), he asked them to send him postcards from wherever they lived. Soon, mail was pouring in from all over the world, filling up the apartment like popcorn in a kettle. Torvalds describes his decision to avoid monetizing his work this way:

> When I originally posted Linux, I felt I was following in the footsteps of centuries of scientists and other academics who built their work on the foundations of others—on the shoulders of giants, in the words of Sir Isaac Newton. Not only was I sharing my work so that others could find it useful, I also wanted feedback (okay, and praise). It didn't make sense to charge people who could potentially help me improve my work.[17]

With that spirit of sharing and cooperation firmly embedded in the terms of the GPL, users of GNU software programs knew that it was now safe to take pieces from that operating system project and add them to the Linux kernel, creating a more or less fully functional complete operating system. For this and many other reasons, it is more accurate to refer to the "Linux" operating system as a whole as Linux/GNU.[18] After all, Torvalds himself has written that "a kernel by itself gets you nowhere. To get a working system you need a shell, compilers, a library etc . . . Most of the tools used with linux are GNU software and are under the GNU copy-left." To this day, as much as 15 percent of the code for the "Linux" operating system is from the GNU project, according to GNU.org, while only about 1.5 percent is code that Torvalds wrote.

With the combination of the GNU pieces and the Linux kernel, the full operating system that Stallman had first envisioned almost ten years prior began achieving wider and wider adoption, with more and more people helping to improve and expand it over the next several years. As reported in *Wired* magazine, conservative estimates among tech analysts in 1997 had Linux/GNU running on at least three million computers worldwide, including the server that had produced a film released that year that would go on to gross more than any other up to that point in history: *Titanic*.[19]

In the fall of 1998, the Linux/GNU operating system was causing such a revolution in the world of software that Microsoft, in leaked strategy papers now famously known as the "Halloween documents," worried internally that "OSS [open-source software] poses a direct, short-term revenue and platform threat to Microsoft . . . Recent case studies (the Internet) provide very dramatic evidence in customer's eyes that commercial quality can be achieved / exceeded by OSS projects." One of the documents concluded with this warning:

> The ability of the OSS process to collect and harness the
> collective IQ of thousands of individuals across the Internet is

simply amazing. More importantly, OSS evangelization scales with the size of the Internet much faster than our own evangelization efforts appear to scale.[20]

The authors of this document were right. By the turn of the century, more than a third of the servers making up the Web were running on Linux/GNU.[21] In a few short years, all of that harnessed "collective IQ" would come to represent the "largest collaborative project in the planet's history," disrupting established wisdom about everything from the roots of human motivation to the social and economic conditions that underlie innovation and development.[22]

Because software is a difficult thing for most of us to appreciate (even when the code is free, most of us don't bother to look at it), consider that if today you were to use TiVo to record and watch a Pixar or DreamWorks Animation movie and then use your Motorola RAZR cell phone or Eee PC netbook to tell your friends all about it, you would be using Linux/GNU-supported technology every step of the way (not to mention that all of this information is available on Wikipedia—another free and open-source project, which we'll come to shortly—via the open-source Mozilla Firefox Web browser).

From a business angle, consider that the total revenue from Linux/GNU-related sales was estimated to have surpassed thirty-five billion dollars in 2008. Or consider that, perhaps most impressive of all, nearly 450 of the 500 most advanced supercomputers in the world run Linux/GNU, including the fastest supercomputer in the world, the Cray Jaguar, used at Oak Ridge National Laboratory, in Tennessee. The Cray Jaguar and similar supercomputers are what allow us to run the highly complex calculations behind everything from quantum physics to climate modeling to nuclear-fusion research.[23]

But how Linux/GNU went from a dark Helsinki apartment and

the dreary labs of MIT to running the world's fastest supercomputers is not a story about the coding expertise of Linus Torvalds or the dogged commitment of Richard Stallman. Indeed, the success of the Linux/GNU system is not so much about *who* (and certainly not in the sense of just a couple of fascinating individuals) as it is about *how*.

A Great Babbling Bazaar

The first clear articulation that the *way* in which the Linux kernel was developed might be more important than the code itself came from hacker-historian Eric Raymond. He presented his essay "The Cathedral and the Bazaar" at a 1997 developers gathering in Germany known as Linux Kongress.

Raymond argued there that until Torvalds came along, software had been unquestioningly developed in the fashion of most large-scale projects: via a centrally managed and closely supervised process that resembled the way one would go about constructing a cathedral. This, he said, had been true throughout the world of software, regardless of whether the effort had been free, like those of the Free Software Foundation, or proprietary, like the systems produced by Microsoft. In contrast, the environment that the Linux kernel had been developed in (after Torvalds had made his first draft public) was more akin to a "great babbling bazaar" where open collaboration occurred across a huge global network.

As Raymond wrote, "Linux was the first project to make a conscious and successful effort to use the entire world as its talent pool." In this way, he added,

> the most important feature of Linux . . . was not technical but sociological. Until the Linux development, everyone believed

that any software as complex as an operating system had to be developed in a carefully coordinated way by a relatively small, tightly-knit group of people.[24]

By steadfastly sticking to three core principles—transparency, flatter hierarchies, and open participation (or as Raymond put it more specifically, "release early and often, delegate everything you can, be open to the point of promiscuity")—Torvalds helped usher in a new era. This approach has come to be known as "open source," not so much for the license terms that the software is released under (as is the case with the free software itself) as for the way in which the software is created.

Indeed, it is a crucial point that the one missing part from the GNU operating system—the kernel—was the most complex of all. And while Torvalds's individual coding talent helped get his kernel project off the ground, he was only able to achieve truly exceptional quality once he started going beyond a small initial group to take advantage of contributions from thousands of people all over the world—the authors of all those postcards. Raymond has dubbed the principle at the heart of this development model Linus's Law, which states, "Given enough eyeballs, all bugs are shallow."

Partly to emphasize this newly emergent approach to creating software and partly to address the trouble created by multiple meanings of the word "free" in the English language (which was forever confounding journalists who tried to explain "free software"), the term "open source" was suggested as an alternative, and it was soon adopted by many, beginning in 1998.

While the two terms are still closely related (and many people consider them essentially interchangeable), there have undeniably emerged two sets of characteristics distinguishing the open-source movement from the free-software movement. And no two people better illustrate this divide than Linus Torvalds and Richard Stallman themselves.

For Torvalds, the primary benefit of the open-source model is that by having so many minds contribute, you usually end up with technically *better* software. If developers of other projects don't want to make their code free, that is simply their choice (although Torvalds thinks that such a choice usually puts them at a competitive disadvantage). Once asked at the end of an interview what message he would like to impart to readers, Torvalds replied, "Unlike Richard Stallman, I really don't have a message. I'm just an engineer. Let's see: Do things well! Do them with heart!"[25]

For Stallman, on the other hand, the driving motivation is not quality or convenience but rather to make as much software as possible free. Unlike Torvalds, he *never* uses proprietary programs on his computer, even when they are far better than the free alternative. For Stallman, it's the principle of the thing.

I learned this when, while requesting an interview over e-mail, I naively suggested to Stallman that we might use the free (as in beer) online video and phone service Skype. Little did I know that it is not free (as in speech) software. The first thing Stallman said in his reply to me was,

> If you want to write about the principles of the Free Software movement, the first crucial thing is to see how they apply in daily life.
>
> For instance, you just suggested use of Skype. That is a proprietary program, so people use it only at the cost of their freedom.

To suggest Skype to someone else means suggesting that he give up his freedom. And that's a really bad thing to do.[26]

Chastened, I have since gained an appreciation for what Torvalds meant when, commenting on the first time he heard Stallman speak, in Finland, he later wrote, "I was interested in the technology, not the politics—I had had enough politics at home." Indeed, while Torvalds has called the General Public License a "brilliant device" and suggested that Stallman "deserves a monument in his honor for giving birth" to it, his praise ends there.[27] While copylefting has worked for Torvalds and his kernel, he describes Stallman with words like "zealot," "preachy," and "irritating" for the way he tries to force the decision to use it onto other software developers. Torvalds writes in *Just for Fun*,

> The GPL is wonderful in its gift of letting anyone play. Just think about what a major advance for humanity that is! But does that mean that every innovation should be GPL'd?
> No way! . . . It should be up to the individual innovator to decide for herself or himself whether to GPL the project or to use a more conventional approach to copyright.

But for free-software proponents like Stallman, *all* software that is published should be free. Considering free software to be in a great battle with proprietary software, Stallman sees things in clear terms of black and white, free and non-free, good and evil.

A *Star Wars* fan, he is probably best described as a Yoda-like figure (though in his size and facial hair he bears more resemblance to Chewbacca). And Stallman has adopted the *Star Wars* analogy, using it to jab at Torvalds's willingness to cash in on his work. In response to his Free Software Foundation receiving an award named after Torvalds, Stallman remarked bitterly that it was "a bit like giving the Han Solo award to the Rebel Alliance."[28] The bottom line is that ever since the flickering flame of free software almost went out during his time at MIT, he has seen it as his life's mission to help keep it alive.

But while Torvalds and Stallman have different approaches and don't much like each other, it would be outrageous to claim that either the free-software or the open-source movement (or both) would ever have become as successful as it has without an emphasis on both of the sets of principles that the two men have come to personify.[29] In this way, the two are like computer-nerd versions of Kobe and Shaq, who likewise have very different approaches and do not like each other very much. Nevertheless, both players were essential to the Los Angeles Lakers' three-year championship run from 2000 to 2002. Similarly, the success of Stallman's and Torvalds's movements has depended on each of their approaches existing in a sort of dynamic equilibrium, a yin and yang for the free- and open-source-software world. Perhaps nothing illustrates the success of that balance more clearly than the story of a certain online-encyclopedia project that began in 2000.

"The Sum of All Human Knowledge"

As the turn of the past century came and went, Jimmy Wales was looking for his next project. Wales had been riding the dot-com wave during the last few years of the 1990s as cofounder of the cheekily named Bomis, Inc. (which semi-secretly stood for Bitter Old Men in Suits). As an Internet start-up, the company took an everything-but-the-kitchen-sink approach to earning a profit in the brave new world of online entrepreneurship, trying its hand at creating everything from an online food-ordering system to a search engine geared toward guys that resulted in something called the Bomis Babe Report, with many projects landing somewhere in between.

The focus (or lack thereof) of Wales's early ventures shouldn't belie the fact that he is also a serious student of philosophy who had previously pursued a Ph.D. in finance at Indiana University. While doing data analysis there on a Unix-based computer system, he happened upon the writings of one Richard Stallman, who at that time was hard at work on the GNU project and spreading the free-software gospel through a series of manifestos.

Stallman's ideas stuck with Wales, and a few years later he became inspired to try to take the idea of freedom as Stallman promoted it beyond software and apply it to written content more broadly. Pursuing a long-held dream of creating an online encyclopedia, Wales came up with the idea of starting a "Nupedia." Itself a play on the GNU name, Nupedia would even come to adopt a form of the GPL called the GNU Free Documentation License (GFDL) at Stallman's urging.

But just as the creation of the GNU operating system was slowed by what Eric Raymond called the cathedral approach, so too was Nupedia. Assuming that they would have to follow the standard model for gathering encyclopedic entries—engaging experts to write and review them—the founders of the Nupedia project adhered to a closely managed, centralized process in which only a chosen few were allowed to create and review the articles. After nearly a year of funneling articles through this complicated process, Nupedia only had a total of *twelve* completed articles to show for it. Clearly, making the license free, as Stallman had suggested, was only part of the equation.

The missing ingredient proved to be the spirit of open source as practiced by Linus Torvalds. That aspect would finally come to the project starting on January 3, 2001, when Larry Sanger, the sole staffer whom Wales had hired to run Nupedia, happened to meet an old friend named Ben Kovitz for dinner at a little Mexican restaurant in San Diego.

As their discussion ranged from life updates to philosophy, Sanger shared his frustration with the slow rate at which Nupedia was producing articles. Kovitz wondered aloud if his friend might gain something from checking out a Web site he had recently come across called WikiWikiWeb, which allowed anyone to edit any page at any time, without having to first get permission. In fact, developed in 1995 by programmer Ward Cunningham, the technology that appropriately gets its name from the Hawaiian word for "quick." By making anyone an editor, it resolved the problem of a long, drawn-out editing process by dispatching it in favor of near-instantaneous content creation and peer review.

In this way, a wiki can take the open-source development model to a whole new level. The principles key to Torvalds's success—"release early and often, delegate everything you can, be open to the point of promiscuity"—are literally built into a wiki's architecture. "Releases" (or edits) happen instantaneously, as soon as you hit the "save page" button. The barriers to contributing are lower than those of open-source-software projects because, while you need to be a fairly sophisticated coder to develop something that will be used in the Linux/GNU operating system, for example, all you need in order to contribute to a wiki is an Internet connection. Lastly, the entire effort happens with the utmost transparency, thanks to the logs that track any and all changes to a wiki page.

Sanger went back to Wales and suggested that they start a trial "Wikipedia" to see if this strange but empowering new method could help speed things up for Nupedia. Although it was started as a side project, as word spread, the new Wikipedia soon surpassed Nupedia. The latter was essentially abandoned within a year. As Wikipedia grew, Wales's original vision, "to distribute a free encyclopedia to every single person on the planet in their own language," no longer seemed quite so outlandish after all. Indeed, it is a realization of something that our democratic process has yet to fully take advantage of: a bottom-up, collaborative effort that functions better and more efficiently than its top-down predecessors.

Explaining Wikipedia's Success

Today, Wikipedia consists of over thirteen million articles in 262 languages, written by people all over the world.[30] In other words, comparing that number to the twelve or so articles that Nupedia produced in its first year, the difference between a closed and an open process proves to be a million-fold.

One of the top-ten Web sites in the world, Wikipedia now covers more subjects (and often in more depth) than the "expert"-authored Britannica and Encarta encyclopedias combined.[31] Impressively, Wikipedia has also managed to match Britannica for scientific accuracy while simultaneously offering articles on topics that the stuffier tome wouldn't dare include, from the "Buttered cat paradox" to the "Chewbacca Defense."[32]

Next to Nupedia, Wikipedia's stunning growth is easy to understand. Because wiki technology allows anyone to begin or edit an article at any time, there is far less of a bottleneck owing to insufficient time and resources. It can be difficult, though, to appreciate how revolutionary this simple idea is. Sometimes, for instance, Wikipedians will come across a commenter who posts a message along the lines of "this is not right" or "someone should do this"—the kind of standard-issue critiques that are so commonplace in our public conversations. But the difference is, on Wikipedia you just can't get away with that kind of passive, complaint-based attitude, as it is completely antithetical to the culture. So in response to such complaints, a standard refrain often appears: "SOFIXIT, it's a wiki after all!"[33]

Moreover, because all changes made to a page are recorded, there is no danger that content will be destroyed or lost. If an edit is not considered an improvement by the rest of the community, the article can always be edited yet again or simply reverted back to the way it was. In short, Wikipedia is designed to enable and encourage a trial-and-error type of participation.

The originator of the wiki concept, Ward Cunningham, recognized this early on, when he wrote that "wiki is *inherently democratic*— every user has exactly the same capabilities as any other user." However, it would be deeply misleading to imply that participation is anywhere close to approaching balanced on Wikipedia. Just because everyone has the same opportunity to contribute doesn't mean that everyone does.

First, there is wide variability in the adoption and use of Wikipedia across different languages. The English edition of the site has more than three times as many entries as the German edition, which claims the second-largest number of articles. In all, even though 262 languages are represented, about 70 percent of the articles are written in one of ten tongues.[34]

Within languages, rates of contribution are even more heavily skewed. While about seventy-five thousand people have signed up as editors of the English version, three quarters of all the edits made have been the work of fewer than fifteen hundred individuals, or a mere 2 percent of all those users.

This general type of pattern, where a small number of people contribute a vast majority of the content, is usually cited as an example of the 80/20 principle, or a power law. Heavily skewed distributions like this are not unique to Wikipedia (or Linux/GNU, where they are also present) but are, in fact, all around us, both in many human organizations and in nature.[35] The presence of power-law distributions helps illustrate why the term "open source" is important. "Open" implies potential, not automatic reality. In a more open-source society, the leaders who are the source of ideas and change will still be those who show up—the 20 percent who do 80 percent of the work, as is the case with Wikipedia. But *who* those 20 percent are and *how* they lead is changing, becoming not only more democratic but also more meritocratic and collaborative.

Consider what happens when a dispute arises on Wikipedia. A transparent, rational debate follows on a discussion page, where, in the words of Jürgen Habermas, "the forceless force of the better argument" is supposed to carry the day. In fact, voting to settle a dispute is widely discouraged on Wikipedia—some have gone so far as to adopt the mantra "Voting is evil." This sentiment, of course, refers not to casting ballots in an electoral context but rather to how the process can threaten the encyclopedic mission of striving for neutrality in all articles. In the latter context, the process of voting can too often and easily be manipulated, as the question at hand becomes less about what is true and more about what is popular.

A Fork in the Road

Speaking of popularity, back in 2002, Wikipedia was growing exponentially thanks to the contributions of a dedicated and expanding core of members. What it had yet to do, however, was reveal a clear way for Bomis, the struggling company that owned it, to turn a profit. While the project was free back then, in both senses of the word, it was still owned by a for-profit private company. In February of that year, facing declining revenue from its other ventures, Bomis was forced to lay off Wikipedia's sole staffer, Larry Sanger.

In a post to the community after this happened, Sanger suggested that his departure might not be permanent if Bomis could find a way to monetize Wikipedia:

> Bomis might well start selling ads on Wikipedia sometime within the next few months, and revenue from those ads might make it possible for me to come back to my old job. That would be great. I've liked this job very much, and I'm willing to do some work to help make it pay for itself.

A frequent contributor to the Spanish Wikipedia, Edgar Enyedy, saw Sanger's message and refused to stand for it. His hurried reply read in part,

> Nobody is going to make even a simple buck placing ads on my work, which is clearly intended for community . . .

And I'm not the only one who feels this way.

I've left the project.

You can see the Spanish Wikipedia development in the last two days and then you may think it over.

Good luck with you wikiPAIDia

Edgar Enyedy
Spanish Wikipedia[36]

While Wales and Sanger tried to backtrack and insist that no decision had yet been made, the damage was done. Enyedy knew that Wikipedia was governed by the terms of a GPL-style free license and that he was therefore entitled to "fork" the project, or copy all the content, move it to a new site, and then continue on as he wished. Finding a host Web site at the University of Seville, he did so, and the new effort came to be called Enciclopedia Libre. Enyedy managed to bring many of the most active contributors to the Spanish Wikipedia along with him, leaving the old site largely inactive for the remainder of 2002.

This incident, known as the Spanish Fork, convinced Wales that a free license wasn't enough to ensure that the ever-expanding community stuck with Wikipedia. To keep more forks from taking place, Bomis gave up all rights to Wikipedia and turned it into a nonprofit organization that to this day refuses to sell advertising on the site.

The Spanish Fork incident illustrates an important aspect of the open-source and wiki phenomenon: The motivation of its participants to contribute goes far beyond what can be understood in simple economic terms.

Of Bakers and Doughnuts

Our employment, or lack thereof, carries much weight in our society. Consider that in conversation once someone knows your name, the next question is often "So, what do you do?" Even many of our last names attest to the professions that defined our ancestors: Think of Smith, Carpenter, Chaplin, Shepherd, Baker, Brewer, or Weaver.[37]

But through wikis—or an open-source development process more broadly—people have become more able to contribute beyond a narrow role in the economy, outside of the profit motive. Yes, this has long been true of hobbies, volunteer and charitable work, incidental favors, and even some forms of economic consumption. But there are key differences that characterize this newer form of amateur involvement.

First, there is the sheer *amount* of this activity that is now enabled. With such low costs of communication and participation, group forming has become, in the words of Peter Kaminski, so "ridiculously easy" that anyone with an Internet connection can now contribute to an endeavor beyond their profession, simply because that's how they prefer to spend their free time.[38] As author Steven Weber writes, "firms and markets only tap into a piece of human motivation—an important piece certainly, but for many individuals only a small part of what makes them create."[39]

With those other motivations now unleashed, we have the privilege of pursuing more of the amazing diversity of things that truly, deeply inspire us as individuals, even if we don't happen to pursue them "for a living." Our reward when this happens is not only the creativity and beauty that can often result, but also a concept of our shared humanity that is far richer than that suggested by the "rational actor" caricature of economic theory, which proposes that we should care about nothing beyond maximizing profit.

Note here that the word "amateur"—that term so often applied to the thousands of unpaid Wikipedia contributors and Linux/GNU developers—has French roots that literally mean "lover of." In this sense, "amateur" could not be a more apt description for individuals like Edgar Enyedy. Clay Shirky picks up on this when he writes in *Here Comes Everybody*, "We are used to a world where little things happen for love and big things happen for money. Love motivates people to bake a cake and money motivates people to make an encyclopedia. Now, though, we can do big things for love." No wonder Enyedy was offended when Sanger suggested placing ads on his work.

Another difference with the kind of volunteerism we are now seeing is that the sum total of all these "extra" contributions can be something that rivals or surpasses the "professional-quality" products of profit-driven companies, as both Linux/GNU and Wikipedia have in their respective fields. Although the potential implications of this new Internet-enabled reality were first, naturally, glimpsed via open-source software, they are now visible across our economy to such an extent that authors Charles Leadbeater and Paul Miller have introduced the idea of a "Pro-Am Revolution" (also the title of their book), a trend marked by "amateurs who work to professional standards" popping up in fields and sectors far and wide.

Perhaps a more apt way of describing this emergent activity is that offered by the author Jeff Howe, who coined the term "crowdsourcing" in a 2006 *Wired* article. He wrote,

The open source software movement proved that a network of passionate, geeky volunteers could write code just as well as the highly paid developers at Microsoft or Sun Microsystems. Wikipedia showed that the model could be used to create a sprawling and surprisingly comprehensive online encyclopedia. And companies like eBay and MySpace have built profitable businesses that couldn't exist without the contributions of users . . . The labor isn't always free, but it costs a lot less than paying traditional employees . . . It's not outsourcing; it's crowdsourcing.[40]

Howe's book of the same name provides a thorough accounting of how and why, in his words, "the Power of the Crowd Is Driving the Future of Business." There's InnoCentive, for example, a network made up of 180,000 independent scientists all over the world that can receive a payday of up to one million dollars for solving research and development challenges that companies like the pharmaceutical maker Eli Lilly can't figure out in-house. If you have ever used a Swiffer duster, you've benefited from InnoCentive's brand of innovation.

But it is not just complicated scientific problems that can benefit from crowdsourcing. Relatively simple products have joined the game too. Threadless.com, for instance, is a site that accepts T-shirt designs submitted by anyone. The owners of the site then print whatever design receives the most votes from the community (which also provides a handy barometer for gauging demand and deciding how many will likely sell). The general practice has become so common in the world of product development that even Dunkin' Donuts recently invited its customers to offer suggestions for the next flavor it should add to its baking racks.[41]

All of this crowdsourced activity, from dusting to baking, is a kind of realization of a prediction that Alvin Toffler made in his

1980 book, *The Third Wave*. Toffler envisioned a breakdown of the separation between consumer and producer. A time would come, he correctly predicted, when "consumers" would take a more active role in the production process, sharing their ideas and preferences to such an extent that they would more accurately be termed "prosumers."[42] The ethic and approach of the open-source-software movement have done just that, and are now extending beyond the world of computers and programmers into our larger culture, increasingly influencing everything from our jobs to how we communicate. Going forward, we will have to develop new models of decision making and participation to accommodate this revolution, recognizing the new and expanded possibilities—and responsibilities—it holds for both our private and our public selves.

This shift is related to the rise of what MIT professor Eric Von Hippel has called, "democratizing innovation." The title of one of Von Hippel's books, the term refers to the way in which "users" are increasingly able to develop new products and services on their own and to make improvements to those they have already purchased. In this way, platforms like the Internet, and the communities it supports, help facilitate a kind of participation in society that goes beyond the standard role of the needy and passive consumer to one in which individuals can outpace manufacturers with innovations better designed to fit our needs and desires—even if those desires are for *less* of what they are trying to sell us.

Indeed, one of the most empowering examples of this form of "consumer" power occurred back in 1986, about as far from the world of technology and software as you can get. While he didn't use open-source software or a wiki to do it, Carlo Petrini modeled the idea of democratized innovation when he protested the construction of a McDonald's in Rome and sparked the Slow Food movement, which has come to reinvigorate appreciation (and demand) for local foods that are "good, clean, and fair." In the years since Petrini's first organized protest, the Slow Food movement has spread beyond Italy's borders to today claim over one hundred thousand members in 132 countries around the world. Although McDonald's may still be ever-present, it is no less true that an alternative, self-organizing, "co-producer" movement has also developed strong roots and begun to flourish.

A key goal of the Slow Food movement is to empower people to understand that our purchases determine what·is produced. If we choose food that is "good, clean, and fair," we can increase demand for it, and become co-producers with farmers, markets, and restaurants. As the Slow Food mission statement notes, "by being informed about how our food is produced and actively supporting those who produce it, we become a part of and a partner in the production process."[43]

I raise the example of Slow Food to make this simple point. The highest purpose of our newfound freedom and power to create (or co-produce) will probably not be that well measured on company balance sheets alone, nor will it be limited to online spaces. I don't mean to imply that business does not or will not have a vital role to play in solving some of our great social challenges. However, owing to their very structure and nature—private and profit-motivated— business enterprises alone simply cannot be counted on to solve challenges that are inherently public: the climate crisis, genocide, access to health care and clean water, etc.

For as neat as it may be to have citizen scientists figuring out how to make a Swiffer, we now live in an age when there are far-higher callings for our citizen scientists specifically and all citizens in general (and we might do well to consider "citizen" to be not an interchangeable term for "constituent" but rather, as George Bernard Shaw once wrote, the "highest rank" in a country, carrying deep responsibilities that extend far beyond voting and paying taxes). Indeed, the true promise of the open-source idea has yet to be realized, and I would submit that working on the great *public* challenges of our twenty-first-century society will give us a more fulfilling opportunity to connect to our deepest desires and abilities than designing a new doughnut (though we're grateful for sour cream and toffee).

Think of the choice this way. Wikipedia has allowed anyone to contribute to a public log of everything that *is* in the world of human knowledge. But when it comes to the next logical step—allowing people to participate in answering questions of what *could* or *should be* in the world—the extension of open source as a development model, or crowdsourcing, seems to have been applied mostly in the realm of private business, on behalf of corporations beholden to no greater interests than those of their shareholders.[44]

Social-change organizing, more effective government decision-making, and public problem-solving seem to me a better match for the idealism that originally inspired the rise of these movements. After all, Wikipedia is a site that dreams of a "world in which every single person is given free access to the sum of all human knowledge." Certainly, we will have squandered the promise and potential of the open-source and wiki movements from which that sentiment arises if we use the tools that come from them mainly as just one more way to hawk product.[45]

Indeed, beyond the knowledge of "what is" lies the wisdom of "what is right," raising the question of what kind of personal and collective action we can take to improve our lives and the world we live in. Surely we can also find a way to "open source" questions of this sort.

I am far from the first person to raise this possibility. For years, law professor Lawrence Lessig has advocated that the basic ideas underlying free software should also be applied to the legal profession, academia, and other realms of our culture and society, and has helped in that very application.

More recently, Beth Noveck has written about using the wisdom of the crowd to help tackle responsibilities that are under the purview of our federal government. In her book *Wiki Government*, Noveck tells the story of how she led the creation and implementation of the Peer-to-Patent process, a crowdsourced initiative that sped up the review of backlogged patent applications. The success of this effort has landed Noveck the responsibility of leading the Obama administration's Open Government Initiative, an effort that we will explore further in chapter 5.

Indeed, the indisputably public goods that are our laws and public policies are probably the last things that could ever be considered proprietary. So it makes sense that the barriers to collaborative problem solving in these areas might be far lower—and the results could be far more fruitful—than in the world of software, where the question of public versus private ownership is more contested. Even some nominally private efforts, like WebMD, the one-stop online site for whatever medical information one could want, are using a kind of wiki approach to create real-world public benefit.

All of these innovations suggest that we are learning to heed Schopenhauer's warning, refusing to take "the limits of [our] own field of vision for the limits of the world." The amazing array of possibilities that this wiki-inspired ethic opens up can be glimpsed when we consider this simple question: If enough eyeballs can make *software bugs* look shallow, what might happen to our great *social* challenges as we tap into and combine the stores of wisdom and will held by each and every one of us? For a look at how this story is already unfolding, let us now turn to the largest, most diverse, and first "digital native" generation in our history: the Millennials.

THREE

MILLENNIALS: THE OPEN-SOURCE GENERATION

Our answer is the world's hope; it is to rely on youth. The cruelties and the obstacles of this swiftly changing planet will not yield to obsolete dogmas and outworn slogans. It cannot be moved by those who cling to a present which is already dying.

—ROBERT KENNEDY

The characteristics of this civic generation will move the debate beyond the question of how to administer government programs to the more fundamental question of how decisions should be made and by whom. Instead of debating how to reinvent government, the country will debate how to reinvent its governance.

—MORLEY WINOGRAD AND MICHAEL D. HAIS

IN MAY of 2005, one of the largest and most successful youth movements in U.S. history took off. Having just graduated from college, I traveled to New York City for the catalyzing event, a convening of representatives from twenty of the leading youth environmental and clean-energy organizations that then made up the bulk of a growing coalition known as Energy Action. So you can appreciate the significance of this gathering and what would soon come from it, first a bit of background.

The Energy Action Coalition came out of the Climate Campaign, a common effort of six of the major student environmental networks that had a presence in the Northeast. The groups began collaboratively organizing their campaign efforts in 2003, after each had independently identified climate change as its top organizational priority. Not long after coalescing, the Climate Campaign organizations started working with leaders of yet more student networks, all over the country.[1]

In an early test of their reach and ability to work together, this expanded group of youth networks planned a joint day of action for "clean energy campuses" in the autumn of 2003. On November 13, groups on sixty five campuses all over the United States held events, blowing away the organizers' initial goal of twenty-five.

The day of action was an early indication that the youth organizations behind the then-nascent youth climate movement were ready to move beyond their contentious history. As Josh Lynch, a cofounder of the Energy Action Coalition, has written, these developments "brought the often fractured student environmental movement together in a way that [hadn't] been seen for years" and "signaled the birth of a new student and youth clean energy coalition."[2]

I first learned about the troubled dynamic in 2001, the year I joined the national governing board of the Sierra Student Coalition, as a high school senior. Still fresh in the memory of older, college-aged SSCers was a story they passed down to us from six years earlier.

In 1995, the four major national youth environmental organizations of the time—SSC, Student Environmental Action Coalition, U.S. PIRG, and Greenpeace—were all on their heels. Newt Gingrich's Republican Revolution had taken over Congress a year earlier, setting up party efforts to gut a series of environmental-protection laws, from the Clean Air and Water Acts to the Endangered Species Act. In response, the youth organizations decided to hold a joint "emergency campus environmental conference," which would take place at the University of Pennsylvania ahead of the twenty-fifth anniversary of Earth Day.

Officially called Free the Planet, the gathering attracted over one thousand students from thirty-five states, all rallying in support of a congressional "environmental bill of rights," to beat back the Gingrich-led efforts.[3] Culminating in a march to "alert the world" to the revitalization of the youth environmental movement in the United States, Free the Planet received national media coverage and was likely the largest student environmental event of the late nineties.

But before any momentum could be gathered from the conference, the coalition of organizations behind it disintegrated just as quickly as it had formed. One of the organizations involved took the list of the one thousand plus conference registrants and spun off a "new" student network named after the event. Going to funders, the Free the Planet group asked for grants to support what it could now call the largest student environmental network in the country. The problem? Its list was mostly made up of activists from the three other groups that had co-organized the conference.

The lesson we were supposed to take from the story was clear: When it comes to funding, don't trust other organizations. And indeed, following that breach of trust between the groups in the youth environmental community back in 1995, each had largely gone about its own business for the next six to eight years. The SSC, for instance, had enough going on internally—running six national campaigns simultaneously—without even considering outside collaboration.[4]

But after the day of action for clean-energy campuses in 2003 and some other successful collaborations, all of the groups involved decided to let go of the past and try to set a different example. Formalizing their collaboration, they created the Energy Action Coalition in June of 2004. The founding mission statement reads,

> To unite a diversity of organizations that will support and
> strengthen the student and youth clean energy movement in
> Canada and the U.S. Together we will leverage our collective
> power and create change for a clean, efficient, just and renew-
> able energy future. We will accomplish this by focusing on four
> strategic areas: campuses, communities, corporate practices,
> and politics.

By the time I came to Energy Action in 2005, leaders like Josh Lynch, Billy Parish, and Liz Veazey had already laid the groundwork for the coalition to move beyond coordinating national days of action, to the point where we could all consider organizing an entire national *campaign* together.[5] The need to decide what that common campaign might look like was the reason we all found ourselves in New York City on May 22, 2005.

The meeting was the first I attended as the SSC's newly hired national director.[6] Also in New York that day were representatives of most of the other national youth environmental organizations, including Josh Lynch, from Greenpeace; Julian Keniry, from the National Wildlife Federation; and a couple of leaders from the Student PIRG chapters. Representatives from the dynamic new regional organizations that were more explicitly climate focused were also there, including Liz Veazey, from the Southern Energy Network, and Josh Tulkin, from the Chesapeake Climate Action Network. Members of the Sierra Youth Coalition, the SSC's counterpart in Canada, also made the trip south to share their expertise. And of course, there was

Billy Parish, who had recently been hired as the Energy Action Co-alition's first coordinator. In all, there were thirty-one of us repre-senting twenty-five organizations, and we met for three days straight.

The motivation for our coming together started with a shared, stark realization: The climate challenge we collectively face is of such an enormous scale that none of our organizations could ever hope to catalyze in isolation a movement broad and diverse enough to meet it. During our time together, we each offered what we thought it would take to mount a campaign big and bold enough to make a real difference. The result was what came to be called the Campus Climate Challenge.

The idea was to take to scale the amazing work that had begun sprouting up at colleges and universities in the United States and Canada in order to make hundreds of our campuses "models of sustainability" for the rest of society. By demonstrating the benefits of moving to clean energy on campus first, we would have the expe-rience and credibility to ask mayors, governors, and presidents, "If we can do it, why can't you?"

When we added up the numbers of what we thought such a campaign would require, a two-million-dollar-a-year budget was up on the projector, spread across our twenty organizations. At that point, I personally felt pretty dejected—how could those of us whose only fundraising experience was asking student-government associations for a couple hundred bucks ever hope to raise an amount like that?

But others were undaunted. As the realization of the enormity of what we were doing started to settle in, Julian Keniry, a leader of youth-organizing efforts going back to her college days in the late

1980s, and the leader of the National Wildlife Federation's Campus Ecology program, provided the words we needed:

> In at least 16 years of professional organizing I have never seen a group come together and respect the vision, the inspiration, the contributions, and the capacity needs of all the organizations involved . . . It's a humbling thing to realize that your organization, your team can't solve this problem working alone. But it's a wonderful thing to know that we can come together and ensure that the whole can be greater than the sum of its parts.[7]

To make Julian's statement true, we knew we couldn't fundraise for our collective campaign in the normal, organization-versus-organization model that had sown seeds of discord in past coalitions. Instead we created a brand-new model that funders had never seen. Before we made a single funding ask, we collectively decided what our overall budget would be and how we would distribute funds to each organization, through a neutral fiscal sponsor of the whole coalition. Organizations could only ask for donations to the whole campaign, to be divided up as agreed upon, not for grants to support their individual work.

Decisions about which organizations should receive what amount were made in a strikingly straightforward way: Those with existing capacity in priority states came first. By virtue of our proven track records and large capacities, the Student PIRGs and the SSC were slated to receive the largest allocations.

In retrospect, the budgeting process we went through prior to fundraising reminds me of the largely nonpolitical process that open-source programmers have described through which they determine what code to include in a release: Their phrase is "Let the code decide."[8] For the coalition, it was something very similar, a kind of "Let the capacity decide." The questions we asked were "How many campuses is your organization already working with?" and "How many and what kind of campaign victories have you already demonstrated?" It was surprisingly uncontroversial.

With an agreed-upon budget and a fundraising plan in place, we set about the work of making our vision a reality. By the end of 2006, we had raised over three million dollars for the Campus Climate Challenge campaign. For a comparison, consider that in 2003, before the Energy Action Coalition was formed, only a little over one million dollars was invested in all campus clean-energy and climate organizing in the United States (and more than half of that was in one PIRG program).[9] This increase in overall investment is certainly part of what Julian meant when she invoked the phrase "greater than the sum of its parts."

But far more important than the amount of money raised is what it has enabled. The results speak for themselves: From 2006 to 2009, the joint effort led to over 660 campuses developing plans to go climate neutral—i.e., zero net greenhouse-gas emissions—complete with signed commitments from their presidents. It's Getting Hot in Here, the blog of the international youth climate movement, was launched by members of the Energy Action Coalition at a U.N. Climate Conference in 2005 and has since gone on to become the "largest youth issue blog in the world."[10]

Perhaps most important, the youth climate movement has helped lead the push for clean-energy and green jobs. In the spring of 2009, the coalition's Powershift conference, in Washington, D.C., attracted over twelve thousand young people from all fifty states.

After days of trainings and panels, the messengers of our future spread out across Capitol Hill for the largest day of lobbying for climate solutions yet to occur in the U.S.

Part of the reason for this growth and success has been a continued faith in our organizing model. The goal was to simultaneously create space for collaboration and relationship building while also respecting the individual creativity and autonomy of each group. Doing so allowed us to build a more powerful and vibrantly diverse new movement: Today, the coalition has expanded to include a wide-ranging array of fifty active and supporting organizations.

The reach of such a sprawling coalition was on full display in early 2007 when our member organizations coordinated a Rising to the Challenge Week of Action, encompassing 587 events across the United States and Canada. Building on previous days of action, such as Energy Independence Day (280 campuses, October 2004) and Fossil Fools Day (130 campuses, April 2004), the week marked an exponential progression of the resonance and power of our distributed organizing model.[11]

In recent years, the power of this organizing model has reached its greatest expression through the organizing of Step It Up and 350 .org, efforts widely supported by the Energy Action Coalition. Step It Up was a day-of-action-focused campaign started in 2007 by the author and activist Bill McKibben and a group of recently graduated Middlebury College students. Their day of action, on April 14, 2007, included fourteen hundred events in every single state in the country. Each gathering used some creative, media-worthy idea to call for 80 percent reductions in carbon emissions by 2050. Whether the event was a political rally, a community potluck, or a film screening— that was totally up to the group putting it on. At each event, organizers held up a banner that read, STEP IT UP CONGRESS: CUT CARBON 80%

BY 2050, referring to the long-term target that climate scientists then said it was necessary for us to reach to avoid destabilizing "climate tipping points." It was not long after the Step It Up events that both Barack Obama and Hillary Clinton—then still battling for the Democratic nomination—decided to make "80 by 50" the baseline of their climate-policy proposals.

More recently, the same core group that organized Step It Up formed 350.org in order to coordinate another day of action, on a global scale. The events of October 24, 2009, were designed to draw attention to the notion of 350 parts per million, the number now demarcating the "safe upper limit of carbon dioxide in our atmosphere."

The result? Millions of people at over five thousand gatherings spread across nearly every country in the world rallied around "the most important number in the world."[12] Events ranged from an underwater government cabinet meeting in the Maldives—designed to warn of what will happen to the country should seas rise as much as is predicted owing to unchecked global warming—to the largest single action of the day: a fifteen-thousand-student march through the streets of Addis Ababa, Ethiopia. All in all, these events were reported by CNN to be "the most widespread day of political action in the planet's history."[13]

McKibben, the cofounder and lead spokesperson of the effort, describes how the amazing 350 day of action was organized:

> Our structure is that we are not an organization. We are a campaign. The reason for that is to make it very porous. It's open source organizing, which is a relatively new idea. Our hope is that everybody grabs a hold of it and brands it with their own logos and does their own thing with it. The globe is too big

for any one organization to actually organize. In essence we are throwing a huge potluck supper and saying here's the date and here's the theme, now you guys cook. We'll try to coordinate just enough to make sure not everybody brings dessert. But that's about the degree to which we can centrally coordinate it. And we will make sure that the results of this big meal are seen around the world.[14]

In fact, as the twenty-five thousand plus pictures from around the world streamed onto the 350.org Web site, many of them were also appearing on the most iconic television in the world: the big screen in Times Square, New York City.[15]

The Climate Generation Gap

Aside from an open-source organizing model (which is another, related book in itself), what exactly is it about the issue of the climate that has inspired such deep passion and widespread action, as evidenced by the Energy Action Coalition, Step It Up, and 350.org?[16]

Certainly, the very scale and the systemic nature of the challenge have served to focus concern like no other issue in the post–Earth Day history of the environmental movement. Indeed, part of the reason for the passion behind the climate movement is that the Millennial generation—roughly, those born between 1979 and 1997, including nearly all of the leaders behind the Energy Action Coalition and a majority of the organizers leading 350.org—generally gives a higher priority to the environment compared to our immediate predecessors.

For instance, in a 2006 CBS News poll asking Millennials, "Which is the most important problem your generation will have to deal with?," the number-one response was "the environment," which was selected more than twice as often as "terrorism and war."[17] This trend continues to show up in more current polling as well, with a December 2009 Pew Research Center poll finding that twice as many voters under thirty view energy policy as a top concern compared to those who view terrorism that way. Compared to older generations, Pew notes, the Millennials are unique in this regard, with "other [non-Millennial] age cohorts generally consider[ing] the issues to be of similar importance or giv[ing] a slight priority to terrorism."[18]

However, it is also undeniably true that Millennial engagement with climate issues is about far more than our high rates of environmental awareness. In fact, I've found that concerns about poverty, hunger, human rights, and other issues have proven to be more of a motivating factor than concerns about "the environment" for many, if not most, of the young people that I've organized with.

Thinking of the climate as something beyond the environmental sphere can be a tough thing for those who have grown up organizing in more or less clearly defined "issue areas"—the environment, education, human rights, etc. But with systemic twenty-first-century challenges like climate destabilization, those categories now have far less meaning. As we come to realize that the climate is not a sub-issue of the environmental movement, we also realize that the expertise needed to solve the problem extends far beyond the relatively narrow arena of environmental-policy making. We need to look everywhere from psychology to farming, economics to building design. The same can be said of how we need to address poverty, genocide, or any number of other dynamic global challenges in the twenty-first century. The old categories just don't apply anymore.

But if the enormity of the issue was enough to bring the youth organizations together around this vision, the same was not true of our parent organizations or "adult" organization counterparts. Nearly to a person, the youth leaders representing organizations in the Energy Action Coalition felt that our primary responsibility was to build a climate movement—embodied in our powerful and diverse coalition—and that our respective organizational interests were secondary.

In contrast, leaders like Carl Pope, then executive director of the Sierra Club, often expressed sentiments such as this: "My number one responsibility is to ensure the success and future sustainability of the Sierra Club."[19] With organizational interests seemingly always taking precedence, groups like the Sierra Club, the National Wildlife Federation, PIRG, and Greenpeace have often worked together toward a common goal far less effectively than their youth-arm counterparts.

This troubling dynamic is often displayed in meetings of "the Green Group," a collection of environmental organizations that meets semiregularly in Washington, D.C., to discuss legislative strategy of mutual interest. What usually emerges is a dispiriting lowest-common-denominator approach, with influence in the hands of those organizations most willing to compromise shared principles in order to claim a narrow win for themselves. The Environmental Defense Fund, led by Fred Krupp, is one of the worst offenders, seemingly always ready to settle for symbolic legislation—no matter how weak or hollow—just so the organization has *something* to report as an "accomplishment" to its donors. Ensuring that the environmental community holds firm together on a basic principle, such as climate-legislation targets being guided by actual climate science, is merely a secondary concern, and sometimes a casualty, of the self-interested, organizational imperative.

Diane Ives, an environmental-grant maker for the past twenty years and an early supporter of the Energy Action Coalition, describes this tendency as "a kind of old-school thinking that's all about self-perpetuation of the institution." As she tells me, "most nonprofits will typically come with a proposal that says, 'This is who we are, this is what we do, yeah, we need to collaborate with folks over there. So give us money, and we'll collaborate with those people over there.' Then their reports will come in when the grant is up for renewal. So often it's 'That group we talked about working with, well, they didn't work with us.' Or 'We had a conference, and they didn't show up.' "[20]

With the Campus Climate Challenge, we didn't like the example being set by our parent organizations and decided to avoid this dynamic from the outset, at all costs. For instance, many established organizations had taken the path of calling for pollution-reduction targets mirroring those in the Kyoto Protocol, even though those numbers were outdated and inadequate. Our first decision, then, was pivotal: We committed to only calling for solutions actually up to the scale of the challenge, with targets firmly based on what science and simple moral responsibility demanded.

That meant (and means) a clear goal of moving to climate neutrality. In contrast to groups for whom setting targets was a negotiable political matter, we set ours by reading countless scientific reports, from Intergovernmental Panel on Climate Change papers to the Arctic Climate Impact Assessment, and only after consultation with leading climate scientists such as Princeton's Dr. Michael Oppenheimer and NASA's Dr. James Hansen, who both made it eminently clear that the science was not negotiable.

Second, and just as important as the clarity and integrity of our science-based campaign goals, we were committed to doing all campaign planning, budgeting, and fundraising in an open, transparent, and collaborative way. Without fostering trust and respect so intentionally—an aim also evidenced by our relatively flat decision-making structure in a council of all organizations consistently striving for consensus—we would never have attracted the range of organizations we were able to.

When Diane became the fund adviser for the newly founded Kendeda Fund in 2006, the failures of coalitions past were on her mind as she first read the Campus Climate Challenge proposal. "Before the Energy Action Coalition and the Campus Climate Challenge campaign, there were certainly coalitions that approached us asking for money," she says. "But with other coalitions I have seen, its component organizations decided to fundraise for their portion of the work individually. Making the decision that you all would *only* fundraise for the whole—and then share funds based on an already-agreed-upon distribution—was a model of joint fundraising that we had never seen before."[21]

Doing everything in this "all for one, one for all" way made potential partners and funders believe that we were something new and different, worthy of their faith and investment. And the approach extended beyond fundraising. Our campaign planning was done at in-person gatherings, before the beginning of each semester. When we couldn't put our heads together on strategy in person, we used Google Docs (a form of wiki) to develop campaign plans that everyone could see evolve in real time and that anyone from any member organization could add ideas to.

Diane again: Prior to Energy Action, we had been hesitant to fund youth environmental work. In the past, really interesting programs would start based on the vision of one or two people, and they would only stay vibrant as long as those people were around, which was often not very long, given the student context. When those founders left, new people came up and wanted to do the work differently, and the effort or organization would usually just get swallowed up or fade away. What made Energy Action and the Challenge campaign different was this idea that every group would sit down together and that it wasn't dependent on any one personality.[22]

In explaining where this approach comes from, the National Wildlife Federation's Julian Keniry offers a generational perspective. At forty years old, she is now a youth-organizing veteran who has seen different organizing approaches ebb and flow as each class of students has graduated. And though she did almost as much as anyone to make the Campus Climate Challenge campaign happen in its early days, she points to other, younger leaders as the reason behind the success of the Energy Action Coalition and the campaign:

"My view is that the Millennial generation is something special. I'm not part of it. There's just this alchemy . . . In the whole time I've been organizing with youth, I've never seen anything like this generation that is about ten years younger than me. Look at the sophisticated ways you all came up with to pay for clean-energy projects on campus—whether it's revolving loan funds, earmarking portions of student fees, or lobbying state legislatures. There's just this fearless, focused attitude of 'Let's roll up our shirtsleeves and get in there and get it done' and not just complain and protest like past generations."[23]

Ted Glick, a veteran social-justice organizer who was part of the antiwar movement in the sixties and seventies, and who now works with the Chesapeake Climate Action Network, also offers a generational assessment when asked what he thinks makes the Energy Action Coalition work so well: "Energy Action uses a much more consensus-oriented model of organizing, and there is much less individual ego from its leadership. During the Vietnam War days, there was just a constant clash of egos between different activists and organizations. Back then, you also had fairly strong, well-organized leftist parties that played a fairly significant role in those coalitions. These parties operated in a very hierarchical, top-down style that created a constant source of tension, leading some groups to drop away."[24]

After talking to Julian, Diane, and Ted, I became curious: If the key to the Energy Action Coalition's success really has been its unique generational ethic, as they say it has, was the same approach present in the other major youth movement that swept college campuses during the same 2005–2007 period?

Darfur and the Rise of the Anti-Genocide Movement

After soccer practice one day in September of 2004, Georgetown University sophomore Erin Mazursky took a short bus-and-metro ride into downtown Washington, D.C., to attend a program at the U.S. Holocaust Memorial Museum. Already well aware of the horrors of the Holocaust from her Jewish cultural upbringing, she was there for a program about the unfolding conflict in the Darfur region of Sudan.[25]

As she left the building after the presentation, Erin was in disbelief, with a lingering thought that she couldn't get out of her mind: "Genocide still happens today?"

At that point, as Erin told me when I interviewed her at a D.C.

pub one afternoon, soccer had been her passion for the past fifteen years. "I was very naive about activism," she said. But her hesitancy about activism turned into motivated anger once she realized that "no one was really doing anything about it." Stepping up to help fill the void as much as she could, during the fall semester of 2004 she cofounded a campus organization called STAND, which then stood for Students Taking Action Now: Darfur.[26]

Around the same time, 130 miles north at Swarthmore College, Mark Hanis was having trouble focusing on his senior-year classes. Having spent a semester in Sierra Leone during 2003, he had been involved there in the Special Court proceedings that charged warlord and former Liberian president Charles Taylor with crimes against humanity. While there, Mark had read Samantha Power's then–recently released book *A Problem from Hell: America and the Age of Genocide.*

Back at Swarthmore in 2004, the message from the book became so seared in his conscience that he had trouble thinking about anything else. "After I read that book," he told me, "it became clear that genocide needs to be treated as a security crisis, not as a humanitarian crisis."[27]

Part of the connection that Mark had to Power's book came from growing up in Quito, Ecuador, where, at his synagogue, he heard the stories of Jewish elders who had survived the Holocaust. His own father's parents had fled to Ecuador near the end of World War II, after being liberated from Nazi concentration camps. So from both family stories passed down through the generations and those he heard at synagogue, Mark knew that the only thing that had prevented the fulfillment of Hitler's Final Solution was the Allied Forces. As he told me, "sending only bags of rice when people are being killed is almost offensive. No one would have given a Jew in Auschwitz only a solar stove and then said, 'That's my response.'"

As he did more research, though, Mark found that such a one-sided response was essentially what was happening in Darfur. Amnesty International, for instance, was recommending that Americans write letters to the president of Sudan—an official whom American citizens have no influence over. "Amnesty does two things well: expose and denounce," Mark told me. "But when it comes to actually putting an end to genocide, asking Americans to write letters to prisoners of conscience or the heads of a foreign government does not work. I mean, Amnesty was even hesitant to label what was happening as what it was: genocide."

In response, Mark and some fellow students decided to found the Genocide Intervention Fund (now the Genocide Intervention Network, or GI-NET), to fill the void and serve explicitly as the "first permanent anti-genocide constituency." From the beginning, they focused on a two-pronged strategy. First, raise money for direct protection, such as funding equipment purchases for peacekeeping forces. Since 2004, GI-NET has granted over half a million dollars for this sort of direct protection.

Second, they wanted to exercise strategic political influence where it could make a difference—here in the United States. By starting the Web site DarfurScores.org, GI-NET made it easier for Americans to hold their *own* elected officials accountable. A comprehensive listing of what each member of Congress has done—or failed to do—to address the genocide in Darfur, the site bases each member's score on a series of votes and whether or not they have traveled to Darfur or cosponsored key legislation. The first thing you notice on the front page of the site is a box where you are supposed to enter your zip code. Type it in, and up pops a page that shows you what grade your representative and senators have earned on the issue (note to those in Connecticut's Third Congressional District: Representative Rosa DeLauro gets an A).

Before I met with Mark, I had come across an article about him and GI-NET in the *Christian Science Monitor* in which he was quoted as saying, "You're willing to help someone if they're in the same room . . . Why does 3,000 miles remove this responsibility?"[28]

The quote struck me. When I was directing the SSC and traveling to campuses all over the country between 2005 and 2007, the only issue besides the destabilization of our climate that was generating similarly intense passion and campus activism was the genocide in Darfur. Response to both issues has been driven by an existential sense of global moral imperative that is powerful, for sure, but is very different from the more directly personal and tangible conflicts that motivated student movements of previous generations (the civil rights battles and the Vietnam draft resistance, to name just two). So I asked Mark what he thought it was that made the climate and anti-genocide movements take off.

His explanation: "The Internet has made geography obsolete." Indeed, for those of us who have grown up with the Internet and its rapid evolution beyond e-mail to Skype, micro-blogging, and video SMS, it is easier to become aware of, *and then do something about*, whatever troubles us in the world. I asked Mark if there was also a generational difference in those whom he saw working to end the genocide in Darfur.

"With GI-NET, our intention was never to limit it to students. It was just that the most active people who responded were young. Look at the Darfur rallies," he told me. The largest of the rallies Mark was talking about occurred on April 30, 2006, when a coalition of hundreds of faith-based, student, and other organizations concerned about Darfur staged a seventy-five-thousand-person rally on the National Mall in D.C., calling for an end to the genocide.

By this time, Erin Mazursky was the new executive director of STAND, the largest student anti-genocide network in the country. In the less than two years since she had given up soccer for organizing, Erin had helped grow STAND to include groups on two hundred campuses. On the day of the D.C. rally, the chapters of STAND set up *eight hundred* student-lobby visits with members of Congress, all to urge the passage of the Darfur Peace and Accountability Act.[29] Six months later, the bill, sponsored in part by Barack Obama, was passed by both houses of Congress and then signed into law by President Bush.

The momentum of the movement kept growing, to the point where STAND surpassed seven hundred student chapters in late 2007. Thanks to increasing awareness of the genocide via online social networks, concern about the issue had spread far across the Millennial generation in particular by 2007. A survey of Millennials that year found that while "24 percent cited the war in Iraq as the most important foreign policy issue . . . 17 percent wanted the United States to first deal with the genocide in Darfur, Sudan."[30] Consider how astounding that is: Darfur was only slightly behind the most controversial American military engagement since Vietnam in participants' minds, even as some of those polled had friends and family fighting in Iraq. As Mark said, "The Internet has made geography obsolete."

Even with the passage of the Peace and Accountability bill, students concerned about the genocide were still not satisfied. For leading activists, it was not enough to get more peacekeeping money into Darfur; they also wanted to get the money that was fueling the violence *out*. Before long, and under intense student pressure, sixty colleges and universities would pass resolutions divesting funds from corporations contributing to the violence in Sudan, such as Petro-China.[31] With twenty-seven states, sixteen cities, and numerous pension funds following suit, Congress would pass the Sudan Accountability and Divestment Act before the year was out. When all was said and done, twelve companies were convinced to pull out of or significantly alter their behavior in Sudan within two short years.

While many organizations, from Save Darfur to the Enough Project, played a critical role in the successes of the anti-genocide movement, perhaps no single factor was as important as the merger that happened between STAND and GI-NET in 2006. With significant start-up funding secured by Mark and a hard-hitting political strategy including tools like DarfurScores.org and 1-800-GENOCIDE, GI-NET had everything going for it except a network of activists. For STAND, the reverse was true: An impassioned collection of student chapters, it lacked nonprofit status, a staff, and a coordinated political strategy. It soon became clear to the young leaders of both organizations that a merger would make them far more powerful together, in better service of their shared mission.

I asked Erin and Mark if there were any other examples of anti-genocide organizations merging to increase their strength. Neither was aware of any. As Erin told me, GI-NET and STAND were "the only anti-genocide organizations with youth leadership at the time. The organizations with adult leadership all stayed separate and were often in competition with each other . . . I don't think that's a coincidence."

Today, GI-NET has a full-time staff of seventeen and a $2.2 million operating budget. As its student division, STAND now includes over one thousand chapters, with most of the increase over the past few years attributable to high school groups. Staying true to its original mission of developing a "permanent anti-genocide constituency," GI-NET is looking beyond Darfur and is now also involved in conflict areas such as Burma and the Democratic Republic of the Congo. In Burma, the group is distributing radios to minority communities that can act as early-warning systems when violence breaks out. Mark's goal is to "get people to go beyond being Darfur advocates and really become anti-genocide advocates," which is related to an even more ambitious goal of "preventing genocide before it happens."[32]

Next Generation Leadership

When I interviewed Mark in GI-NET's D.C. office, he had recently finished reading Jim Collins's book *Good to Great: Why Some Companies Make the Leap . . . and Others Don't.* The book is based on a massive research project seeking out the factors that set the most successful and sustainable companies apart from the rest. Collins initially tried to avoid leader analysis, Mark told me, but he couldn't escape a clear conclusion of his own study: Leaders matter.

But it's not just any kind of leadership that makes the difference, and certainly not the kind of loud, commanding corporate leadership—à la Donald Trump—that our popular culture is so familiar with. Instead, Collins found the most effective leaders, "Level 5 leaders," are those who, in Mark's words, "put the movement or . . . sector ahead of the organization or individual." Indeed, Collins's research found humility to be a leading indicator of effective corporate leadership.

As Mark told me, this is the kind of leadership that he believes he and Erin strove for as they first started discussing a merger of the two organizations. His navigating the growth of GI-NET with this kind of broader, movement-wide vision has not gone unnoticed. Over the past four years, Mark has received three fellowships—the Echoing Green, the Draper Richards, and the Ashoka—in recognition of his "social entrepreneurship," and has invested all the money back into GI-NET. Billy Parish, the first coordinator of the Energy Action Coalition, has been similarly recognized for his movement-building, entrepreneurial approach, also receiving the Ashoka Fellowship, a year before Mark.

In yet another generational analysis, *New York Times* columnist Nicholas D. Kristof calls social entrepreneurs like Mark and Billy, "the 21st-century answer to the student protesters of the 1960s."[33] He writes,

> In the '60s, perhaps the most remarkable Americans were the civil rights workers and antiwar protesters who started movements that transformed the country. In the 1980s, the most fascinating people were entrepreneurs like Steve Jobs and Bill Gates, who started companies and ended up revolutionizing the way we use technology. Today the most remarkable young people are the social entrepreneurs, those who see a problem in society and roll up their sleeves to address it in new ways.

But if individual leadership has been key to the growth of these two youth movements, it's a different kind of leadership than is usually lauded in the business world. As Jane Wei-Skillern, a professor of social entrepreneurship at Harvard Business School, and Sonia Marciano, of New York University's Stern School of Business, have written of leaders like Mark and Billy (and also Erin and Energy Action's most recent coordinator, Jessy Tolkan),

> Unlike traditional nonprofit leaders who think of their organizations as hubs and their partners as spokes, networked non-profit leaders think of their organizations as nodes within a broad constellation that revolves around shared missions and values.
>
> Most social issues dwarf even the most well resourced, well managed nonprofit. And so it is wrongheaded for nonprofit leaders simply to build their organizations. Instead, they must build capacity outside of their organizations. This requires them to focus on their mission, not their organization; on trust, not control; and on being a node, not a hub.[34]

Sound familiar? It is the exact same model of leadership as that behind the open-source movement. Similar in nature to operating systems and encyclopedias, the social challenges that have most motivated the problem-solving energies of Millennials are global, complex, and systemic. And just as the quality of online open-source projects like Mozilla and Wikipedia surpassed that of proprietary projects like Microsoft Explorer and Britannica, networked, on-the-ground organizing is now proving more effective than the isolated-nonprofit or -issue model that defined a previous generation. Creating meaningful and lasting change in the twenty-first century will require avenues of participation for more and more people, at a scale and of a diversity that no one organization's membership roll will ever be able to capture. In short, the net-worked model is better suited to the problems we now face and is also more appealing to those who increasingly want to help solve them.

The Millennials

Generations are tricky things. Perhaps the best-known writers on the subject, Neil Howe and William Strauss consider the Millen-nial generation to be made up of those of us born between 1982 and 2003. But while their term has gained widespread acceptance since they first used it in their 1991 book, *Generations*, not everyone who now invokes the Millennial label agrees on exactly whom it in-cludes.[35] The Center for Information and Research on Civic Learning and Engagement (CIRCLE), for instance, uses the birth years 1985 and 2004 to bookend their interpretation of the generation. Mean-while, groups like the New Politics Institute and the Center for American Progress consider the much earlier 1978 to be the year of the first Millennial birth.[36]

Millennial is also far from the only name that has been used to describe this generation. The author Don Tapscott uses "Net Genera-tion" to categorize those born between 1977 and 1997. Meanwhile, renowned pollster and author John Zogby uses "First Globals" to describe the group born between 1979 and 1990. As if that weren't enough already, PBS titled a documentary about our generation *Gen-eration Next*, a label that the Pew Research Center (1981–2000) now uses interchangeably with Millennial in its polling reports.

To add to the confusion, there are other, earlier terms such as "Gen Y" and "echo of the baby boom," though none has caught on in quite the same way as "Millennial." This is largely because Millennial was a self-selected name, chosen by members of the generation from a list of options, as part of polling conducted by Howe and Strauss. The unique name proved far more popular than anything that defined us merely in relation to a preceding generation, whether our older Gen X cousins or our boomer parents.[37]

At any rate, dividing people into distinct generations is an inexact science, and, as evidenced by all those competing birth-year spans, generational theorists rarely agree on details like where one generation begins and another ends. Further complicating generational theory, individual members or large subsets of one generation will often exhibit traits or values ascribed to another. And of course, you can always find individual members of a generation who do not fit the ascribed general pattern at all. To move through this thicket, responsible demographers and generational theorists often try to distinguish between the kinds of influences that create generation gaps in values and opinions, and gauge whether they are likely to be lasting or more fleeting.

On the fleeting side is the life-cycle effect, which is perhaps most famously referenced in Winston Churchill's, patronizing old cliché: "Show me a young Conservative and I'll show you someone with no heart. Show me an old Liberal and I'll show you someone with no brains." This is the idea that people will let go of their ideals as they advance into adulthood and have to play different societal roles.

However, there are two other generational influences that can prove to be more lasting—"cohort" and "period effects"—and these are what really matter in predicting the impact a generation will have on our society. According to Pew, cohort effects are the "unique historical circumstances that members of an age cohort experience during adolescence and young adulthood, when awareness of the wider world deepens and personal identities and values systems are being strongly shaped."[38] For Millennials, think of broad trends such as growing up as digital natives, with the ever-present possibility of writing a blog, articles for Wikipedia, or an app for Facebook. Cohort effects, then, are those deep historical forces that shape a generation and then persist throughout the lives of its members.

Related to cohort effects but more distinct are period effects. These are the specific events that define an era—think of September 11, 2001, and early-September 2005, post–Hurricane Katrina. While all generations, of course, experience the period effects of historic events simultaneously, the lasting impact is usually more pronounced among younger generations, whose values and worldviews are still being shaped, than among older generations, for whom those are already more or less established.

With this in mind, I consider the period from 1979 to 1997 to be the range of birth years that best captures the Millennial generation. Those years include those of us who were both old enough to be aware of and young enough to be especially shaped by the unique and historic social trends and public occurrences (i.e. cohort and period effects) of the past ten-plus years, both in America and beyond.

These include the period effects of the attacks of September 11, 2001; Hurricane Katrina and its aftermath in 2005; and the election of Barack Obama in 2008. They also include longer-term cultural and technological trends, or cohort effects, such as the rise of major open-source projects like Wikipedia, peer-to-peer social-networking sites like Facebook and MySpace, and Web 2.0 innovations like YouTube and Twitter. All of these were enabled in part by the proliferation of the personal computer, the Internet, and cell phones. Beyond technology, the increasingly dire existential threat posed by the collapse of the world's climate is a cohort effect that this generation has been experiencing ever since we first started learning about it in elementary school science classes.

The clearest impact of all these combined historical circumstances is seen in opinions on the proper role of our government, the issue that Pew says is where "young voters differ most from older voters."[39] Indeed, 69 percent of Millennials "favor an expanded role for government, agreeing that it should do more to solve problems." This represents an incredible *twenty-five-point* polling gap between us and older generations, none of whom break 50 percent agreement with that statement.[40] As I write this, Republican Scott Brown has just won a U.S. Senate seat in Massachusetts, supposedly for promising to provide the forty-first vote against government health-care-reform efforts. Tellingly, Millennials were the only age group to vote against him by a wide margin, preferring his opponent to him 58 to 40 percent.[41]

I believe that this general divide is due to the unique period effects, or events, that have shaped the time during which we have come of age. As we have seen our government fail to effectively respond to events like Hurricane Katrina, unchecked climate destabilization, and human rights abuses like the genocide in Darfur, one of the things that has come to define our generation most of all is a visceral sense of the need for a more *active* government.

This is in stark contrast to the preference among boomers and Gen Xers for less government, as evidenced by the two-time election of Ronald Reagan, the candidate who famously said that "government is the problem." Note, too, that this was also the case throughout the 1990s and 2000s.

Indeed, when exposed to the evidence of young people's voting patterns over the past three general elections, Sir Winston's remark looks as though it has lost any modern relevance, if it ever had any. Gen Xers, those born in the sixties and seventies, were *already* fairly conservative when they were young. In the 2000 election between Bush and Al Gore, for instance, when eighteen-to-thirty-year-old voters were nearly all from Gen X, support for the two candidates was split right down the middle. In 2004, though, when half of eighteen-to-twenty-four-year-old voters were from the Millennial generation, their votes were enough to overcome Gen X conservatism and give Kerry a ten-point margin of 54 to 44 percent; it was the only age group he would carry. Most recently, in the 2008 presidential election, eighteen-to-thirty-year-old voters—who were all Millennials—backed Obama 66 to 32 percent over John McCain. Millennials will again make up the entire eighteen-to-thirty voting group for the next two presidential elections.

For Millennials in 2008, the Bush presidency in general and the aftermath of Hurricane Katrina in particular seared into our consciousness the failure of conservative, limited-government ideology. Seeing the saga of New Orleans unfold on live TV, we learned of the real human consequences of turning government programs (like those devoted to levee repair) into shells of their former selves, so they become "small enough to drown in a bathtub," as reactionary conservative and anti-tax activist Grover Norquist has called for. We learned that, rather than affecting some impersonal "government," the tragic results of such a goal impact our neighbors and fellow citizens. While the actions of our government may not always please us, we know that investing in its success is better than leaving our fate to the same unchecked private whims that gave us the subprime-loan crisis and the recession that officially began in December of 2007.

More important than the size of government, though, is what it accomplishes and how. Specifically, we Millennials, as citizens, want to play a more direct and active role in helping solve public problems and creating positive social change, in partnership *with* our government. For instance, Millennials volunteer at far-higher rates than Gen Xers ever did at our age: In 2006, sixteen- to nineteen-year-olds volunteered at *twice* the rate that teens in that age range did back in 1989.[42] But beyond those numbers and perhaps even more important is the finding that fully a third of Millennials express interest in "internet-based collaboration *with* government," and that half of us express an interest in working for federal, state, or local government—levels also significantly higher than for older generations.[43]

In short, then, the focus for Millennials is the *method of governance*. As Michelle Conlin wrote of youth voters in 2008,

> They understand the power of networked humanity. So a candidate who says, "Vote for me and I'll create a lot of programs," leaves them cold. One who says, "Join me, and together we can change this country and the world," takes a page right out of Web 2.0 and summons them to action.[44]

I think this shift also has something to do with the fact that the stakes of government failure in our time are qualitatively (and quantitatively) different for Millennials than for those who are not as likely to be around to deal with the consequences. For those in the Millennial generation, "the year 2050" conjures up not visions of some far-off fantasy future that we will not live to see, but rather a date when we'll only be in our fifties and sixties, not even ready for retirement. A simple Google search of the term "by 2050" reveals the kind of world we will have to learn to try to live in by then, from the apocalyptic—the number-one and -four headlines of my search result were BY 2050 WARMING TO DOOM MILLION SPECIES, STUDY SAYS and EARTH 'WILL EXPIRE BY 2050,' respectively—to the downright unfortunate and troubling (FORECAST: SEX AND MARRIAGE WITH ROBOTS BY 2050.)[45]

The worldview of those of us who will witness such things has been shaped in a fundamentally different way than that of previous generations (and, for that matter, those who will follow us). To be clear, it is not some magic gene that only showed up for an eighteen-year period that sets us apart, but rather the events and culture of our formative years, which provided us with unique lessons, values, and principles. Those in turn define who we are now and how we are likely to interact with one another and the world at large for the rest of our lives.

For regardless of the exact range of birth years (or the term you choose to use), it is indisputable that those now generally in their teens, twenties, and early thirties have proved to be profoundly different from preceding generations. As pollster John Zogby reports in his prescient book *The Way We'll Be*, "When we break our survey results down by age, First Globals [his term] often appear to be sui generis, a world unto themselves."[46]

Indeed, from poll after poll and book after book on the subject, a picture emerges of a generation distinguished by a set of common traits and values, which I list in the box below.[47]

Distinguishing traits and values of Millennials[48]

- Desire open avenues for participation and customization
- Favor flatter hierarchies and decentralized networks[49]
- Demand transparency: Process matters
- Favor cooperative and collaborative approaches
- Think in terms of systems and prefer global and interdisciplinary education
- Have a global outlook and are open-minded and tolerant of difference
- Are empowered by a familiarity and ease with using digital communications mediums and other technologies
- Are the largest generation in the United States by size and economic influence
- Are culturally and racially diverse[50]
- Seek common ground and do not contain many culture warriors[51]
- Prefer a more active and collaborative government
- Are politically active, with high volunteerism rates
- Are politically progressive/lean Democratic
- Are bearing the brunt of the current recession/have high levels of debt

---

What stands out most to me about this list is how similar the principles and characteristics that distinguish Millennials are to those that underlie the open-source movement. Notice how the first half of the list could just as easily be describing the foundational principles of the open-source movement. So, to the long list of alternate names for the Millennial generation, let me suggest adding one more: the Open Source Generation.

Identifying a familiarity and ease with digital communications technologies as something that sets this generation apart is hardly new. Author Don Tapscott suggested that "growing up digital" was the primary factor shaping the rising Net Generation as early as 1997. Marc Prensky authored the book *Digital Natives, Digital Immigrants* in 2001, suggesting that being surrounded by the digital environment from birth is akin to growing up speaking a language rather than having to go through the more difficult and time-consuming process of learning it as something "foreign" later in life.

However, because these terms say little about what *kinds* of digital technology we are drawn to, or about how we use them, they are somewhat limited in their descriptive power. On the other hand, open source and the unique Web 2.0 principles and values it has spawned mirror the Millennial philosophy almost perfectly. This is true not only as it speaks to our preferred way of using the net and other digital technology—via open, transparent, peer-to-peer formats—but also with regard to how we interact with one another and seek to engage with the wider world offline.

Millennials, for example, are the most tolerant generation in America and are more likely than the generations that came before us to support the ideal of equality of opportunity. Specifically, since 2008 a variety of polls have consistently found Millennial support for gay marriage to be between 58 and 61 percent, with opposition at about 35 percent. With older generations, those numbers are reversed, with 60 percent opposed to allowing gays to marry whomever they wish and only 33 percent in favor. This gap is so pronounced that the Center for American Progress predicts that simple generational replacement (older generations passing away and younger Millennials reaching adulthood) should result in a working national majority in support of gay marriage as early as 2018.[52]

Similar, though somewhat less pronounced, gaps appear with regard to opinions about women in the workplace and interracial dating.[53] In a 2009 Pew poll, for instance, one out of every three people born before 1946 and nearly one out of every five baby boomers reported that they do not approve of interracial dating. Compare this to the near-unanimous 93 percent of Millennials who approve of people dating whomever they wish, regardless of race.[54]

Why does all this matter? Just as with the open-source movement, opening up the *opportunity to participate* to all people—whether that be the opportunity to write code or simply the opportunity to live and love the way they wish—forms the bedrock foundation of the Millennial value system. From there, the core principles of the open-source movement and the Millennial generation are even more interwoven.

Linux, powered by global cooperation and collaboration, first came to mass attention in the late 1990s, just as use of the World Wide Web was becoming more widespread and the first Millennials began graduating from high school. As is true with the evolution of open source post–Linus Torvalds, the global outlook of Millennials is a major piece of what sets them apart from preceding generations.

In 1995–1996—the last year before the first Millennials began entering college—fewer than 90,000 American students opted to leave home and study abroad. However, as Millennials took over campuses through the next decade, learning in and from another country became incredibly popular, with the number of study-abroad students increasing by over 8 percent a year, to the point where a decade later the annual rate had more than doubled: 220,000 students received credit for studying abroad in 2007.[55] Even for those who stay in the United States throughout their undergraduate education, there is now a wider breadth to what they study. As the *Los Angeles Times* has reported, "U.S. Department of Education statistics show an 85% rise in the number of bachelor's degrees with double—and the relatively rare triple—majors over the last decade."[56] Thus, even when students are not physically going abroad, they are still trying to broaden their knowledge with multiple and interdisciplinary majors that do not limit them to one narrow field of study.

The global impulse of Millennials also appears beyond college campuses. Of the eighteen- to twenty-four-year-olds surveyed by Harvard in 2007, 59 percent reported that they had already traveled outside of the United States.[57] That same year, 56 percent of eighteen- to twenty-nine-year-olds reported having family or friends living outside of the United States, which Zogby compared to elder generations by saying, "No other age cohort approached that [Millennial] number."[58]

It's not just going abroad that contributes to American Millennials' global outlook; it's also having peers from other countries who have come to study in the States. In a 2006 speech titled "Globalization and the University," Yale president Richard Levin shared that "over the past three decades the number of students leaving their home countries each year for study abroad has grown at an annual rate of 3.9%, from 800,000 to 2,500,000."[59]

Much of that increase is thanks to the increased use of the Internet generally, and some of it, to the adoption of open-source principles more specifically. For instance, since 1991 the Los Alamos National Laboratory, in New Mexico, has hosted a free online archive where anyone in the world can submit and read papers. In 1996, an undergraduate physics student from the Czech Republic named Luboš Motl decided to post the results of his research in the subfield of physics known as string theory. His groundbreaking paper came to be seen by a physics professor from Rutgers University, in New Jersey, just one among the millions of views that papers submitted to the archive attracted each week. Not long after, Motl was offered a scholarship to Rutgers, where he would go on to earn his Ph.D.[60]

While individual stories like this may be rare, the broader lesson of what is now possible is powerful. Consider that fully 85 percent of the faculty at Richard Stallman's own MIT now provide their courseware freely, enabling anyone with an Internet connection to see syllabus reading lists, browse articles, and watch lectures. Over the last eight years, MIT has been joined in this effort by over two hundred universities across the world, which together form the Open Courseware Consortium. In sum, today's young people are simply no longer bound by geography—whether in education or in activism—to the degree that their parents and grandparents were. As Zogby concludes about Millennials, "for First Globals, the American Century is already over, and the Whole Earth Century has begun."[61]

Perhaps no event made this more clear than the election of Barack Obama—a man whose father had studied in the United States as an exchange student from Kenya and whose candidacy was rooted in large part in the promise of global cooperation.

2008: The Millennial Election

Barack Obama was the candidate of the Millennial generation. On Election Day, 2008, America saw the highest turnout of any general election since 1960.[62] Accounting for 60 percent of the increase in voters nationally, Millennials favored Obama to such an overwhelming extent—*66 to 32 percent*—that if they alone had decided the election, McCain would have carried a paltry eight states and fifty-seven electoral votes.[63]

In comparison, voters over thirty only very narrowly favored Obama, 50 to 49 percent. As Pew reported following the election, the difference between age groups represented "the largest gap ever seen in a presidential election between the votes of those under and over age 30." [64]

Though Obama would still have won the general election without the youth vote, it did make the difference in the states of Indiana and North Carolina. Nationally, young voters turned what would have been a close election into the landslide that occurred.

More important, without younger votes Obama would never have made it to the general election. In Iowa, the state that made people believe he was electable and gave him crucial early momentum, it is virtually certain that he would have lost the caucuses without the under-thirty vote.[65] Throughout the rest of the party nomination process nationally, his one-million-voter advantage over Clinton among youth more than accounted for the 150,000-popular-vote margin that he held at the end of the Democratic contest, not to mention the margin in delegates that allowed him to formally secure the nomination.

Perhaps of greater importance than young voters themselves were the young organizers who made sure their peers turned out, either for their candidate specifically or to vote in general. Indeed, on the Obama campaign, the online social-networking platform MyBarackObama.com was headed up by a then-twenty-three-year-old online strategist named Chris Hughes, while the candidate's deeply resonant message was crafted in large part by then twenty-six-year-old head speechwriter Jon Favreau.

Outside the campaign, nonpartisan groups adept at young-voter registration and turnout efforts, such as the United States Student Association and the Student PIRGs, also helped contribute to the surge in youth voting. The groundwork had actually been laid with earlier pioneering efforts such as 2004's New Voters Project, which helped increase under-thirty turnout nationally in that year's election by eight percentage points over 2000 (from 41 to 49 percent).[66]

But 2008 saw a whole new level of youth enthusiasm, and it was due most of all to Barack Obama himself. It is difficult to imagine a candidate better tailored for our generation. As David Von Drehle wrote for *Time* in his prescient article "The Year of the Youth Vote,"

> What concerns many [Millennials] is the nature of politics: the perceived gridlock of parties, conniving of special interests and shallow biases of the media. When Obama talks broadly about changing those dynamics, what strikes some older ears as airy and substance-free hits younger voters as the chime of insight. Washington University senior Matt Adler, 21, puts it this way, "What Obama brings to the forefront is the issue of process. It's not just what gets done but how it gets done; the morality of the process matters. *Being honest, open and inclusive is an issue in itself.*"[67]

Or as Michelle Conlin put it in an article for *BusinessWeek* titled "Youthquake," "Millennials are mobilizing around the idea that the federal government's *operating system* is in dire need of a sweeping update. Iowa and New Hampshire [where youth turnout increased 200 percent and 25 percent, respectively] proved that candidates ignore these voters at their peril."[68]

Indeed, the issues that motivate Millennials are qualitatively different from those that defined a previous generation of politics.

After extensive surveys of the Millennial generation, the Center for American Progress, for instance, has come to the following conclusion:

> One likely consequence of the Millennial generation's rise is an end to the so-called culture wars that have marked American politics for the last several decades. Acrimonious disputes about family and religious values, feminism, gay rights, and race have frequently crippled progressives' ability to make their case to the average American . . . Millennials support gay marriage, take race and gender equality as givens, are tolerant of religious and family diversity, have an open and positive attitude toward immigration, and generally display little interest in fighting over the divisive social issues of the past.

Perhaps some of this desire to move beyond culture wars comes from the very multicultural makeup of the Millennial generation. One in five Millennials has at least one parent who is an immigrant, and by 2016, the date by which all Millennials will have entered adulthood, the percentage of racial minorities of voting age will have risen to 43 percent.[69] Compared to today, a larger percentage of that total will also be multiracial, as "those under 18 are twice as likely as adults" to be classified as such.[70] Indeed, it is in large part because of Millennials—and the decisions that we are anticipated to make about having children—that whites are predicted to move from being a racial majority to being a racial plurality as soon as 2042.

This shouldn't be taken to mean that support for Obama among Millennials came only from racial minorities. Much to the contrary, 54 percent of white Millennials voted for him, compared to only 41 percent of whites from all other generations. Millennials often have more in common with one another, regardless of racial differences, than they do with members of older generations, even if they look just like them.

Obama is also an ideal candidate for young people because there are fewer Millennials at the poles of public opinion. The radical and reactionary extremes are represented more by our parents (or crazy uncles) than by us. As the Center for American Progress found in another study, "the ideological distribution among young people is both more progressive overall" and "*more compressed* than the ideological range among the total population."[71]

This preference for pragmatism over pure ideology goes beyond public opinion to influence the way Millennials go about social-change organizing. In summing up what she has learned while working with STAND and in the years since, as she has continued to do youth-empowerment work with movements around the world, Erin Mazursky told me, "Our generation moved from being activists to being advocates. We push on and engage systems of influence rather than attempting to create parallel ones with fewer resources. We connect the dots rather than trying to be the whole dot. And rather than attack public officials, we challenge them and then make them our allies."

Regarding the similarities between genocide and the threat of climate destabilization, Erin said that each is "about a moral imperative that anyone can understand." While the climate has unfortunately become a somewhat partisan issue for older generations (likely because of Democrat and former vice president Al Gore's lead role as a climate-solutions spokesperson), among Millennials making clean-energy investments and intervening to end genocide are both issues that attract broad bipartisan support. In fact, as I organized for clean-energy solutions, I noticed that many of the most deeply committed activists were socially conservative people of faith who felt called to care for creation.

To be fair, Millennials only have the ability to organize in this way, to move beyond the culture wars and focus on these global issues, because of the amazing progress created by generations before us. If there was still legalized racial segregation or if eighteen-year-olds did not yet have the right to vote, I am sure those causes would be top priorities of Millennial activists. Instead, because of the dogged commitment of activists who came before us, we have grown up in a more progressive world. Additionally, the infrastructure—namely, the Internet—allowing us to work in a networked and collaborative way was built by members of past generations to whom we also owe an enormous debt of gratitude.

I should reiterate that many young people today bear little resemblance to the larger Millennial portrait presented in this chapter. Similarly, there are many members of older generations who exemplify so-called Millennial characteristics and impulses as much as, or even more than, many twenty-year-olds. Such older people who embody some of the best qualities seen across the Millennial generation remind me of the words of Robert Kennedy, who said on June 6, 1966, in South Africa,

> The cruelties and the obstacles of this swiftly changing planet . . . [demand] the qualities of youth: *not a time of life but a state of mind*, a temper of the will, a quality of the imagination, a

predominance of courage over timidity, of the appetite for adventure over the love of ease.

On a still swiftly changing planet, a new generation—and those with the qualities of youth who would join it in common cause— now has the opportunity to build on the progress of those who came before it and create its own generational legacy.

That will mean far more than electing one good president who, as talented as he is, can only do so much on his own. More important, we should continue redesigning our social-change-organizing and government-decision-making models to engage far more people in solving all of the great problems of our society. For although our challenges can seem mind-boggling, so too is the amount of un-tapped wisdom and will we have at hand as a society. As Don Tap-scott writes in *Grown Up Digital*, "a billion people in advanced economies may have between two billion and six billion spare hours among them, every day."[72]

To help unleash that potential, the central political question of our time must cease to be about ideology and policy as we have tradi-tionally understood them and instead focus on *who* has the power to make decisions and *by what means*. For instance, is it liberal or con-servative to advocate for a more active government, but one that in-volves us in governing rather than trying to solve our problems for us? In truth, it is not "either/or" but rather "both and more," with the "more" being most accurately described as Millennial. It's not about issue ends or left versus right ideology; it's about how we get where we need to go as a society and who can help get us there.

In one sense, it's an old debate: The question of who has the power to participate in a democracy has always challenged us, from the Emancipation Proclamation to women's suffrage to the

Twenty-sixth Amendment, which gave eighteen-year-olds the right to vote. But this is less about who participates and more about whether that participation is substantive or superficial. Voting and giving money to candidates will no longer satisfy us in an age when we have information, tools, and values that call upon us to engage deeply in decision making and implementing public policy. With that, let's meet the leaders who are showing us how to do exactly this, through Web start-ups, the federal government, local and national decision making, and much more.

FOUR

DISPATCHES FROM THE FRONTLINES OF A NEXT GENERATION DEMOCRACY

When geometric diagrams and digits
Are no longer the keys to living things,
When people who go about singing or kissing
Know deeper things than the great scholars,
When society is returned once more
To unimprisoned life, and to the universe,
And when light and darkness mate
Once more and make something entirely transparent,
And people see in poems and fairy tales
The true history of the world,
Then our entire twisted nature will turn
And run when a single secret word is spoken.

—NOVALIS

ONE DAY in the late fall of 2007, a twenty-seven-year-old Web designer in New Haven, Connecticut, named Ben Berkowitz noticed some graffiti on his neighbor's wall. Unfortunately, it wasn't, as he says, "the cool kind. It was just crap . . . so bad that dogs would bark at it." After about a month of having to stare at the graffiti, Ben eventually decided to call city hall. Put on hold and transferred between multiple departments, he finally said to himself, "There's got to be a better way to solve this." Specifically, Ben envisioned a

Web site where people could post local problems on a map, with a message board to help citizens and government officials communicate transparently and efficiently.

Meanwhile, Ben's friend Miles Lasater was looking for a way to put his technology skills to use on behalf of social good. Searching for examples that married the two, he was, appropriately enough, on his honeymoon when he first heard of a London-based Web site called FixMyStreet. The site allows users in the United Kingdom to post reports of things like illegal dumping and graffiti (or, as those activities are known across the pond, flytipping and flyposting), which are then sent on to the local council for attention.

So when Ben called Miles to see what he thought of his idea, Miles immediately remembered the site and suggested that they give it a look. They both thought that FixMyStreet worked well and was similar to what they had in mind . . . but would building something comparable be worth their time? Would they be able to earn enough money to support themselves in the process?

With these questions still in his head over the Thanksgiving holiday, Miles sat down to dinner and shared the idea with his family. His father loved it and told him, "You have to do this!"

Back from the holiday break, Miles, his brother Kam, a software developer, and Ben all gathered at three one afternoon and made a deal: "If we can come up with something we like in four hours, we'll keep going." Just in time for dinner with friends, the three managed to build some code on top of a just-released Google Maps interface that allowed them to report issues. They also created a database where all reports could be stored. Within hours, the initial workings were far enough along that their friends tried it out after dinner, reporting some potholes and graffiti that were bugging them.

For four months, the three kept at their project, which they named SeeClickFix, devoting any free time they could find. An early, pivotal decision was that they didn't want the site to be a mere complaint board directed at government, like FixMyStreet. Instead, the SeeClickFix guys wanted to build in the capacity for feedback and collaboration *with* government and to enable people to volunteer to fix problems themselves. Another key difference between SeeClick-Fix and FixMyStreet is that, built on Google Maps, SeeClickFix is a platform designed for use anywhere in the world—or, as Kam Lasater likes to say, is "local everywhere." Comparatively, FixMyStreet is specific to the United Kingdom, both because of the limits of its mapping application and because the funding it receives—from a U.K. government ministry—explicitly limits it to this role.[1]

Soon the three SeeClickFix guys would enlist their friend Jeff Blasius, an application developer who was then Yale University's systems administrator, and the core team of founders was set. By March of 2008, an alpha version of SeeClickFix was ready. Not only did the early site enable users to report a non-emergency issue that was bugging them—say, a pothole or a clogged storm drain—but users could also create a "watch area," to get e-mail alerts whenever anyone reported a problem that included a keyword they were interested in (say, "light out") or that was in their neighborhood, however they defined or mapped it. Crucially, in addition to allowing anyone to create a watch area and sign *themselves* up for alerts, the site let users sign *others* up (provided they had an e-mail address for them). Finally, to help particularly important issues get more attention, the SeeClickFix guys added the functionality of voting for and/or leaving a constructive comment on any issue.

Ben used the watch-area function early on to create a "graffiti" keyword alert for New Haven's Livable City Initiative (which, as he eventually learned, is one of the departments tasked with handling spray-paint-related problems). Just to make sure, he also set up a similar keyword e-mail prompt for a "merchants association clean team" also responsible for removing graffiti.

The moment when Ben finally knew that all their efforts had been worth it came early one morning in the spring of 2008. Driving his wife to work at seven, he noticed eighteen buildings along his street that had been spray-painted during the night. As soon as he returned home, he reported the issue on SeeClickFix. When he went out to get some dog food at the gas station (one of the places that had been tagged) a few hours later, there were already city workers painting over the graffiti outside. As Ben soon found out, they had been dispatched almost immediately after the city had gotten the e-mail notification following his post.

An hour later, Ben got a call from his alderman, Roland Lemar, who had also gotten the e-mail alert because the graffiti had happened in his ward. When Ben picked up the phone, Lemar started saying, "I called city hall about this and am trying to get through to people—" until Ben interrupted him to say, "They're already out there!" The same thing happened when the merchants-association team called Ben a few minutes later to say that they would come and clean it up tomorrow—no need.

Interestingly, this early incident prompted the city's Livable City Initiative and a local business improvement district to realize they had overlapping roles, motivating them to get together and divide up responsibilities. Now one removes graffiti at ground level while the other focuses on cleaning up paint sprayed on second stories and above. In this way, an online, nongovernmental organization has not only helped augment city services but has streamlined them too.

More important, many people besides Ben started using the site to report their own issues—issues that went far beyond potholes, graffiti, and clogged storm drains. With problems all over the city, the site soon started to fill with posts. It became a place to report everything from drug dealing and prostitution to the need for a new public transit line and a supermarket in an underserved area of the city.

From the beginning, Wikipedia's model of distributed empowerment was an inspiration and model for SeeClickFix. As Ben says, "there's no way we could, or would want to, write all the content for every issue or sign up every government official for alerts . . . so we crowdsourced the reporting and the watch areas from the very beginning. In terms of moderating what is written, we allow anyone in the community to flag something as inappropriate."[2]

Indeed, Ben says that the most exciting thing about the evolution of the site has been watching all the ways in which SeeClickFix is being used that its founders never anticipated. Early on, for instance, multiple complaints were posted about Yale Shuttle buses speeding through residential New Haven neighborhoods and running red lights (as in many university locales, New Haven and Yale have a long history of strained "town-gown" relations). "At first, I wasn't so sure SeeClickFix was the best place to try to fix that, but we consider the site public space, so we generally let the community use it however they want," Ben says.

In one of my favorite examples of how SeeClickFix has empowered New Haven residents to challenge aspects of Yale's culture and practices that bother them, a wonderful SeeClickFixer reported the headquarters of the university's famed secret society Skull and Bones for blight. More maddening and far less humorous was the post that read, "[Y]ale shuttle sped through a light that had already turned red, almost hitting two pedestrians, one was a small child"[3]

In response, and to Ben's surprise, the very first comment on that post read,

> Please send as much info as possible on this incident to Donald, who runs the Yale transit system:[e-mail address]. Based on exact time of day, driver description and other info, he should be able to track down the details and investigate. Yale uses a GPS system on its fleet.

When a similar issue occurred a month later, it was clear that a protocol had been established, with quick responses from the university.

> Juli—a representative from [Y]ale just called and said the driver has been disciplined, and this situation has been used for training purposes and a reminder to the bus company that "there is no quota that they need to fill. slow down. there is no rush." . . . He also reiterated that recording the bus number, time and place are crucial in dealing with these issues.

There has been one drawback, though, to bus speeds slowing down thanks to the vigilance of SeeClickFix users and the cooperation of Yale's administrators. "My neighbors are now cursing me out for having to drive behind slow buses," Ben says.

Most regular school buses don't have GPS systems that allow managers to track driver speed. But SeeClickFix users have nevertheless figured out a way to report non-GPS buses too. One New Haven citizen took a video of a speeding school bus, managing to get the bus ID number, a reading from an electronic radar speed sign, and the posted speed limit sign all in the space of one ten-second YouTube video.[4]

Although some of these issues might seem relatively minor in the grand scheme of things, Ben believes that starting with things that improve your everyday quality of life can be the "gateway drug" to greater civic involvement. Say someone reports a speeding bus one day, and the next day the same driver goes by their house under the speed limit—that kind of tangible difference can be very empowering. Or as Ben says, "while reporting a pothole on a Web site might not seem like it's the ultimate act of good citizenship, it's a sign of the end of apathy and the beginning of giving a shit."[5]

Fixing something, he tells me, feels so good that it's kind of addicting: "It starts to make you think about things you haven't been doing but could." After using SeeClickFix, Miles Lasater's sixty-year-old dad—the one who insisted they give the site a go—started picking up trash he saw on the street for the first time in his life. It's a habit Ben has gotten into as well: He'll pick up an abandoned pair of glasses and put them on top of a parking meter or reposition a traffic cone that's been knocked out of place.

In isolation, such behavior may not sound terribly impressive, but just imagine the possibilities when whole communities experience this transformation. Say the person who reported the speeding bus decides to clear a clogged storm drain because they now feel more of a sense of ownership and responsibility for their street—that's one less work order for an already overworked Department of Public Works. Multiplied across a whole city like New Haven, such acts can make a big difference, especially at a time when public budgets are stretched dangerously thin.

The Reach of SeeClickFix

As of March 2010, over three thousand people were receiving watch-area alerts from SeeClickFix, and the site was getting over two hundred thousand views a day. Most of the views come via news companies that have embedded the SeeClickFix tool on their local news sites, including Gannett's *Tennessean*, Hearst's *San Francisco Chronicle*, and Tribune's *Baltimore Sun*.

Indeed, SeeClickFix has quickly spread beyond New Haven to become a national and even global phenomenon. Those who use the site are no longer mostly located in Connecticut, but rather in northern New Jersey and the Philadelphia area. Dallas; California's Bay Area; Louisville, Kentucky; and Minnesota's Twin Cities, Minneapolis and St. Paul, have also become some of the most active metropolitan areas. Ten cities, from Tucson, Arizona, to Lansing, Michigan, benefit so much from using SeeClickFix for municipal services that they pay for expanded "pro" or "plus" versions.

In total, upward of two hundred local news sites feature it, including Charlotte, North Carolina's WBTV, which runs a weekly "See Click Fix" television segment reporting on whether and how posted problems are being fixed.[6] Further speeding its adoption, there are SeeClickFix apps for every major mobile device, allowing anyone with an iPhone, a BlackBerry, an Android, or some other version of mobile Web to see, click, and fix right from their phone.

The site is also used from Australia to Argentina. Other countries with active user communities include Canada, France, Italy, and Bulgaria. Fully translated into six languages, the site also has translations in progress for three more languages as I write.[7] To learn more about how all this came about, I interviewed Ben on one of the few days he was in New Haven between his frequent trips around the country.

When Ben and I first talked, we met at SeeClickFix's newly rented offices. Appropriately, the building they're in is across the street from the construction site for a future grocery store in a neighborhood that was known as a "food-desert" before SeeClickFix and its legion of Fixers helped bring attention to the problem.

The first thing you notice about Ben is his engaging, easygoing personality. For the head of a start-up company, he seemed incredibly relaxed (though there was much more gray in his hair than you'd expect to see at only thirty years old). Short and fit, he greeted me wearing a simple T-shirt and jeans.

As he showed me inside and gave me a tour of the offices, he told me that they'd gotten the place for a deal, after the previous tenants had left without paying, putting the landlord in a tight spot. Luckily for SeeClickFix, the situation had left them with a random assortment of furniture, including a useless but fun old metal pay phone, at no extra cost. Except for the leftover furniture, a fresh coating of bright orange paint, and—interesting considering the Web site's history—a few pieces of art from a local graffiti artist, the place was pretty bare.

Once Ben was sitting down and telling me his story, his infectious enthusiasm carried him along for close to three hours, only ebbing once he got hungry enough to suggest that we go grab a slice of pizza. After just a few minutes with him, he struck me as the kind of guy who was probably always getting in trouble in high school, but then just as easily getting out of it too. Creative and hip enough to make money selling original T-shirts (including the popular "marriage is so gay" design), he has nevertheless devoted most of his energy to two things that ten or twenty years ago would likely have been considered quaint and nerdy: civic betterment and Web development. In today's Millennial world, though, doing good through innovation is attracting the savviest of young entrepreneurs.

Ben is following in a long tradition of innovation, civic and otherwise, to come out of New Haven. I quickly learned this from Andy Horowitz soon after moving to the city in the late summer of 2009. Horowitz is well known around town for his oral history projects and being one of the few Yale history Ph.D.s who actually grew up in New Haven.[8] Describing his city as having "invented the hamburger and perfected the pizza," Horowitz rattled off with pride that New Haven is also known as the home of Eli Whitney, who developed the cotton gin here; Walter Camp, "the father of American football"; and the world's first telephone exchange.[9]

But more visible and far more lasting than its role as a host to individual ingenuity has been New Haven's role as a laboratory for public experimentation. From 1954 to 1970, the city's mayor, Richard Lee, was a tireless advocate of "urban renewal." During his tenure, the city spent nearly three times as much money for that purpose, per capita, as any other in the United States.[10] From his position of power, Lee had whole residential neighborhoods torn down and rebuilt with the offices and shopping malls of his imagined "model city." With enormous amounts of federal money directed to the city, projects of the time also included sections of Interstates 91 and 95, which were laid down in a way that divided poor, predominantly African American neighborhoods, all in a centralized, high-modernist effort to make New Haven "the first slum-less city."[11]

Out of the ashes of some of the over-centralized failures of that period have come public innovations based more on community engagement. Seeking to address poverty and crime more comprehensively, for instance, New Haven realized that relationships and individual empowerment can be just as important as bricks and mortar. In the late 1980s, the city instituted one of the first community-policing programs, with police captains meeting face-to-face with neighborhood groups.

Just a few years ago, New Haven also instituted the first "resident card" in the country, allowing all of its residents (even those who came to the United States illegally) access to an ID card. Now less afraid of being profiled or arrested, many residents are now choosing to do simple things like open their own bank account. With fewer residents having to carry all of their cash on them, the city has seen a decline in muggings and robberies.

New Haven does have some particular attributes that facilitate such innovation. For one thing, its size—150,000 people—makes it an ideal "beta-test city." As Yale president Richard Levin is fond of saying, New Haven is small enough to be friendly and large enough to be interesting. And with the possibility of knowing most of the political players in town, creating change is more imaginable than in more impersonal cities with large bureaucracies and greater institutional inertia. At the same time, innovations in New Haven, a multiracial city with vast economic disparities, carry weight with larger cities facing similar demographic dynamics.

Yale also plays a role in making New Haven an especially fertile place for innovation, though not in the ways you might expect. Most of all, Horowitz tells me, with the university employing ten thousand residents, there is a degree of economic stability that helps the city weather economic shifts that might hit other places harder. The situation is similar in other college and university towns, and places that have a similarly stable large employer, such as a hospital or a government research agency.

Indeed, the biggest shift in the city's civic life over the past couple years has had less to do with the fact that there happens to be an Ivy League university here than with the kind of distributed citizen empowerment that SeeClickFix has helped unleash. Building on the community-policing efforts of the 1990s, for instance, New Haven's police force now gets SeeClickFix alerts for the different areas of the city covered by its lieutenants. More important, officers have contributed to the site's message boards to give residents tips on how to safely report more serious issues, such as mobile, car-to-car drug dealing.

Police department engagement with the community hasn't been limited to the site's message boards either. After a spate of muggings and robberies in the city's Wooster Square neighborhood, neighbors who had posted about the crimes on SeeClickFix decided they should start meeting in person to see if there was anything they could do.

I attended the third meeting of the group at a school library one evening in September of 2009. About a dozen people turned out, and the agenda opened with introductions all around. When asked how many had been using SeeClickFix and who had found out about the group through the site, everyone raised their hands.

As the meeting got going, Officer Pete Krause from the New Haven Police Department was in attendance to give an update on recent criminal activity in the neighborhood. "Compared to a few months ago, it's been pretty tame over the last month. I really think it is because of community vigilance and people making calls," he began, going on to sum up the numbers. "Only three thefts from motor vehicles, three reported burglaries—none while the home owner was there—no forced entries."

One of the women in attendance had come because her sister

had been mugged nearby a couple months earlier, so Krause offered some suggestions about how people could avoid being a target. "Most victims of street robberies are victims before they are victims, because they are not paying attention," he told the group. "Your behavior matters: Don't walk down the street with your eyes down. Walk with your eyes looking around and your chin up. People with self-confidence have an air about them. If you want, there are also self-defense classes you can take down on Wooster and Warren." When the meeting concluded, Krause gave everyone his personal cell phone number and told them to call if there was ever anything he could do to help.

As the formation of the Wooster Square group shows, it doesn't make sense to talk about "online" and "offline" as though the two were disconnected from each other. SeeClickFix serves as an online platform for offline action. And the real power of the site, which is like a more problem-solving-focused version of Meetup, is that it's set up to encourage self-organizing of the kind the Wooster Square group has done.

Other examples abound. One day, a New Haven jogger came across some large pieces of a fiberglass boat that had been dumped along a trail. Rather than bother the city about it, an all-volunteer group called Friends of East Rock Park decided to meet up over the weekend and drag away the trash.[12]

Like Wikipedians who will say "SOFIXIT" to those who do nothing but complain or suggest things that *other* people should do, SeeClickFix does not encourage passive participation. Granted, a few of the issues posted on the site make you want to roll your eyes, things like "my neighbor won't pick up his trash." But for many of SeeClickFix's users, it has become a rule of thumb that you shouldn't complain about an issue that you yourself can fix (say, by talking to your own neighbor). And as Ben told me, "there's a real advantage for government in having a citizen say to another citizen, 'Why ask for a Department of Public Works officer when you can do it yourself?'"

As Ben suggests, the complaint-based, parent-child relationship we tend to have with those we elect—the kind where we ask them to solve problems for us and expect to give nothing in return except some taxes and maybe a vote and a campaign donation—is especially ripe for change. In the age of open source, not only is such a model inefficient, but it also borders on insulting to the many people who are ready to solve problems themselves, if only they are given the opportunity to do so.

Take Brian Tang, for example, one of the top Fixers in New Haven. The first time Brian learned about the site was at the beginning of his freshman year at Yale, when he volunteered to help plant some trees along a roadway. "The thing that drew me to SeeClickFix is that it helps me create the type of place where I want to live," he told me over coffee. "If government is not responding to get things done, why not just find a way to make our neighborhood better ourselves . . . In the end, we might be more capable anyway."

Brian's pragmatic, solutions-oriented approach became even clearer when he told me, in prototypical Millennial speak, "It's kind of like the opposite of protesting. With SeeClickFix, I can focus on what I want to happen, not what I don't want to happen." And is there ever a lot that Brian wants to see happen. Since he started contributing to SeeClickFix in 2008, he has posted 76 issues, voted for 31 others, and made 372 comments, earning "He-Man" status with 7,840 "civic points" as of January 2010.

After he started using SeeClickFix, Brian said, he experienced a "distinct change of mind-set." Instead of thinking, "This is what I want done; you should do this," he started focusing his thinking more on questions like "What needs to happen in order for something to change . . . and what is my own responsibility to help make that happen?"

One of his answers to that question was his decision to stay in New Haven for the summer after his first year of school so that he could intern with the city. Interested in improving road infrastructure, expanding bicycle access, and figuring out ways to serve people's transportation needs beyond cars, he learned from city engineers. He said that the internship taught him things like "how even jaded, skeptical engineers can be engaged if you learn to sympathize with their concerns."

His time working for the city also changed the way he contributes to SeeClickFix. "I am definitely much more careful about what I write now than before . . . You realize that 'government' isn't this faceless thing, that it is made up of real people," he said. "It's better to respect and collaborate with them rather than just complain at them."

Indeed, not content to live in the bubble of his assigned residential college, Brian, now spends most of his time out of class volunteering in New Haven with friends he's made beyond the walls of the university, including Ben. As Ben (who, like most of New Haven's residents, did not go to Yale) told me, "Brian is what I would like every Yale undergrad to be like—totally connected to New Haven. He's helped with road design, drawn up ideas for how to improve public spaces, and has helped out at a few festivals."

Brian's main focus has been what's known as the Humphrey Street underpass, which divides the neighborhoods Upper State Street and Jocelyn Square. Amazed by how separate the two adjacent areas can seem due to an interstate underpass, he made a school project out of figuring out ways to help unite them. In the ensuing months, his project brought together local community activists, who decided to focus on public artwork and community events that might help bring the underpass to life and make travel between the two neighborhoods more inviting.

Spending so much time on the project, Brian has formed a kind of bond with the underpass: "It's this totally neglected place. But I've seen it in the morning light and at night . . . the way its concrete has aged, the way the trees on the embankment contrast with the trucks overhead . . . it can really be beautiful." His short film about the underpass is perhaps the most powerful way to express the results of his work (check it out by searching for issue number 3909 on www .seeclickfix.com). But in lieu of pop-up video, consider the "artist's statement" that Brian wrote to accompany his film:

> This is a film about two lonely neighborhoods, separated by Interstate-91. It is about longing. Longing to come together. Longing for friendship, for a sense of place. Wanting to belong.
>   This is a film for those who share that vision, who are ready to build a neighborhood, a place where people can live and connect.

And that's the beauty of the story of SeeClickFix and Brian Tang. In a high-speed world of such frenzied pace, it has been an Internet start-up, of all things, that has helped increase community involvement and, in the process, made relationships and place-based connection less tenuous for some of its users.

I asked Brian what he thought he might want to do after college. Only in his sophomore year, he nevertheless told me that he has dreamed of saving up enough money to buy an abandoned factory on Upper State Street and make it into a green-building supply store, some kind of workshop for manufacturing cargo bikes, or perhaps something like Pike Place, the famous Seattle market from the region where Brian grew up, the Pacific Northwest. "I don't know if I would ever do that," he said. "I'm always dreaming about different things . . . But at least now my dreams have a specific location—New Haven. I've found a place that feels like a home."

Heart & Soul Community Planning

Brian's sentiment is one that Lyman Orton knows well. A seventh-generation Vermonter and third-generation storekeeper, he is the co-proprietor, with his three sons, of the Vermont Country Store.

After graduating from Middlebury College in 1963, Lyman moved back to his hometown of Weston to help run the family business and was also soon appointed to the Planning Commission. In the late sixties, within months of the commission's updating the Town Plan and Zoning ordinances, an out-of-state developer came up with the dubious idea of building an amusement park called the Wildlife Wonderland in Weston, at about twenty-five hundred feet of elevation.[13] The park, the developer boasted, would attract visitors with large African animals and carnival rides.

Because the park did not fit into the Town Plan in any ecological, cultural, or historic sense, the Planning Commission opposed it. Weston's residents, however, were more divided, and to Lyman's dismay, they turned on one another in a battle that would leave scars for years to come. On appeal, the developer suggested using farm animals instead of African megafauna, and the Animal Farm got its permit, opening for business in 1973 (and staying open for five whole months before going bankrupt).

Come the 1980s, the entire state was in the midst of a surge in commercial development and second-home construction. With ski areas being built up and down the spine of the Green Mountains, Lyman observed residents' surprise at the resulting changes to their towns that were never anticipated in their town plans. He began questioning the ability of town plans to truly shape these communities' futures and finally became convinced that significant changes were necessary to enable residents to do so. In 1995, he decided to devote profits from the Vermont Country Store to establishing the Orton Family Foundation with his friend Noel Fritzinger.[14]

"The problem with planning as it is normally done," Lyman says, "is it's often guided by a town plan that will sound good on paper—Mom and apple-pie stuff—but that lacks specificity. With little in the way of guidelines or touchstones to understand what the citizens of the town really want, decision makers end up approving proposals on the narrow metric of what it will do to 'grow the economy' or 'expand the tax base,' forgetting every other part of the town that matters."[15]

To help communities better understand the impact of such decisions, the Orton Family Foundation's first order of business was developing a piece of software for 3-D visualization and impact analysis that they called CommunityViz, a kind of SimCity for the real world. Today, it is the most widely used tool of its kind, helping thousands of communities weigh alternate futures by illustrating the impact of different planning scenarios. By providing a sense of how different kinds of growth will likely impact interconnected issues such as traffic patterns, availability of affordable housing, downtown walkability, environmental quality, and public-infrastructure costs, CommunityViz allows towns and cities to make more-informed planning and growth decisions.

Helping to heal ideological divisions, the tool has allowed communities to move past the simple dichotomy of growth versus no growth. As Lyman says, it's time to "get beyond that idea that we're going to stop growth or have NIMBYism [not in my backyard] rule the day. Change and growth, yes, they are going to occur . . . but let's hang on to those things that are these essences of the community. Those are the things that I think should be the basis for planning, the foundation upon which we start planning processes."[16]

But can communities capture their "essence" with a 3-D-visualization tool alone? No. As the foundation soon learned, quantitative measures of things like traffic flow and demographics are certainly necessary for good planning, but they're far from sufficient. So Lyman and the rest of the foundation set about finding ways to include what they call "the intangibles—[the] shared values, beliefs and quirky customs—that make a community."[17]

With that vision in mind, the foundation has since evolved beyond producing software tools and is, in addition, now pioneering a whole new model of community planning. Based on the belief that citizen involvement should happen at the very beginning of the decision-making process, Heart & Soul Community Planning is an approach that engages the residents of a place through community gatherings and events where people are asked questions like "What keeps you here?," "Why did you move here?," and even "What would cause you to leave?"

With events that encourage residents to share stories about what matters most to them, communities build trust and respect from the outset of a planning process. Eventually, the Heart & Soul approach comes to help communities identify the unique things about their place that its people most value and therefore most want to preserve and/or use as a foundation for future growth.

As Lyman explains it, when a community identifies the various elements that it collectively holds dear, cherishes, and loves—and produces a Heart & Soul document that clearly articulates these elements—it's in a position to help elected officials drive decision making about the town's future based on its heart & soul.

In Steamboat Springs, Colorado, for instance, local workers value what's known as "the powder clause." Though it's not written in employment contracts, most employers know and honor the rule, which goes like this: If the five A.M. snow report says there is eight or more inches of new powder, it's OK to head to the mountain and be a few hours late for work. But as a friend of Lyman's recently told him, "with all of the shifting of local ownership . . . to remote places somewhere else, I worry that the powder clause is going to be cause for getting fired." Losing the clause may not sound like a huge sacrifice to many, but for people who stayed in a place or moved there precisely because of their love of skiing, it means a lot.[18] And while the powder clause itself may not become a basis for town planning, the broader principle that it highlights—the importance of locally owned businesses that understand the local culture—certainly could.

Once specific values and attributes are identified—whatever those may be—communities are able to make planning decisions based on a common set of transparent and agreed-upon priorities. And beyond helping communities to arrive at better planning decisions, the Heart & Soul approach also allows them to get past the old government-versus-citizens dynamic in which the only time the voice of the people is heard is when citizens react angrily in protest of something they don't want—usually at a "public hearing," or what my friend Ed McMahon of the Urban Land Institute describes as "one of the fun places in America today where almost nobody listens to what is said."

Whether alternative, meaningful, grassroots engagement happens online via SeeClickFix or in a school gymnasium during a Heart & Soul event, it is an approach to public decision making and problem solving whose time has come. As Matt Leighninger writes in his visionary book, *The Next Form of Democracy*, "citizens seem better at governing, and worse at being governed, than ever before . . . We are leaving the era of expert rule, in which elected representatives and designated experts make decisions and attack problems with limited interference, and entering a period in which the responsibilities of governance are more widely shared."

As important as the models of SeeClickFix and Heart & Soul Community Planning are, it would be wrong to think that such engagement is only feasible at the local level.

Legislation 2.0

During the summer of 2007, U.S. senator Dick Durbin posted an open letter the likes of which had never before gone out from the staid and formal chamber of Congress he hailed from. It read, in part,

> I write this open letter to invite you to participate in an experiment—an interactive approach to drafting legislation on one of the most significant public policy questions today: What should be America's national broadband strategy?
>
> Starting next Tuesday, July 24, I will be engaging in a series of four nightly broadband policy discussions with the online community. During those four nights, I am looking for the best and brightest ideas on what Congress should do to promote and foster broadband."[19]

In conclusion, the letter read, "As I said at the outset—this is not the traditional way legislation is written in Washington. Some people think that by giving people other than policy experts and special interest groups a seat at the table, this process will never work. I believe differently and I have a feeling that next week, we'll prove them wrong." The person tasked with coordinating this "Legislation 2.0" experiment and helping to prove the senator's prediction true was a grad student named Russell Newman, in D.C. for a summer fellowship focusing on telecommunications and broadband policy.

As Russell told me, one of the major goals of the effort was for Senate staffers who are "hungry for new information and ideas" to break out of the pattern of going to the same folks for advice over and over again. To get a sense of what exactly it was about the normal policy process that the senator and his staff wanted to get away from, I asked Russell to describe the way legislation usually comes to be introduced in Congress.

The first thing I needed to understand, he told me, was "how few people are responsible for handling such a mind-boggling array of policy issues." A House office, for instance, will usually have only six people working on all of the issues that the congressperson needs to know about and vote on. To cover all that ground, each legislative assistant, or LA, will be given a basket of as many as fifteen significant issues. Needless to say, it's nearly impossible for one person to become an expert on all of the intricacies of all of the pieces of legislation that surround one issue, let alone fifteen. So staffers are forced to improvise.

Once the congressperson gives some initial direction on the broad outlines of what they would like to see in a bill, the staffer has to fill in the rest. Usually, Russell told me, whoever is charged with handling the issue will then call everyone they know who has a position on it—whether for or against—and ask them for their ideas on what should and should not go into a bill. Usually these people are fellows and policy experts at think tanks. One might think that academics could or should have a role here, but Russell told me that academic articles generally "give you too much . . . You just don't have time to sift through it all. With a limited amount of time, you end up relying on think tank briefs instead." The extent to which members of academia are involved in policy-making processes depends on efforts, either by their home institution or by a surrogate activist group, to make their materials "digestible" and get them publicized. Often this just doesn't happen, exposing a major weakness in need of significant attention from both academic and policy leaders.

Anyway, Russell continued, as soon as any idea gets floated, even before a draft of the bill has been written, "affected industries will get a whiff of it and ask for a meeting." After meeting with all the lobbyists who have a position to share, the LA will then go to the staff lawyers and ask them to draft legal language to reflect whatever set of goals has emerged from the meetings. With a draft in hand and the congressperson's approval, the staffer will call other staffers on the hill, pass language around, and then start asking other legislators to join as co-signers of the bill.

All in all, it's a fairly clubby process, with a predictable set of inside players participating over and over again. Consider that even when "open" hearings are held in Congress—which are supposed to be open to the public, first come, first served—lobbyists will stop at nothing to make sure that only their voices are heard. "Early in the morning," Russell told me, "I'd pass by lobbyists who would be paying homeless people to stand in line all day for them. Ten minutes before the committee hearing would start later that afternoon, those same lobbyists would come back and take the place of the guy they paid and walk into the hearing room to take their seat."

This is part of what Senator Durbin's office was trying to break free of with the Legislation 2.0 experiment. Partnering with the well-known progressive blog OpenLeft and its founder, Matt Stoller, the senator's office arranged for four straight nights of live blogging. The topics would run the gamut of issues to consider in crafting a comprehensive broadband bill. The last such bill to pass in the Senate was the Telecommunications Act of 1996, which was signed into law just as the Internet was beginning to be part of the mainstream.

On the first night, July 24, Durbin sat down with some staff along a wall of computers just outside his office and typed in a welcome message. Over the next six-plus hours, 150 comments were made by forty-three participants, from all over the country.[20] The discussion was so wide-ranging and detailed that at one point one of Durbin's staff exclaimed, "The citizens are out-wonking us!"[21]

Perhaps surprisingly, the discussion was incredibly well focused. A knowledgeable few—eight people wrote more than half of the comments—guided the discussion, with comments trickling in until one thirty A.M. Given the nature of the topic, both specific and serious, and with participation open to anyone yet naturally self-selecting (who wants to write something that exposes their ignorance in front of a senator?), spam and off-topic comments were minimal to nonexistent. And the structure of the comment threads—responses to an original post appeared together—also served to make the discussion somewhat navigable.

Over the next three nights, outside experts with a range of opinions on the various issues related to broadband policy were invited by Durbin's office and Stoller to host their own live-blogging discussions on OpenLeft.

After the opening run on OpenLeft, conservatives rightly started complaining to Durbin's office that limiting the discussion to a left-leaning blog was leaving out other voices. In response, a week later Durbin did another round of live blogging on RedState, a conservative blog, with similarly successful results.

At the end of nearly two full weeks of soliciting ideas from two of the most active sites in the blogosphere, Durbin and his staff had a number of options to sort through. As Russell told me, the main point of the live-blogging effort was to "fish for ideas" and "bring in folks for an open, honest debate." The senator was not disappointed; as he wrote at the conclusion of the Legislation 2.0 experiment,

> I figured at the outset that if I gave the broader public a chance to comment on these issues, a few good ideas would emerge. I was wrong. What I found instead was a significant number of well-reasoned perspectives and ideas that I had not previously considered. These ideas covered the gamut of policy areas, including net neutrality, incentive programs, spectrum policy, and community broadband.[22]

With the heating up of fellow Illinois senator Barack Obama's presidential campaign, however, Durbin's focus shifted to more pressing matters. Amid the demands of serving as national co-chair of Obama's campaign and majority whip in the Senate, momentum behind the Legislation 2.0 experiment began to fade away.[23] To this day, Durbin's office has yet to sort through all of the ideas that were suggested in the live-blogging sessions and draft legislation. As Russell, who left the office after that summer to finish his Ph.D., told me, "Legislation 2.0 got only about a quarter of the way through idea-generation stage, then stopped. I hardly consider what we did to be the pinnacle of what's possible . . . We offered a discussion and took comments on it, but that's a far cry from open policy making."

In some ways, it's only possible to guess what might have happened had the effort been seen through to completion. In the limited experiment that took place, challenges were already apparent. "The way policy gets made relies on a small circle of trust based on relationships formed over time," Newman said. "It's very difficult for bloggers to develop that from afar . . . When you have some random screen name post something like 'Support net neutrality or else!,' it just doesn't come across with the same gravitas as when a staffer is asked politely by someone in a suit, in the flesh."

Russell also believes that there is likely a limit to how far the usefulness of blogs can extend across the policy-making process: "As far as soliciting ideas for new legislation, this approach works. But if you want to get into all the ground-up pork, chicken, tofu, indigestible plastic matter, etc. that makes up *existing* legislation, it would be almost impossible for a blog or a wiki to be able to take that apart and make it work."

The sheer complexity, he told me, is mind-boggling. Often, only a small handful of people have studied a piece of legislation closely enough to know what it all means and the implications of how it fits together. "The way that legislation, particularly major legislation, such as 'universal service' provisions in telecom law, is written, there are so many interlocking parts—you know, 'If section 27.4 is true, then section 87 holds . . .' It's like a Choose Your Own Adventure book, except without the fun."[24]

If this confusion arises with relatively straightforward policy issues like broadband, how can we meaningfully engage citizens on the really large and complex issues, such as climate change or health care? For that, we will need far more than blogs.

The Deliberatorium

In recent years, there has been an explosion of online efforts designed to tap into the wisdom of the crowd for problem solving and idea creation, or "ideation." Google's 10 to the 100th project, for instance, attracted 150,000 submissions after the company committed ten million dollars for up to five ideas that would "change the world." To pare down the list, Google asked three thousand of its employees to sort through the sea of submissions. The process was so complicated that the project fell nine months behind schedule. By the end of 2009, sixteen broadly outlined proposals (one of which is essentially a description of what SeeClickFix is already doing) had been patched together from multiple submissions of the same or similar ideas.[25]

Other, more government-facing projects have included those of Change.org, Change.gov, and the Better World Campaign, which all held open contests seeking to influence President Obama at the beginning of his term. The most popular question that emerged from Change.gov was whether or not Obama would support the legalization of marijuana. The Better World Campaign—"after a year of debate, over 5,000 ideas submitted, and close to one hundred thousand votes"—was hardly any more serious, the top suggestion for the new president's inaugural act in office being almost purely symbolic: that he plant an organic garden at the White House.[26]

Mark Klein, a principal research scientist at MIT's Center for Collective Intelligence, says that for all their promise, idea-sharing sites like these often fall prey to multiple, recurring problems. From redundant posts crowding out other, more unique ideas to early lock-in because of self-reinforcing popularity (when people vote for only the issues that they see already at the top), these sites may be democratic in the strict sense, but they are often so poorly organized that they fail to be either representative or effective.

As Mark writes about the organic-garden idea that emerged from the Better World Campaign, "that vast investment of collective effort resulted in selecting a tiny, purely symbolic, gesture . . . Surely that amount of effort could have been used to compose a smaller number of more deeply-considered ideas, rather than many shallow ones."[27] To address these problems, he has created a tool he calls the Deliberatorium.

"Before I came up with the Deliberatorium," he tells me, "I looked at what was already out there allowing people to deliberate and share ideas in a public forum. Chat rooms, blogs, and wikis were certainly good for getting lots of people to weigh in on a problem . . . but they can be a mess. You'll get a huge amount of input, only for the gems to get buried."[28] Indeed, the double-edged sword of blogs is that by allowing anyone to participate in whatever manner they wish, innovation is often pushed aside by ignorance and irrational bias.

Further, when it comes to complex problems in particular, you often get what Mark calls, "multiple, disjointed, balkanized discussions" that fail to add up to any kind of coherent, comprehensive solution. Because tools like blogs are organized by time—the most recent post appears at the top or bottom of a page—it can be almost impossible to follow a complex argument along any rational path. Even with wikis, which have the benefit of being more topic-focused and less arbitrarily organized than most blogs, controversial topics lose out. With sites like Wikipedia explicitly set up to showcase consensus on an article page, issues on which there is disagreement are resolved via lowest-common-denominator opinions, with arguments relegated to bloglike "talk pages." As my friend Ben Towne says, Wikipedia is great at telling us "what is" but not "what should be."

Thus, in order to improve both the quality of the participation and the value of solutions made possible by social-computing tools, Mark has added the structure of "argument mapping" to create the Deliberatorium. Argument mapping is based on the idea that the elements of any argument, no matter how complex, can be categorized using only four consistent descriptors: issue, idea, pro, and con. From those, you can make an "idea tree," with an issue always being the trunk; ideas, branches; and pros and cons, the leaves that grow from each branch.

Many benefits result from providing a logical structure for all contributions. First, all related content appears together in an organized fashion, regardless of when it is posted. Also, since each unique issue, idea, pro, and/or con only shows up once, needless repetition disappears. Last, by virtue of the visual presentation of the map, the pros and cons for each idea—or lack thereof—are clearly visible.

Posts on the Deliberatorium are governed by the "live-and-let-live rule." As Mark writes, "if you disagree with someone, add a 'con' argument or a competing idea, but do not edit their posts to undercut them. You should only edit a post if your goal is to strengthen it." From there, people can rate any idea they wish. A discussion board allows anyone to raise questions about or suggest improvements to an author's original post. Throughout the process, moderators are available to help authors submit and edit their posts in the correct format, but are required to remain strictly content-neutral.

What's amazing about structuring people's contributions in this way is that it allows us to move beyond mere knowledge sharing and into a richer realm of actual problem solving. Mark calls this process "collaborative deliberation," "the synergistic (additive or even super-additive) channeling of many minds towards solving complex and controversial problems."

Few challenges are as complex and have as many stakeholders as the issue of water use in the American West. When you compile the number of federal agencies that have some jurisdiction or interest in the matter, the result resembles an argument map. There's the Army Corps of Engineers, the National Oceanic and Atmospheric Administration (NOAA), the Environmental Protection Agency (EPA), the Department of Agriculture (USDA), and the Forest Service, among yet more. In the Department of the Interior alone, there are at least three agencies with a stake in the issue: the Fish and Wildlife Service, the Geological Survey (USGS), and the Bureau of Reclamation (which manages all of the large federal dams west of the Missouri River).

As Beaudry Kock, a colleague of Mark's at MIT, tells me, "there are so many agencies that you can never get them all in one room, let alone on the phone at the same time."[29] To better allow inter-agency collaboration and dialogue, Beaudry, who does contract work for the Bureau of Reclamation, suggested that the agencies try utilizing Mark's Deliberatorium.

The initial goal of the cross-agency deliberation was to develop a list of the most significant factors that will affect water use and availability in the West in coming years, in order to enable more accurate long-term forecasting. The list was varied and long, including factors such as irrigation practices and the intensive use of water for agriculture and energy production. Policy factors included everything from federal legislation such as the Clean Water and Endangered Species Acts to state and local legislation and Native American water rights. Those are all complicated and interconnected enough, but even they were only the tip of the iceberg.

"As we debated in the group," Beaudry tells me, "someone would say, 'I think this affects water demand this way,' and someone else would riff off of that and add another component." Some ideas were added to the map directly by whoever offered them, while others were added by note takers participating on inter-agency conference calls. "By the end of this thirty-person, ten-agency process," he says, "we had an incredibly thorough mapping of factors to consider."

Asked what the greatest benefit of the Deliberatorium has been, Beaudry says, "Federal policy making is such a tortured process. It can be very difficult to have open dialogue under normal circumstances. Even when people want to work together, computer systems, applications, and protocols are different across agencies and sometimes even within. The Deliberatorium is a neutral third-party tool that is quick to set up and easy for everyone to use. Most of all, its structure—which forces discussion towards systematic analysis—has been efficient and effective, something that very busy people with multiple demands on their time are very appreciative of."

As a research project funded by federal government grants, the Deliberatorium was free for the agencies to use. And, as you might expect, all of its code is open source. In that spirit, Mark's great hope is that the Deliberatorium will "allow us to tap, in ways not previously possible, the skills and knowledge of large numbers of people in service of solving complex multidisciplinary challenges . . . those truly wicked problems of our time."

Making Hope and History Rhyme

That Mark has come to have this much faith in humanity is an amazing story in itself. His parents, originally from Poland, were both survivors of the Holocaust. His mother lived in hiding in the cellar of a sympathetic Christian family for several years, while his father ended up as one of the "living skeletons" in the Mauthausen camp, finally saved by American forces. Needless to say, Mark tells me, "both were deeply damaged" by the horrific experiences they endured.

Unfortunately, life in Canada, where Mark grew up, was not the total escape from hardship that they had hoped for. When he was twelve years old, his mother succumbed to cancer, passing away right around the time that his father was losing his money to a thieving business partner.

By the time Mark enrolled at Dartmouth College in 1977, he already knew the question that would provide direction to his studies: "I wanted to figure out what was wrong with people, both individually and collectively . . . and also what was right." Majoring in biochemistry with a focus on neuroscience, he also started working with computers for the first time, toward the end of his undergraduate experience at Dartmouth. Soon Mark discovered the field of artificial intelligence (AI), which he saw as a way to "try to understand how people think . . . and why they end up thinking and doing things that are really hurtful." Continuing that search, his master's degree focused on creating an "AI model for emotion."

As Mark tells me all of this, I am reminded of lines from Seamus Heaney's lines from *The Cure at Troy.*

Human beings suffer,
they torture one another,
they get hurt and get hard.
No poem or play or song
can fully right a wrong
inflicted and endured . . .

History says, Don't hope
on this side of the grave.
But then, once in a lifetime
the longed for tidal wave
of justice can rise up,
and hope and history rhyme.

So hope for a great sea-change
on the far side of revenge.
Believe that a further shore
is reachable from here.

To help the world reach such shores, Mark doggedly continued his studies in distributed AI. Earning a Ph.D. for his dissertation about the "dynamics necessary for complex, collaborative decision making," he also started creating a software agent to "help with conflicts and . . . enable collectives to arrive at better results." Eventually, Mark ended up working for Boeing, in Seattle. As a huge corporation utilizing large-scale collaborative design and complex work-flow systems, it was an ideal place for him to gain insight into coordination challenges.

"When I worked there," he says, "there was a joke that everyone told: 'An airplane is five million parts flying in close formation.' When a company starts outsourcing that work rather than doing it in-house, the process becomes even more complex. Instead of *building* an airplane, you are *assembling* an airplane. With each one of those five million parts requiring a specific plan for how it is designed, manufactured, and outsourced . . . making it all come together at the end is amazingly challenging."

Starting in earnest during the 1920s, ideas popularized by Frederick Taylor about the "scientific management" of labor began to dominate the organization of work in many corporations. Throughout the twentieth century, Taylorism—essentially, the practice of treating workers as mini-machines on a stopwatch—spread far and wide, especially in large corporate environments. At a company like Boeing, for instance, there are a number of tasks that involve multiple steps happening in sequence. Influenced by Taylor's ideas, the company developed computer programs to automatically pass a completed task on to the next person in the process. As Mark tells me, instead of having each employee understand the whole system for something like insurance approval, each person would just know their individual piece, watch their in-box, do the task, and click "done." Then the document would get passed along automatically to the next person in line by the computer system.

Or so the theory went. In reality, as Mark quickly learned, "very few processes run the same way twice. The Tayloristic approach draws a sanitized version of a much messier reality." At Boeing processes frequently broke down because of these obvious facts: Workers are humans, not robots, and human systems are often too complex to capture in any computer system. This helps explain why technological advances should not be lauded in the abstract. There are technologies that can encourage our best human impulses and also those that will suppress them. Our task is to identify the former, in service of social good, while avoiding the latter.

While Mark was having this realization, he was also beginning to question the value of his work at Boeing. Disillusioned by the "extremely dysfunctional, Kafkaesque, *Waiting for Godot* quality" of his workplace, he found refuge in nature, especially Mount Rainier.

Listening to him describe the beauty of Seattle and the Pacific Northwest is less like listening to a computer science whiz and more like listening to a latter-day Thoreau.

"Seattle for much of the year is this glorious profusion of green," he says. "Mount Rainier hovers off in the distance amidst a soft blanket of clouds. It kind of beckons to you. Then when you get out of the city and begin climbing, you quickly leave the realm of vegetation and plants and are hiking among ice crevasses. The air is thin, the cold is sharp, and the view is clear. It really is a spiritual experience."

After his weekends of climbing, Mark would descend the mountain and slowly make his way back to the city for another week at Boeing. It was a gradual, and draining, transition. He rode his bike to work, passing blackberry bushes and parks until he eventually arrived at Boeing's square glass cube of a building and entered a "gray" world. Putting his badge on to get past security, he sat down in a cubicle amid a sea of separators and punched in so the company could track his labor in fifteen-minute increments.

"There were two things happening simultaneously for me," he says. "First, there was the realization that artificial intelligence is not mature enough to do anything more than specialized little contributions. Meanwhile, the messy problems that are kicking our butt as a species are 'wicked problems' that AI is simply not within light years of being able to help solve. At the same time, there was an intense contrast between my experience of nature on Rainier and the Kafkaesque corporate environment I was in. At Boeing, it constantly felt as though we were chopping wood with the wrong end of the ax. Some of us tried, some cynically milked the system, and some just gave up. For me, there was a poignant moment when I finally decided, 'I want to have a productive research career, and I want it to connect my work to the stuff that really concerns me, issues like sustainability.'"

Leaving Boeing, Mark started developing the Deliberatorium. At the same time, he was gradually becoming aware of the open-source movement and sites like Wikipedia. Through the emergence of social media, Mark saw a way to turn his expertise in computers and AI toward social good. With widespread evidence that people "are immensely willing to selflessly contribute to help make the world a better place," he had found a "hugely inspiring counter-example to the dominant view we are taught of humans as selfish utility maximizers." Mark, a black belt in karate and an instructor of tai chi chuan, intuitively knew that a powerful leverage point could be gained if he were to help develop tools to expand this enormous reservoir of largely untapped potential even further.

In 1997, he moved to Cambridge, Massachusetts, in order to work with Dr. Thomas Malone, the founder of MIT's Center for Collective Intelligence. The two have worked together for the past thirteen years, most recently developing a tool called the Climate Collaboratorium, which marries Mark's deliberation tool and climate-simulation models that can predict the real-world impacts of different policy choices.[30]

The idea echoes the open-source development model, in which developers will run a module for a proposed new application to see both if it will work and how it will impact the rest of the operating system. As powerful a tool as the Collaboratorium is, however, it is still dependent on policy makers being susceptible to rational arguments.

As we saw in Copenhagen with the U.N. Climate Conference (and see in the U.S. Congress on almost any issue), policy making just doesn't work that way. While I was interviewing Russell Newman about Senator Durbin's Legislation 2.0 effort, I mentioned the Deliberatorium and asked him if he thought it might be a better way to structure citizen input on policy issues than using blogs like OpenLeft and RedState. He told me that although he is intrigued by the Deliberatorium, and although it might indeed be an improvement, the simple truth of the matter is that "the rational side only goes 10 percent of the way in D.C." Clearly, using the Deliberatorium alone is not an adequate solution for all or even most of the issues that confront us, especially those that involve more value-based decisions and require the addition of more interpersonal, democratic venues.

Yet together the stories of SeeClickFix, Heart & Soul community planning, Legislation 2.0, and the Deliberatorium provide encouraging glimpses of how we might combine different elements from each so as to take government out of the hands of an elite few and attempt to realize the true promise of what President Lincoln spoke of during his Gettysburg Address: "government of the people, by the people, and for the people." Doing so will not be easy. Indeed, solving the larger, systemic problems that currently block such participatory and deliberative methods from guiding our public decision-making will be the challenge of a generation.

But if the open-source movement, the Millennial generation, and new forms of technology-enabled empowerment prove anything, it is that change can happen rapidly, overturning conventional wisdom faster than anyone would have believed possible. Exploring how to enable this next transformation to happen is the purpose of this book's final two chapters.

FIVE

A SYSTEMS APPROACH TO CHANGE

*In this election, the greatest risk we can take is to try the same old politics
with the same old players and expect a different result. You have shown
what history teaches us—that at defining moments like this one, the
change we need doesn't come from Washington. Change comes to Washington. Change happens because the American people demand it—because
they rise up and insist on new ideas and new leadership, a new politics for
a new time.*

—BARACK OBAMA

*There is absolutely no inevitability as long as there is a willingness to
contemplate what is happening.*

—MARSHALL McLUHAN

AS BARACK OBAMA campaigned for the Democratic nomination and
then for the presidency, he told the country that his campaign was
about, more than anything else, creating "change we can believe in."

Even before he announced his candidacy, it seemed that
Obama was different from the majority of senators and representatives who have time and again proved so willing to shirk the responsibility of governing in favor of scoring short-term political
points. In 2006, he penned these words in his book *The Audacity of
Hope*:

What's troubling is the gap between the magnitude of our challenges and the smallness of our politics—the ease with which we are distracted by the petty and the trivial, our chronic avoidance of tough decisions, our seeming inability to build a working consensus to tackle any big problem.[1]

More than that, Obama claimed to understand the larger, systemic challenges that blocked such large-scale reform and progress in Congress. Once he declared his intention to run, addressing the root problem of the American political system—the influence of money and lobbyists in both campaigns and policy making—became a core component of his candidacy.

He started off well. Throughout the entire campaign, he refused to accept money from any registered lobbyists. During an April 2, 2008, speech in Pennsylvania, he called "fictional" the idea "that someone can fight for working people and at the same time, embrace the broken system in Washington, where corporate lobbyists use their clout to shape laws to their liking." He went on, "If we're not willing to take up that fight, then real change—change that will make a lasting difference in the lives of ordinary Americans—will keep getting blocked by the defenders of the status quo."[2]

Only a few weeks later, Obama put the goal of "fundamentally chang[ing] the way Washington works" at the center of his campaign. During an April speech in Indiana, he made this bold proclamation:

> Unless we're willing to challenge the broken system in Washington, and stop letting lobbyists use their clout to get their way, nothing else is going to change. And the reason I'm running for President is to challenge that system.[3]

As the campaign progressed, it became clear that if he were elected, health care reform would be Obama's number-one domestic priority. To prove his commitment to changing the system, the candidate promised that he would not go about fixing health care in any old way. Instead, to model the fundamental change he was talking about, he outlined an entirely new approach for passing major legislation. Here's Obama speaking in Virginia, in August 2008:

> People say, "Well, you have this great health care plan, but how are you going to pass it? You know, it failed in '93." And what I've said is, I'm going to have all the negotiations around a big table. We'll have doctors and nurses and hospital administrators. Insurance companies, drug companies—they'll get a seat at the table, they just won't be able to buy every chair. But what we will do is, we'll have the negotiations televised on C-SPAN, so that people can see who is making arguments on behalf of their constituents, and who are making arguments on behalf of the drug companies or the insurance companies.

The idea was not a new one for Obama. Indeed, it was one of his most frequent talking points throughout both the primary campaign and the general election. As early as January 2008—a full seven months before the Virginia speech cited above—Obama had committed to the "big table on C-SPAN plan" during a debate in Los Angeles. Outlining the idea, he had summed up his reason for wanting such unheard-of transparency and openness: "What we have to do is enlist the American people in this process."[4]

Fast-forward to one year later. On the very first day of his presidency, Obama signed a memorandum directing all federal agencies to "break down barriers to transparency, participation, and collaboration" between citizens and their government.[5] It was a historic step, and the day-one timing of the call signaled that he just might be serious about what he had said throughout the campaign.

Indeed, Obama seemed primed for that moment, having assured the country from the outset of his "improbable journey" that *this* time would be different. At his announcement speech in Springfield, Illinois, he had envisioned a clear break with the past. "Too many times, after the election is over, and the confetti is swept away," he had said, ". . . promises fade from memory, and the lobbyists and the special interests move in and people turn away, disappointed as before."[6]

To help guard against that eventuality, Obama continued to take important and meaningful actions throughout the early days of his presidency. He created the position of chief information officer for the federal government and appointed Vivek Kundra, a pioneer in the democratization of government data, to fill it. Kundra's task is massive. As he shared during an open forum in March of 2009, there are ten thousand different information systems used across the federal government—many of which are incompatible with one another and as much as twenty to thirty years old—and upward of twenty-four thousand Web sites.[7]

Kundra, however, has significant resources at his disposal to achieve his stated vision of "bak[ing] the open philosophy into the architecture and purchasing" of the entire federal government. With billions of dollars in infrastructure spending from the stimulus bill, he and his office are already making sure that the public has increased access to "democratized data" across the federal government, via new Web sites like Recovery.gov and Data.gov. Providing access to data that is generated or held by the federal government, these sites allow for the creation of Web applications based on the free information. And by enabling in-depth and real-time research, they give citizens the ability to track public information, such as how Recovery Act dollars are being spent, and then report potential waste, fraud, or abuse if they find it.

Other transparency improvements have included, for the first time in history, publishing the name of every visitor to the White House and speeding up Freedom of Information Act (FOIA) requests by making transparency the default presumption rather than an exception to the rule. Indeed, by making much data open by default—such as White House staff salaries—the administration is reducing the need to make some FOIA requests in the first place.[8]

By May of 2009, Obama had followed up on his initial steps by launching the Open Government Initiative, an effort to make his day-one pronouncement about "transparency, participation, and collaboration" stick. To head up the initiative, he selected Beth Noveck, the author of *Wiki Government* and the force behind the crowdsourcing effort Peer-to-Patent, which helped speed the review of applications at the U.S. Patent and Trademark Office. At the same March 2009 forum where Kundra spoke, Noveck outlined a goal of engaging as many minds as possible to "innovate the way we make policies to bring about the most effective solutions."

Thus far, however, the only prominent example of the president engaging the public has been his Open for Questions "town hall meeting."[9] Hearing promises that Obama would answer whatever questions Americans deemed most important, ninety-two thousand people logged on to the White House Web site to suggest a question and/or cast a vote on what issues the president should address.

The result was an embarrassment. As Politico reported,

The top four questions under the heading of "Financial security" concerned marijuana; on the budget, people voted up questions about marijuana to positions 1-4; marijuana was in the first and third positions under "jobs"; people boosted a plug for legalizing marijuana to No. 2 under "health care reform." And questions about decriminalizing pot occupied spots 1 and 2 under "green jobs and energy."

While many pundits saw this as a cautionary tale of what happens when you allow more direct forms of democratic participation, the result actually vindicated serious thinkers who have tackled the issue in depth, including *The Wisdom of Crowds* author James Surowiecki.[10] In that book, Surowiecki outlines three conditions that must be met in order for the quality of the collective judgment of the many to exceed that of an expert few.

First, Surowiecki writes, the group must represent a broad diversity in its thinking. Second, each participant should have a degree of independence from other group members. Neither of these conditions was truly present in the Open for Questions experiment, even if the third—the ability to aggregate "local" opinions for all to see—was.

On the diversity question, consider that self-selecting groups are rarely, if ever, broadly diverse in their thinking. Totally open forums tend to pull in not a representative sample of people, but rather people on the poles of public opinion, with intensely held views. Furthermore, open polls that encourage online voting rarely attract independent thinkers. Instead, these polls bring forth unrepresentative groups of people who are notified by an e-mail alert or blog post from an issue group or opinion leader pushing a preferred position.

Consider, for instance, that the number of questions posted to the White House site was just over 100,000, yet the number of *votes* cast to rate those questions was over *3.5 million* (an average of thirty-eight ratings per participant).[11] It is a relatively small group of Americans who have the time to sit at a computer for hours on end, clicking "refresh" to vote over and over, forty times or more, for their pet questions. With the architecture for participation set up in this way, it should come as no surprise that a bunch of super-dedicated pot advocates were able to hijack the whole thing.

This brings us to the number-one limitation of applying the open-source model to citizen engagement in public affairs. On Wikipedia, it may not really matter if the person who writes, for instance, the date on which Ethan Allen led the capture of Fort Ticonderoga is white, black, rich, poor, straight, or gay.[12] It's the same information no matter who provides it. The same can be said of good computer code. While it may not be ideal that the participants in these communities are 87 to 93 percent male—as is the case on Wikipedia—the product that results from such a community can always be peer reviewed against a backdrop of facts.[13]

But with politics, having 90 percent men—or 60 percent marijuana-legalization advocates—decide issues for all of society is another matter entirely. Again, dealing with facts about "what is" is very different from dealing with opinions about "what should be." The latter task involves value judgments that will differ depending on various factors affecting one's experience of the world—say, one's income, race, gender, or sexual orientation. Therefore, when it comes to public engagement in government decision making, achieving *representative participation* is necessary in order to ensure the legitimacy and integrity of the process.

Yet rather than learning from its early mistakes and trying to provide for more meaningful and structured forms of public participation, the White House has since neglected the "participation" plank of the Open Government Initiative, shifting almost all of its focus to the safer realm of open data and government transparency.

As the New Democrat Network has noted, the Open Government Directive "does a lot for the 'Transparency' part . . . but not much for the 'Participation' or 'Collaboration' portions . . . To really get the full benefit of the wisdom of the crowd, the government's next step will have to ensure the dialogue is truly *two-way*."[14] Indeed, the danger that comes with focusing almost exclusively on transparency—a vital yet insufficient goal—is that we may end up seeing the failures of our government but being left with little recourse for doing anything about them. Transparency without avenues for real participation seems a bit like watching a police interrogation from behind a two-way mirror. While you can see what is going on, you have little ability to do anything if something goes wrong.

And in any case, transparency has run aground as well. Abandoning his pledge to do health care around a table on C-SPAN, the president consented to a process of congressional wheeling, dealing, and capitulation to special interests, personified most by senators like Ben Nelson and Joe Lieberman. Once the House and the Senate finally passed their divergent bills, the White House—in a rush to sign a bill—gave its blessing to skipping the conference-committee process and conducting negotiations to reconcile the two bills in private, among Democrats alone.

As PolitiFact.com, a Pulitzer Prize–winning watchdog project of the *St. Petersburg Times*, reports, "Obama promised—repeatedly— an end to closed-door negotiations and complete openness for the health care talks. But he hasn't delivered. Instead of open talks on

C-SPAN, we've gotten more of the same—talks behind closed doors at the White House and Congress." The Web site concludes, "We rate this Promise Broken."[15]

Thus, instead of getting a meeting of representative deliberation on C-SPAN, Americans were left to watch "health care town halls" unfold over the summer of 2009. And here, please grant me one quick aside: As a Vermonter who grew up with the tradition of real town hall meetings—the kind where citizens actually make decisions for their town, directly—I am continually amazed at how distorted the notion of town halls has become in our national media.

It was presidential candidates who first obscured the tradition into some elaborate Q & A session, in order to look folksy for voters in the New Hampshire primaries. But like those events, the "health care town halls" were not set up to productively solve any problem, as is the true tradition of New England town hall meetings. Rather, they were media circuses where people behaved irrationally and with belligerence—for the benefit of producing theater, not solutions. It may have made for good ratings—particularly on Fox News—but it wasn't serious, nor was it worthy of American democracy.

Sadly, such absurd examples tar an otherwise potent idea. Consider the case of Wisconsin senator Russ Feingold. Back in 1992, as an underdog running against millionaire opponents, Feingold painted five promises to the people of Wisconsin on his garage door. Perhaps the most consequential was his commitment to hold a "Listening Session" in every one of Wisconsin's seventy-two counties each year.

Since first being elected, Feingold has kept his word. In the intervening eighteen years, he has held more than *1,250* Listening Sessions. What's unique about Feingold's approach is that he holds the meetings not to give speeches but to genuinely listen, and then, in contrast with the Tea Party folks, engage in serious dialogue with his constituents. The sessions have even produced many ideas for legislation, some of which Feingold has worked with constituents and local groups to pass into law.

In his book *Feingold*, biographer Sanford D. Horwitt relays a particularly powerful story the senator told him about a Listening Session that occurred in a small Wisconsin town called Aurora:

> "There are only about thirteen people," Feingold says, including an old man. "I won't say curmudgeonly, but he hardly said a word. And we go through this meeting; it takes about forty-five minutes." And then Feingold repeats what the man said: "I just want to say something. I can't believe that you would come here and sit down and listen to us here like this." And, Feingold says, the man began to cry. "The way he said it," Feingold remembers, "made me realize that this is almost like a vision for people of what democracy should be."

Barack Obama had similar visions when he first decided to run for public office. Running for the state senate in Illinois in 1995, he shared an unconventional view of democracy in an interview with the *Chicago Reader*. Drawing on his experience as a community organizer on Chicago's South Side, Obama said,

> What if a politician were to see his job as that of an organizer, as part teacher and part advocate, one who does not sell voters short but who educates them about the real choices before them? As an elected public official, for instance, I could bring church and community leaders together easier than I could as a community organizer or lawyer. We would come together to

form concrete economic development strategies, take advantage
of existing laws and structures, and create bridges and bonds
within all sectors of the community. We must form grass-root
structures that would hold me and other elected officials more
accountable for their actions.[16]

Obama did follow up on the idea shortly after being elected to
the state senate, announcing that he would begin "organizing 'citizens' committees' to help him shape legislation."[17] Yet the initiative
quickly faded away. As Ryan Lizza reports in the *New Yorker*, "I
asked a longtime Obama friend what ever became of the committees. 'They never really got off the ground,' he said."[18]

The idea may have more staying power today. With all that is
enabled by the age of open source and Millennials, this vision of politicians as conveners, facilitators of change, and community-network
nodes makes far more sense than ever, and it should replace the ex-
clusive "I'm the decider" model of a previous era. When people in
positions of authority say, "Don't worry, I'll take care of it for you," or
"Vote for me and I'll fix your problems," they do a severe disservice to
those they are trying to serve. When they fail to engage the concern
and talent of citizens (beyond asking for their money or vote), how
much potential simply withers on the vine for want of harvest?

The authors of the book *Getting to Maybe* suggest a different
approach: that politicians run for office with the goal of "fostering
learning" and dialogue, rather than promising specific end results.
Essentially, this would mean campaign platforms outlining ways to
open up and improve the very process of societal problem solving,
rather than listing the same big issue goals over and over again, and
disillusioning people when the problems aren't fixed in two or four
years (or twenty years, as in the case of meaningful action on climate

destabilization) because of the underlying inadequacies of our system of governance.

While individual public servants like Obama and Feingold offer us varying degrees of inspiration for how to help fix our situation, the truth is that we desperately need to get beyond analysis of change that is dependent on a single leader. If we are going to change our system of governance, it must come from "we the people," not be handed to us by some benevolent official. In reality, there is only so much any one person—even the president—can do to reform our broken government without the collaboration of other branches of government and sectors of society.

Indeed, we would do well to remember the crucial part of Obama's Springfield speech that followed his warning that "too many times . . . promises fade from memory, and the lobbyists and the special interests move in and people turn away, disappointed as before."[19] For in the very next breath, he reminded us,

> That is why this campaign can't only be about me. It must be about us—it must be about *what we can do together . . .* This campaign has to be about *reclaiming the meaning of citizenship*, restoring our sense of common purpose, and realizing that few obstacles can withstand the power of millions of voices calling for change.[20]

A couple of years into the Obama presidency, we are now confronted with the stark realization that truly transformational progress will not be made on any major social challenge until the underlying dysfunction of a "pay to play, keep the people at bay" system in Congress is addressed. It is painfully clear, as it has been for some time, that the way our political system is currently set up—from the selection of our candidates and how their campaigns get financed to the formulation of public policy without any substantial public involvement—allows for little more than incremental change, even as we know we need historic leaps in human progress. Obama will not and cannot change this alone.

Where might we look for progress instead? I believe that to get at the root blockages of transformational progress, we must address the disenfranchisement of the American and global public from the decision-making institutions of our society. As author Don Tapscott has written, "real change seems glacial . . . What the current system lacks are mechanisms enabling government to benefit on an ongoing basis from the wisdom and insight that a nation can collectively offer."[21]

Indeed, while the defining ideological debate of the previous generation concerned the proper *size of government*, for the Millennial generation the pressing question should be the nature—open versus closed, collaborative versus zero-sum—of our very *process of governance*.

What comes next sets up the conclusion of this book. Too often, the suggested solutions to large, systemic problems are naive, belligerent, or both. In recent years, the antiwar and Tea Party movements, arising mostly from the left and right, respectively, have provided clear examples of this. With this book, which is ultimately about how change happens, I seek to steer clear of such simplistic, dead-end paths.

At the same time, there is also the unfulfilling route of offering trite solutions to huge challenges—the "just vote for me" or "sign this online petition" refrain that is all too familiar. So although I am not one for grand schemes, I am also wary of applying Band-Aids to wounds that cannot be treated so simply. To help chart a sensible yet sufficiently serious way forward, let me share a short story.

Lessons of a Vermont Farmhouse

A few years ago, my dad was ready to stop renting and finally buy a house of his own. With a limited income, he settled on a two-hundred-year-old two-bedroom farmhouse in rural Vermont, the state where my family has lived for ten generations. Being in Vermont, the location is, of course, beautiful: On one side of the property is the Waits River, and on the other is one of the most photographed churches in New England. The house itself, however, needed a ton of work.

The previous owners had lived there for fifty-five years before their children sold it to my dad. As the couple had gotten older, repairs had clearly been neglected. There were old outbuildings that hadn't been used for years—a falling-down sugar shack and a rotting chicken coop. These and the house's peeling paint were the first things I noticed about the place. Indeed, just looking at it, one might have thought that step one should have been to tear those outbuildings down and put a fresh coat of paint on the house. Luckily, my dad saw something more pressing.

What he noticed was that the foundation of the barn and the back end of the house were both sinking. They weren't about to fall over, but it was bad enough that if you set a baseball down on the floor in the front end of the kitchen, it would roll downward all the way to the back end. Very quickly, Dad realized that the problem was water seeping down from the property above us on its way to the river, compromising the foundation.

After he bought the house, the first thing Dad did was to rent a backhoe and dig a French drain around the property in order to divert the water around the house. With the foundation-weakening water taken care of, he then jacked up the barn and the back end of the house and poured new concrete foundations.

In the last couple years, we've also taken down the outbuildings and their concrete foundations, replacing them with a large vegetable garden. Dad has also built a new chicken coop.[22] Even after all he's done, though, the one thing he still hasn't wanted to do is paint the house. "That'll come last, after everything else is taken care of," he says.

Even if he wouldn't say so himself, my dad is a great example of a systems thinker. He knows intuitively that his house is an interdependent system, where some interventions are more effective than others. For instance, it makes no sense to build an addition (let alone paint it) until the foundation on which it is going to rest is sound.

Now, just as a thought experiment, consider all the other ways in which a house is a complex system. It's wired for electricity, phone lines, and (sometimes) cable television. It's piped for plumbing. The internal temperature is regulated by exposure to sunlight, insulation, and seasonal weather—and then radiators, thermostats, and window-unit air conditioners. This is all just the tip of the iceberg too. Making a change to the house, like building an addition, may require expertise in a dozen fields, not to mention the approval and cooperation of construction and zoning professionals. The point here is not that we don't know how to replace our own lightbulbs, but to remind us just how much it takes to get one to turn on.

Applying this thinking to our political system, it becomes clear that while action in the public interest is certainly benefited by having a good president in office, that alone is far from sufficient: a bit like putting a new roof on a house (and Senate) that is structurally deficient. The roof can help keep the rain and snow out in the short term, but over time its integrity is dependent on the support structure, physical and otherwise, that holds it up.

This is pretty straightforward stuff. For although whole academic disciplines devoted to the study of systems theory have emerged in the last ninety years, the basic insight of systems science is often conveyed with figures of speech far older than that.[23] Whenever we speak of a need to "get to the root of the problem," or to "look at the big picture," we are expressing the wisdom of systems thinking. Likewise, if we do not want to "tinker around the edges" or be stuck with a "Sisyphean task," we will "teach a man to fish" rather than give him one or make sure we are not trying to "fill the bathtub while the plug is out."[24]

The same is true in thinking about our government. Analysis dependent on individuals, such as the president, can only get us so far. Thinking more broadly and historically, consider that many of the assumptions that our government was formed on two hundred plus years ago—including a cost of communication so high that it prohibited more direct forms of democracy, except at the local level—no longer hold true to the extent that they once did. This creates a new operating reality and therefore new possibilities for *who* makes decisions on society's behalf and *how* those decisions are made. This is true not just on the local level of SeeClickFix and the Orton Family Foundation, but on the state and federal levels also.

Purely representative state and federal governments with strict divisions of responsibility between average citizens and elected officials might have made sense in an age when there was far less transparency of information and access to education than there is today. But with those limiting factors now becoming more and more obsolete, it's about time that we reconceive fundamental aspects of how our state and federal governments are set up, not just whom we elect to fill them.

With the success of the open-source movement—based on the ideas that "we" are smarter than "me" and that passion can be a better motivator than profit—we can glimpse what it might be like to live in a world where many more of us could help build the society we want. But instead of drawing on citizens' immense stores of wisdom and ability—as the open-source development model suggests we should—our current governance system allows for little substantive public involvement in policy making. In other words, we've got a lot of work to do on this old house, but the people who would help are fenced out.

To bring them in, we must do two things simultaneously: decrease the power of private and corporate money (the folks behind the fence) and increase the number of avenues whereby citizens can help solve our public problems. At root, this is about switching the currency of our democracy from quantities of money to the quality of people's ideas. In the final chapter, let me introduce you to two of the leaders who are showing us both why this should happen and how it could.

SIX

REALIZING DEMOCRACY'S PROMISE

I am not an advocate for frequent changes in laws and constitutions, but laws and institutions must go hand in hand with the progress of the human mind. As that becomes more developed, more enlightened, as new discoveries are made, new truths discovered and manners and opinions change, with the change of circumstances, institutions must advance also to keep pace with the times.

—THOMAS JEFFERSON

The first stage in a movement can be described with some precision, I think. It happens when isolated individuals make an inner choice to stop leading "divided lives." Most of us know from experience what a divided life is. Inwardly we feel one sort of imperative for our lives, but outwardly we respond to quite another. This is the human condition, of course; our inner and outer worlds will never be in perfect harmony. But there are extremes of dividedness that become intolerable, and when the tension snaps inside of this person, then that person, and then another, a movement may be underway.

—PARKER PALMER

THE FIRST TIME I saw Frances Moore Lappé, she was telling the story of a woman named Deb Simpson, now a state senator in Maine. I walked into the back of a packed room, where a rapt audience was listening to Frances, known to her friends as Frankie, recount how

Simpson, a waitress and a single mother, was elected to Maine's House of Representatives and then went on to chair the chamber's Judiciary Committee. Many aspects of Simpson's campaign were remarkable, but what enabled her to compete in the first place was Maine's pioneering "clean elections" law, passed in 2000, which gives candidates who demonstrate significant popular support access to public financing for their campaigns, freeing them from the need to court wealthy individuals and corporate donors.

Beyond Maine, Arizona and Connecticut also have clean-elections laws making public financing available to candidates for any legislative or statewide race. With a smaller list of offices eligible, clean elections also exist to a more limited extent in North Carolina, Vermont, New Mexico, and New Jersey.[1] Altogether, clean elections have enabled hundreds of candidates to run for public office based on the quality of their ideas and character rather than the quantity of money they raise. How Frankie came to be promoting clean elections, an integral component of a larger concept she calls "living democracy," is an amazing story in itself.

For those of you for whom Frankie's name is familiar, it's likely that you know her as the author of *Diet for a Small Planet*, which was published in 1971 and went on to become a three-million-copy bestseller. It was the first American book to bring the benefits of a "plant- and planet-centered diet" to mainstream consciousness, and its influence is evidenced by Frankie's place on *Gourmet* magazine's 2008 list of "The 25 People Who Changed Food in America," where she appeared alongside Thomas Jefferson, Upton Sinclair, and Julia Child.[2] Worthy and accurate as it is, though, this popular portrait of Frankie is nevertheless woefully incomplete.

Born in 1944, Frankie spent most of her childhood in Fort

Worth, Texas. As part of the Bible Belt and the segregated South, the city saw its share of both conservative religious dogma and racism. Around the age of four, according to family folklore, Frankie came home from Sunday school one day to ask her parents, "What does 'hellfire and brimstone' mean?" Their answer to that question— "It means we have to start a Unitarian church"—was to have a profound impact on her.

The first meetings of the fledgling fellowship were held in a downtown hotel, with members attracted by ads the Moores had placed in the local paper. Within a few years, the group had become robust enough to purchase and remodel an old Baptist church, which became the home for the congregation now known as First Jefferson. Most important, as Frankie tells me, the church was the first in the terribly segregated city—the neighborhood that her family lived in when they first moved to Fort Worth was (and still is) called White Settlement—to welcome African American parishioners and become a racially integrated congregation.

"I remember the organizing meetings they held," she says. "They would usually meet in our kitchen, and so there would always be this hum of activity emanating from there. I remember thinking, 'That's what adults *do*. That's what it means to grow up and to live a good life—talking with your friends and, in your own unsung way, trying to solve problems and be a part of history.'"

Frankie's father, John, was a meteorologist for the government, but his interests varied far and wide. Aside from helping to found the Unitarian congregation, he was an amateur historian, writing an article for a military journal about the provisioning of troops during the Civil War that was published while Frankie was growing up. And after his death on July 4, 2002, Frankie found correspondence between her father and the Federal Reserve, the letters covering intricate details of monetary policy. "What a gift to give a child," she tells me, "to show that if you care enough about something, of course you can learn what you need to learn to have an opinion and then do something about it."

Later, Frankie also had a transformative experience while attending college at Earlham. To this day, one class stands out among all the others she took. More than forty years later, she recalls, "It was a course on the history of scientific thought taught by Ted Benfey, and we read Thomas Kuhn's *The Structure of Scientific Revolutions*." That book helped Frankie realize how "people invent all sorts of ways to justify a false paradigm—until it finally crumbles. That's when it really dawned on me that what really matters is the lens through which we see the world, from our view of human nature to democracy and economics."

After graduating from Earlham and attending a Quaker-led community-organizing school, Frankie moved to Philadelphia to try to put the ideas she had been studying into practice. She was hired by the city's housing authority to work on a "Neighborhood Renewal Program," which was funded as part of President Lyndon Johnson's War on Poverty.

Frankie worked in the northwestern part of the city, in a neighborhood called Germantown. After passing an exam to become a housing inspector, she began going door-to-door, meeting women, almost all of whom were African American, who were renting from slum landlords. Frankie's goal was to make sure they were aware of both the living conditions they were legally entitled to and their right to make their landlord bring their apartment up to code. But her bigger goal was to help the women come together to realize their rights under the welfare laws and to protect those rights. Soon, Frankie and a group of about ten women from the neighborhood began organizing meetings to create a chapter of the National Welfare Rights Organization.

The person she bonded with most during this time was a woman in her early forties named Lilly. Although, like all the other women in the neighborhood, Lilly faced the challenges of poverty, she nevertheless retained her spirit and brought life and verve to the meetings. She inspired the group with her energy in the face of hardship. Then, within a few months of the formation of the group, Lilly had a sudden heart attack and died, leaving her grade-school-age children without their mother.

After the funeral, trying to understand how Lilly could have died so young, Frankie became convinced that she had "died of poverty." As Frankie tells me, "she always had to worry about having money to put food on the table. She was stressed about the health of her kids, since they had asthma from the coal used to heat the apartment. I think living with those fears and in those conditions is what caused her death."

Not long after Lilly's death, Frankie's then husband was offered a postdoc position at UC Berkeley. After the move, she enrolled in the school's master's program for social work. By working on fair-housing issues in Oakland, she was able to continue her community organizing too. But thinking about Lilly, Frankie started to wonder if her studies and organizing were actually relating to the real underlying causes of suffering in the world. As she puts it, "I came to a point where I had to know that what I was doing with my life related to the root cause of her death."

It was at this point that Frankie made what she calls the most important decision in her life, aside from having children. "I decided to stop doing anything so I could make the space to ask questions," she says. She dropped out of her master's program and stopped organizing. "I wanted the chance to think about why, why, why . . . so I could at least develop a working hypothesis about the roots of suffering in the world. I realized that if I didn't figure that out, I might end up at the end of my life with no idea of its meaning." The phrase she now uses to describe the ever-reactive feeling of those who try to do good through direct service or some forms of community organizing is "random acts of sanity." Not content with this disorganized approach, Frankie made the brave choice to just stop doing it and try to find a more effective path.

Her decision to "follow her intuition" has been identified by David Bornstein, author of *How to Change the World*, as a common event in the lives of leading social innovators around the world. He writes,

> In short they [a]re able to marry reflection and action. This is rare. We live, by and large, in a culture that divorces contemplation or reflection from action. We go to school, a time of contemplation, to prepare ourselves for action. Those who never wish to enter the world of action remain in school, as academics, or become monks, writers, artists. Those who spring into action rarely find time for contemplation, for standing still—except on vacation, when they collapse from overwork.[3]

The most effective social-change leaders, Bornstein suggests, are those, like Frankie, who are able to make space for reflection and action at different points throughout their lives, often finding ways to balance the two simultaneously, as Frankie has for most of her life.

But first, Frankie had to create space for reflection alone. When she decided to leave her master's program, the debate about hunger in the world was raging. A year earlier, Paul R. Ehrlich's book *The Population Bomb* had been published, predicting mass starvation in the 1970s and '80s and calling for immediate measures to curb human population growth around the world. A year before that, the sensationalist book *Famine, 1975! America's Decision: Who Will Survive?* had been written by the Paddock brothers.

Amid this atmosphere of a predicted hunger crisis, Frankie resolved to start with what to her was the most basic question of all: food. "I remember thinking, 'Gosh, if we can't feed ourselves, then what?'" she says.

She started spending most of her time at the library, reading widely and going to lectures. "I tell academic audiences that my true learning began only after I left graduate school," she says. "That's when I developed the research technique that has served me so well for all these years—following my nose. Because I had beginner's eyes, I wasn't afraid to start with square-one questions."

With that mind-set, Frankie decided to see if the assumed reality—that there was not enough food in the world to feed people—was actually true. Spending hour after hour in Berkeley's Agricultural Economics Library, she pored through reports by the United Nations' Food and Agriculture Organization (FAO) and the U.S. Department of Agriculture. Using her father's slide rule, she literally added up all the numbers to figure out the world's food supply.

What she found was that there was actually more than enough food in the world to make us all overweight. The problem was that a third of the world's grain (now closer to 40 percent) was being fed not to people but to livestock, a terribly inefficient allocation of calories and resources. Frankie felt compelled to share this information with people, so she created a flyer that she thought she'd post around Berkeley. But then she thought, "Well, I should know more before I say anything," and that one-page flyer turned into a couple-page handout, then a booklet, and then a bigger booklet.

She tackled the next logical question: If there is enough food in the world, what about protein? On average, Frankie found, we eat more than twice as much protein, mostly from meat, as our bodies can actually use and store. In fact, we can get all the protein we need from plants as long as we eat a variety of whole foods. For a young woman who had grown up in Texas on mashed potatoes and meat loaf, these truths did not come naturally and were met with some skepticism. But for her, the conclusion was inescapable: "You cannot blame hunger in the world on nature's inadequacy . . . It's a product of human-made systems," she says. "Our grain-fed, meat-centered diet is a symptom and symbol of an economic and political system that creates scarcity out of abundance."

Having received a D on her first English paper in college, the last thing Frankie saw herself as was a writer. Up to that point, she hadn't published anything, not even a letter to the editor. But after a friend shared her booklet with an editor in New York, Frankie received an offer to publish it as a book, with the suggestion that she add recipes throughout. The rest is gastronomic history.

Yet Frankie has never been content with what has come before. With her own career as with social change, she is always looking for truer, more lasting progress. In fact, I would argue that her most important work has been produced over the past two decades, during which she has come to focus more and more on democracy, power, and participation—the issues that underlie not only what we eat but also how we act and govern ourselves more broadly. She explains, "I don't want to be stuck on any one issue. I want to go beneath all the issues . . . to go to the process of democracy itself." As she concluded in a recent speech,

> What is the real crisis? When I began thirty-five years ago or so in my mid-twenties, it seemed clear that the real crisis was hunger in the world. The real crisis was devastation of our earth. And as I've aged, I've realized, no, none of these are the real crisis. The only real crisis we have to worry about is our own sense of powerlessness . . . The only thing we have to worry about is our own feeling of insignificance in the face of these global problems.[4]

This may be particularly true for members of the Millennial generation. Consider the conclusion of a recent study on youth and politics prepared by the Kettering Foundation, an independent, nonpartisan research organization:

> The report's chief recommendation is that the problems of information overload, confusion over formal politics and uncertainty over ways to achieve social change could be mitigated if students have more opportunities to discuss current issues and experiences to stimulate meaningful discussions in various *"open" and "authentic" settings—those not dominated by institutions.*[5]

Such opportunities are increasingly hard to come by. With a system of representative democracy in which members of Congress have gone from representing about sixty thousand people each in 1790 to representing more than six hundred thousand today, citizens receive less and less representation, while moneyed interests receive more and more. Indeed, more than two dozen registered lobbyists now roam the halls of Congress for each elected representative we send there.[6]

Though she doesn't use the term "open source," Frankie nevertheless sounds like an open-source evangelist when she offers the helpful frame of contrasting this kind of "Thin Democracy" with what she calls "Living Democracy." She writes,

> The centralized power of Thin Democracy leaves most of us feeling powerless, robbing the planet of just the problem solvers we most need. It encourages us to look to the "market" or to CEO's or to government higher-ups for answers, but our problems are too complex, pervasive, and interconnected to be addressed from the top down. Solutions depend on the insights, experience, and ingenuity of people most affected—all thwarted when citizens are cut out and manipulated, and when decisions get made secretly by the few . . . Put very practically, Living Democracy means infusing the power of citizens' voices and values throughout our public lives and removing the power of money from governance.[7]

But the crucial point here is that her concern for the health of our democracy has not come about in spite of her passion and concern for sustainable food, but rather because of them. She has found that progress on hunger, poverty, or climate—or whatever your primary concern is—first requires that our democracy become beholden to the public interest. "As long as we tolerate a democracy in which those funding the process have inordinate voice," she says, "we aren't going to make real progress on any of the vital challenges before us. We have to stop kidding ourselves."

In fact, it seems that nearly every serious thinker who comments on current events and public affairs eventually comes to a similar conclusion. Consider these related excerpts from three leading thinkers and publications.

Fareed Zakaria, from his book *The Post-American World*:

As it enters the twenty-first century, the United States is not fundamentally a weak economy or a decadent society. But it has developed a highly dysfunctional politics. What was an anti-quated and overly rigid political system to begin with (now about 225 years old) has been captured by money, special interests, a sensationalist media, and ideological attack groups. The result is ceaseless, virulent debate about trivia—politics as theater—and very little substance, compromise, or action. A can-do country is now saddled with a do-nothing political process, designed for partisan battle rather than problem solving.[8]

William Greider, from his book *Who Will Tell the People*:

The empty space at the center of American democracy is defined ultimately by its failed institutions. At the highest level of politics, there is no one who now speaks reliably for the people, no one who listens patiently to their concerns or teaches them the hard facts involved in governing decisions. There is no major institution committed to mobilizing the power of citizens around their own interests and aspirations.[9]

James Fallows, in the *Atlantic*:

Yes, the problems are intellectually and politically complicated: energy use, medical costs, the right educational and occupational mix to rebuild a robust middle class. But they are no worse than others the nation has faced in more than 200 years, and today no other country comes close to the United States in having the surplus money, technology, and attention to apply to the tasks. (China? Remember, most people there still live on subsistence farms.) First with Iraq and now with Afghanistan, the U.S. has in the past decade committed $1 trillion to the cause of entirely remaking a society. We know that such an investment could happen here—but we also know that it won't.

That is the American tragedy of the early 21st century: a vital and self-renewing culture that attracts the world's talent, and a governing system that increasingly looks like a joke.[10]

In the time since the great democratic experiment of American self-government began, over two hundred years ago, we have seen near-exponential progress in science and technology, from medicine to communications, among countless other fields. But in the same period of time, our government's ability to connect, co-ordinate, and act on that increased knowledge has failed to keep pace, particularly in the last forty years.

So although the twentieth century was so much about hierarchy and separate fields of study and knowledge, the twenty-first century offers another possibility. Having so far produced a generation more interested in open, collaborative networks, we can now connect knowledge and ideas in ways that address the dynamic and comprehensive nature of the growing challenges of our time.

To do so, we will have to reform a political system that is like a dog chasing its tail (the analogy fits whether you consider the tail to be money or the other party). Democracy in America today is simply not worthy of a people who, from very humble roots, resuscitated the very form of government after the American Revolution and then preserved it with countless sacrifices in two world wars.

As Frankie knows, our democracy underlies everything else we care about. So before we can make innovative progress on nearly any large-scale challenge before us, there must first be bold reform of the process by which we make decisions as a society. That means doing two things simultaneously: decreasing the power of money in politics *and* increasing the opportunity for the public to participate meaningfully in problem solving. For a leader working on that vital second task, let us turn to the story of Carolyn Lukensmeyer.

America*Speaks*

Born in Hampton, Iowa, as World War II was coming to a close, Carolyn Lukensmeyer was raised in a traditional farming community by parents who imparted both a large dose of Midwestern sensibility and a "strong sense of responsibility to make the world a better place." One of the most formative experiences Carolyn had while growing up was being part of a fundamentalist Christian church that had no ordained ministers and was led by a lay congregation. "That's when I first observed the capacity for self-governance," she tells me. "We were a congregation of twenty-five families who all helped take care of each other."

At the University of Iowa during the tumult of the 1960s, Carolyn was a politically moderate elected student leader whose natural mediation skills allowed her to play a constructive role in the wake of debilitating protests. Acting as a facilitator between the students, the administration, and the faculty, she helped the university in its efforts to create new governance processes. This experience played a key role in Carolyn's decision *not* to go to Harvard

Law School (despite being one of only three women the school admitted in 1967) and instead to begin Ph.D. work in organizational behavior at Case Western Reserve University. After finishing her Ph.D., she started her own management-consulting firm in 1974, with a focus on creating change in large, complex systems.

In 1986, Carolyn made the jump to government with some very unusual support. In searching for a new chief of staff, Ohio's recently reelected governor, Richard Celeste, found that the same woman (Carolyn) was being recommended to him by both steel-company executives and the leadership of a radical women's collective. As Carolyn tells the story, "Celeste said to himself, 'Anyone who can be recommended by old-white-guy CEOs *and* radical feminists has to at least be interesting!'"

When he picked Carolyn for the position, Celeste chose not only the first woman ever to be chief of staff for the state, but also the first person to have studied and applied organizational-effectiveness theory in depth. With her background, one of her major priorities as chief of staff was to break down barriers to collaboration among the twenty-eight agencies that reported to the governor through her. Hoping to enable the state government to engage in problem solving around crosscutting issues, Carolyn wanted to find ways to get agencies out of their silos. Working from the idea that major, multifaceted challenges cannot be the province of one department alone, she pioneered the practice of cross-agency "clusters," wherein agency heads work together to develop budgets and tackle shared challenges.

Describing the Celeste administration's approach to economic development in Ohio, she says, "If the only people responsible . . . are the people in the Department of Economic Development, then you won't get any real out-of-the-box thinking. So we made an economic-development cluster that actually shocked some people because of who was in it. The Department of Youth Corrections, the prison system, all the public-safety agencies were in it. We realized we could save a lot of money—say, the thirty thousand dollars a year it takes to incarcerate someone—if we invested in entry-level workforce-development programs that helped reduce recidivism."

Celeste was term-limited out of office in 1991. Shortly after leaving her position, Carolyn co-authored a white paper with one of the cabinet members, outlining how the "cabinet cluster" idea could be applied to other executive offices and how the approach provided "leverage points" when used to address crosscutting issues like economic development.

Still mulling over what was next for her, several weeks after Bill Clinton's election in 1992, Carolyn read an article in the *Washington Post* that mentioned the formation of something called "cabinet clusters" by the presidential transition team. "I immediately called Pam Hyde [the co-author of the cabinet-cluster white paper] and said, 'You're not going to believe this, but Warren Christopher [the director of the Clinton transition team] is actually creating cabinet clusters!'" she recalls.

Another week or so later, Carolyn got an unexpected request to fly to the president-elect's campaign headquarters in Little Rock, Arkansas, to "consult on personnel issues." When she got there, she discovered that a member of the transition team had, in fact, read a copy of the white paper and had forwarded the idea on to Clinton and Christopher.

After a couple weeks of helping the president-elect's transition team and demonstrating her expertise in organizational effectiveness, Carolyn was asked by Vice President–Elect Al Gore to help plan and facilitate the first cabinet retreat, to be held at Camp David prior to the inauguration. With Jane Hopkins, from Gore's team, she set about interviewing each member of the cabinet, along with White House staff, to put together an agenda for the retreat.

One of the major goals of the Camp David session was for members of the new administration to develop connections by getting to know one another as people and sharing information about themselves beyond their résumé. As cabinet members and staff opened up personally, Carolyn thought, "If only the American public could hear [incoming Secretary of Commerce] Ron Brown say this—if only the American public could hear any of these stories." "But," she notes, "if the media had been in the room, they would have put a cynical twist on these personal stories that would have destroyed their meaning."

Nevertheless, those who were there knew the meeting had been a major success. It laid the groundwork for the cabinet's being able to speak in a single voice during the contentious federal-budget process that followed in 1993. Soon after the retreat, Vice President Gore asked Carolyn to serve as the deputy director for management of the National Performance Review, better known as the Reinventing Government Taskforce. From this vantage point, she began to observe in close detail how our government's decision-making system worked.

"Within ten months," she says, "I started saying to people, 'I'm sitting here at the nexus of our major national institutions—where the executive branch, Congress, the media, corporate special interests, and the big Washington think tanks make all of our politics and governance happen, and I can see clearly that not one of them has the slightest interest in bringing the public in. Every single one of them wants to speak *for* the public, or replace the public entirely.'"

Time and again, Carolyn tells me, failure to create any kind of major reform was in large part due to the fact that the public couldn't get a word in edgewise—couldn't demonstrate its will to these governing institutions. Even if you have political capital to do something meaningful—as Clinton, and now Obama, did—she explains, the system is designed so that interest groups can array against it and either neutralize it or kill it. "We were trying to have a serious debate about health care reform, while vast amounts of money were being spent on marketing efforts that would swing the debate in one direction." The now-famous "Harry and Louise" TV ads, she notes, cost the Health Insurance Association of America $14 million in 1993–1994 (equivalent to $20.4 million today).[11] As a point of comparison, during the 1992 presidential campaign that preceded this ad blitz, Republicans raised a total of only $12.5 million in soft-money contributions, while Democrats raised $20 million.[12]

At that point, Carolyn began thinking, "What if instead of being captive to the influence of special interest groups, we could engage the public directly?" Around the same time, Jonathan Rauch published *Government's End*, which is still today the most revealing and apt critique of what is wrong with our present governing system. He writes,

> The standard kind of political thinking makes matters worse, not better. Liberals and Conservatives still think they can bring the interest group spiral under control if they can just beat the groups on the other side . . . What few on either side have figured out is that they are all trapped together in a self-defeating mind-set . . . The more you try to beat the other guy, the more the game expands.[13]

Carolyn understood this. As someone who didn't much care for partisan politics, and who just wanted to help get things done, she wasn't susceptible to the siren call that real change was just another election or singular candidate away. "Bumping up against the dysfunction of the overall system on a daily basis," she tells me, "leads you to one of two choices: You either deaden yourself . . . or you seek another way."

And so she sought another way. Deciding that it would be best to tackle this challenge from the outside, Carolyn took her leave of the White House. Less than a year later, she founded an organization called America*Speaks*, whose mission would be to engage citizens in governance. Having experienced a significant and persistent gap between the public and its elected officials at multiple levels of government, Carolyn wanted to find a way to create direct and tangible links between public will and political will.

Over the ensuing fifteen years, that's exactly what she and her team have done, developing their signature 21st Century Town Meeting to tackle public problems in a transparent and publicly credible way. This model was the one used to successfully move the Unified New Orleans Plan forward in the post-Katrina chaos. In fact, America*Speaks* has used the model all over the country, and internationally, on a range of pressing public policy issues. Over 150,000 people have participated in a 21st Century Town Meeting.

As Carolyn tells me, "we are living at a time in which our collective individual consciousness is ahead of the consciousness embedded in our institutions." Part of our task, then, as she sees it, is to redesign our institutions so that they reflect the collective will of the public, and can glean the best ideas and solutions that exist across our society at any point in time.

Along the way, Carolyn and America*Speaks* have had to take on a number of critical challenges to ensure that tapping into the public's views via large-scale deliberation would yield credible and actionable results.

A Democracy for the 21st Century

The idea that many minds are better than a select few is as old as human civilization. Political philosophers from ancient Greece all the way up to modern-day deliberative-democracy theorists have espoused the myriad benefits that can be gained from group deliberation. But reality can be messy. In *Infotopia*, Cass R. Sunstein recently concluded that deliberation is not necessarily always desirable. He writes,

> Does deliberation actually lead to better decisions? Often it does not. Group members may impose pressures on one another, leading to extremism or to a consensus on falsehood rather than truth. The idea of "groupthink," coined by Irving Janis, suggests that groups may well promote unthinking uniformity and dangerous self-censorship, thus failing to combine information and enlarge the range of arguments. Countless groups do badly not in spite of deliberation but because of it. The problem is that deliberating groups often do not obtain the knowledge that their members actually have.[14]

Aside from the issue of self-selection among participants that can (intentionally or inadvertently) skew a group (e.g., Obama's Open for Questions—about pot—"town hall"), Sunstein highlights two particularly critical problems that frequently foil deliberations: framing the choices too narrowly, and thereby setting up a false dichotomy that pits people against one another, and creating an environment in which people feel they must censor their ideas or opinions for fear of ridicule. In either scenario, potentially valuable information will often stay hidden and unusable.

Thankfully, challenges such as these are what America*Speaks* has spent fifteen years figuring out how to overcome. For example, to ensure that preordained, limited choices aren't "baked into" a 21st Century Town Meeting, the design of the event allows participants to prioritize among a range of options—including those they put on the table themselves. In addition, discussion guides, which help participants make their way through complicated material, are developed in partnership with organizations and leaders representing a diversity of views. Further, participant discussions are led by trained facilitators who are specifically charged with making sure that all voices at a table are heard. Networked laptop computers operated by volunteer note takers at each table serve as electronic flip charts to record ideas, which are then sent to a centralized Theme Team that identifies commonalities.

The sum of these collective views is then projected onto a huge screen in the middle of the convention center or similarly large venue (America*Speaks* meetings usually run into the thousands of people). Finally, each meeting participant has a keypad-polling device with which to anonymously express opinions on the issues under debate. The anonymity ensures that, after being exposed to multiple options and arguments, every participant can share their preferences honestly, without worrying about peer pressure or backlash.

To address the problem of possible overrepresentation among self-selecting interest groups, America*Speaks* takes many steps to ensure that its meetings are composed of a representative sample of

the affected public: conducting targeted outreach, providing supports that help people participate, etc. In addition, although experts
help craft the discussion guides and keypad-polling choices, there is
no official-stakeholder-group participation in the events themselves. Analysis of participant demographic distributions and then
assigned table seating also prevent organized groups from trying to
influence the process.

The true power of the America*Speaks* model, then, is that it
combines the great strength of the open-source idea—engaging
many minds in service of solving problems—with the political legitimacy that results from deliberation among participants who
represent a true cross section of the public.

The participants of America*Speaks*'s 21st Century Town Meetings aren't direct decision-making bodies, since results do not automatically become law. However, the meetings are intentionally
designed to ensure that the effort is not wasted. For starters, the
sheer number of participants in a meeting makes the development
of citizen views on the issue at hand a major news event. If elected
officials ignore the results, they can pay a heavy price. In New Orleans, for example, the participation of thousands of representative
citizens in the development of the Unified New Orleans Plan gave
Mayor Ray Nagin and the city council little choice but to embrace
the results. At the same time, well-publicized public agreement on a
way forward in a difficult situation can provide leaders with significant "cover" for tough political decisions.

A related but distinct way of creating political breakthroughs
was demonstrated by the example of the North Dakota Consensus
Council. In 1990, private and public leaders in North Dakota came
together to create a private, nonpartisan, nonprofit group that would
act as a "neutral convener" to help work out solutions to issues

stalled in the normal political process. The governor and the state legislative bodies each appointed representatives to the council, each of whom signed a legal document in which they agreed to abide by whatever decisions resulted from the council's deliberations and promised not to challenge the outcome in court.[15]

Such "multi-stakeholder dialogues," however, usually only convene the "parties to a conflict," putting folks who represent narrow interests in a bargaining environment that can result in a lowest-common-denominator solution that few if any of the participants are happy with and that often fails to represent the broad public interest. The big difference between this approach and 21st Century Town Meetings is that although America*Speaks* engages affected parties to help craft the discussion guides and keypad-polling choices, the public—selected at random—holds ultimate sway rather than aggrieved or self-interested representatives with a narrow goal.

"Nonprofits, corporations, the media—even elected officials or snapshot polls—have all proven that they cannot function as adequate stand-ins for the public interest," Carolyn says. "The good news is that we are now finally able to design processes and utilize tools that allow the public to 'represent' themselves directly."

Not every issue is appropriate for a 21st Century Town Meeting. As Carolyn tells me, the best issues are salient enough that most people are familiar with and concerned about them, yet they are also in a "stalled" state and in need of fresh momentum. Finally, there must be a researched and well-articulated set of possible solutions to draw on so that participants have a strong starting point from which to make decisions over the course of a full-day or weekend-long meeting.

Carolyn mentions the issues of health care reform, immigration, and climate destabilization as the kinds of challenges that could work well with the America*Speaks* model. Indeed, as this book went to press, America*Speaks* was gearing up for a "national discussion" on our nation's fiscal future, aimed at engaging tens of thousands of citizens—in as many as twenty cities across the country—in deliberations about specific reform options for our short-term economic recovery and our long-term fiscal health as a nation.

America*Speaks* believes that our country can and should hold a national discussion like this, on a critical issue, every two years. During the 2008 presidential election, the organization and a coalition of other deliberative-democracy advocates outlined their vision this way:

> Our ideas rest on a set of shared convictions about what democracy ought to mean. We envision an America that encourages the maximum levels of voter turnout, practices people-centered governance, and actively seeks and genuinely values everyone's participation. To this end, we must build an infrastructure of participation and governance that welcomes everyone, while also taking steps to ensure that the voices of the powerful are not unduly elevated . . . The next President should signal a new kind of governance by calling on the American people to take part in a series of national discussions, each engaging one million Americans or more, on the issues of highest public concern, such as the economy, health care, foreign policy, energy and climate change. The national discussions will provide policy makers with an independent, nonpartisan means of assessing the informed opinions and collective priorities of the American people and forge a stronger link between Americans and their government.[16]

To gather participants for such an event, America*Speaks* proposes a system akin to our current jury-duty process. After all, if we are willing to select random members of the public and give them the responsibility of life-and-death decisions in court, why not entrust them to step in where legislatures and our money-saturated political process are failing?

Joe Goldman, America*Speaks*'s vice president, tells me that this "institutionalization challenge" is the next step in America*Speaks*'s evolution. "Our goal is to transform institutions that engage the public, not just to act as a consultant for specific participatory processes. For the last ten to fifteen years, we have done extensive R&D, in partnership with others, showing how this model can work at truly large scale. But to make it happen, we have to get beyond demonstration projects and create an integral place for it in our governance system."

Some of the infrastructure necessary for this kind of institutionalization already exists. America*Speaks*, for example, has been working with the American Library Association to engage libraries as they rewrite their mission statements for the next decade. As Carolyn points out, many libraries are naturally well suited to act as public gathering spaces. By setting aside certain rooms for public discussion, libraries could be the connecting points for communities across the country that are participating in guided deliberations via telecast. This series of deliberations would then become, in effect, a national conversation.

Goldman adds that intentional, place-based participation like this is crucial to the success of the process. "If the only approach you take to citizen engagement is decentralized and viral, you get a self-selecting, Web-savvy audience that is not representative of the public at large. Because of the digital divide, if we don't augment that approach with on-the-ground recruitment and face-to-face meetings, these deliberations won't be as diverse and representative as they need to be."

Because there are various barriers to the participation of working-class people, parents, youth, those without Internet access, and others, America*Speaks* expends significant resources to recruit participants constituting a demographically representative sample of the larger population. As Goldman tells me, "if you try to do public involvement on the cheap, you will get a self-selecting group that has different priorities than the population at large. To make a process legitimate in the eyes of the public, you've got to pay for it." The cost of America*Speaks* gatherings can run into the hundreds of thousands of dollars for a one-day meeting, with a significant portion devoted to the outreach and support services—such as transportation and day care—that enable a truly representative group to participate.

Yet in light of the breakthroughs that can result—as happened in the wake of the Unified New Orleans Plan meetings—the investment seems a bargain. As Carolyn tells me, "for example, our government just invested $5.7 billion in a National Service Act, which is very important . . . but why not expand this? For a fraction of that amount of money, we could also do real public participation. If we took public engagement in decision making seriously, it could lead to unbelievable progress on a range of problems that have bedeviled us for decades."

America*Speaks*'s 21st Century Town Meeting model is not the only way to directly engage citizens in governance. Much more prevalent is the use of ballot initiatives or referenda, which are legal in more than half of America's states. Through ballot initiatives, proposals can be voted on by the public at large, bypassing the legislature. This approach, though noble in intent, suffers from a series of serious problems that need to be addressed.

First, the wording of ballot initiatives is often confusing or misleading, with the framing of the issue usually driven by whichever wealthy individual or corporate interest had the money to pay signature gatherers to get the initiative on the ballot. Further, because ballot language is determined at the outset, there is little to no opportunity for the initiative to benefit from public ideas and input of the kind that can arise in a more deliberative process—it's just an up-or-down vote. And with the only real public debate about the pros and cons of a ballot initiative happening via thirty-second "yes" or "no" ads, it is incredibly difficult to foster any kind of genuine public learning or awareness about the impact its passage would have, not to mention the impossibility of considering a third (or fourth) option.

But there is another way to engage citizens that avoids many of the problems of a normal ballot initiative while also drawing on the strengths of the AmericaSpeaks approach. Known as "citizens' assemblies," the model first took root in the Canadian province of British Columbia. It was there, in the election of 1996, that the New Democratic Party ended up with a majority of seats in the provincial legislature even though its main rival, the Liberal Party, took the popular vote.[17]

Such results are endemic to electoral systems that use the common "first past the post" method of deciding elections, whereby a candidate can win with less than majority support as long as they receive a plurality of votes. This was the case in my home state of Vermont during our election for lieutenant governor in 2002, when Republican Brian Dubie won the office despite receiving a mere 41 percent of the vote. Because supporters of the Democratic and

Progressive party candidates split their votes 32 and 25 percent, respectively, and there was no system in place for a runoff or instant-runoff election, the will of the public was obscured without a way for the top two finishers to compete head-to-head.

In British Columbia, Gordon Campbell, the leader of the Liberal Party, promised—should his party win the election—to create a "citizens' assembly" that would consider reform of the provincial electoral system, suffering from this same kind of problem. When his party did come to power in 2000, Campbell and the Liberals followed through on that promise.

The result was an unprecedented event in the history of direct and deliberative democracy. For the first time ever, a body of randomly selected citizens was empowered to recommend changes to an electoral system, with the assembly's final proposal placed directly on the ballot as a popular referendum.

Here's how it worked: 160 citizens—one man and one woman from each of British Columbia's seventy-nine electoral districts, plus one aboriginal man and one aboriginal woman—made up the assembly and were charged with figuring out the "best possible electoral system for British Columbia."[18] Meeting over the course of eleven months, the assembly heard from thousands of people, experts and regular citizens alike, during fifty open public hearings. Further, it considered in excess of sixteen hundred written submissions of factors to examine in coming to a decision.

In a way, Campbell's move was incredibly politically savvy. By empowering an independent group to consider the issue of electoral reform, his party was able to avoid the conflict-of-interest charges that would have resulted had it taken the matter up itself. This is a particularly convincing reason why, in tacking issues on which political parties cannot be trusted to act disinterestedly—such as, in addition to electoral reform, the issues of campaign-finance reform and redistricting—the citizens'-assembly method is far preferable to the normal legislative approach.

There was one major flaw in Campbell's original charge, though: The threshold for reform was set at 60 percent support required for passage (rather than, as is usually the case with ballot initiatives, a simple majority). Thus, when it came time to vote on the *near-unanimous* recommendation that came from the assembly's members—a move to the more representative single-transferrable-vote system—British Columbia voters fell short, mustering only 57 percent support for the proposal, three points short of passage.

As we've also seen in the U.S. Senate, getting 60 percent support for *anything* is nearly impossible in this day and age, raising the very fair question of what level of support actually constitutes public will. In most cases, I would argue, a simple majority is appropriate. Even for political-process reforms, where a strong argument can be made for the desirability of supermajority support being present, one would think that achieving a double-digit gap between supporters and opponents—anything over 55 percent—would adequately meet that criterion.

Nevertheless, the groundbreaking example of the British Columbia citizens' assembly has managed to have a lasting impact. Inspired by the original effort, fellow province Ontario and also the Netherlands have since completed similar efforts, and momentum for the approach continues to grow.[19]

Imagine if instead of settling for ballot initiatives driven by private wealth and thirty-second ads, a few pioneering states were to adopt the citizens'-assembly model—based on collective wisdom and careful deliberation—to consider reform of their electoral and campaign-finance systems.

Such a path would not only be in the public interest; it would likely also be politically advantageous. Consider this finding from polling done to decipher attitudes on political reform in the Midwest. An impressive 62 percent of respondents were "more interested in a political candidate who believes it may not be possible to improve education, create jobs, and cut taxes without first reducing the role of money in politics and the influence of lobbyists, than in a candidate who focuses solely on the issues (35%)."[20] With more and more process-oriented Millennials coming of voting age, such a sentiment is sure to only become more common.

Nor would we have to completely abandon our own issue cares and concerns in service of such reform. Each of us can still be advocates for the vital concerns of a clean-energy future, health care reform, improved education, or whatever else motivates us. The crucial point is that, in doing so, we must now realize that the larger interest of each of those causes (and more) will only ever be met if we simultaneously band together to reclaim our democracy and upgrade it for the twenty-first century.

That means not going all in, as so many of us are wont to do, for one personal cause or favorite candidate. As a public, we often fall into the trap of saying or believing things like "If only [insert current president] would do this one thing for [insert personal cause], then everything would be fixed." Such notions have become the cotton candy of our political system: Bright and enticing at the outset, narrow-issue advocacy and individual candidates nevertheless almost always fail to sate our hunger for real change (and very often leave us feeling sick after the first few bites).

To enable more meaningful and lasting progress, it's time to take a step back from individual issues and candidates and instead focus on the systemic question of how we go about societal problem solving and decision making. This requires a shift in thinking away from doing one thing incrementally now (like health care reform) to doing the kind of *process* reforms that can enable us to address lots of issues more effectively over the next forty or so years.

I see the task before us as twofold: *saving* our democracy from the corruption of money and influence while *upgrading* it with more meaningful avenues for participation such as SeeClickFix, Heart & Soul Community Planning, America*Speaks*, and citizens' assemblies. While none of these provides a stand-alone blueprint for a new model of societal problem solving, each nevertheless offers tantalizing glimpses of what a more open-source-inspired form of democracy could look like.

If you take any message from this book, then, I hope it will be this: Less important than finding some silver bullet policy solution is finding ways to empower as many problem solvers as possible to contribute as much as they can, in as many different ways as possible.

Nevertheless, there are specific federal-level solutions that can and should be advanced. The Fair Elections Now Act, for instance, would create a national version of the clean-elections laws in Maine, Arizona, and Connecticut. Promoted by vital groups such as Change Congress, the Center for Responsive Politics, and Common Cause, the bill would provide voluntary public financing for House and Senate candidates who met a threshold of qualifying small-dollar donations. Candidates who accepted public financing would forgo all private donations in excess of one hundred dollars. However, every donation of one hundred dollars or less would be matched by a public fund four times over.

Further, recognizing that more than half of the total cost of competitive campaigns for federal office can be attributed to highly priced television advertising, the bill provides for "free airtime" for qualifying candidates. Since the airwaves are a public resource held in trust by broadcast companies, we can require that they devote airtime to topics in the public interest, as they already do with educational programming and public service advertisements.[21]

Getting a broken federal system to fix itself is not going to be easy. Even some of its most powerful players have decided the task is too much, as Indiana senator Evan Bayh conceded when he decided not to run for reelection in early 2010. Following his announcement, Bayh explained his decision this way:

> In my father's day, there was a saying in the Senate, you're legislating for four years; you campaign for two. We now have perpetual campaigns. They never stop. My first day in the Senate, and the first discussion was let's talk about the next election. That was two years away. Part of that is driven by the constant need to raise funds. If you're just out there fundraising all the time, then things political are on your mind. And that does not help.[22]

Thankfully, though, we can work to advance the effort to save and upgrade our democracy on multiple fronts at once, many beyond Washington, D.C. In the words of former Supreme Court justice Louis Brandeis, our state legislatures can act as "laboratories of democracy," passing innovative or politically difficult laws to help clear the way for other states and the federal government to follow suit.

In the past century, for instance, states such as Wisconsin, California, and Vermont have consistently acted as trailblazers for other states and the federal government. Wisconsin can claim credit for the first income tax laws, as well as for having woven some of the first strands of the social safety net that is now standard in most states and nationally. For its part, California has long been a leader in passing environmental-protection legislation, particularly clean-air efforts. Most recently, fourteen states have followed California's lead in adopting clean vehicle-emissions standards (known as "the Pavley law," for the state legislator who initially led the effort), pushing the federal government to increase national standards to be in line with leading states.

In Vermont, this type of leadership goes back to the state's earliest roots. Our state constitution was the first in America to outlaw slavery, give voting rights to non-property-holding males, and guarantee public access to primary and secondary education. That tradition of bold civil rights initiative continues today. Having passed the first civil unions bill in 2000 (with nine other states following suit since then), the state recently led the way again, becoming the first to enforce full marriage equality by legislative means in 2009, with more states sure to follow in coming years. As has been proved with clean-elections laws, the same "laboratory federalism" approach can be utilized to advance democratic reforms in a more bottom-up fashion.

Whether working locally or nationally, there are important roles for each of us. As the late senator Paul Wellstone once said, "there are three critical ingredients to democratic renewal and progressive change in America: good public policy, grassroots organizing, and electoral politics."[23] Each of those spheres—often referred to and represented visually as the "Wellstone Triangle"—needs our attention. Whether by focusing our work for democracy in one area alone, say, as a professor, community organizer, or candidate for public office, or by living a life that somehow manages to combine all three (as Wellstone himself did), we can each be a vital part of the renewal of our democracy and society.

With this book, I have endeavored to provide a creative spark and an inspirational touchstone for that journey. A creative spark for what our democracy might be with stories of the efforts of SeeClickFix, America*Speaks*, and more. And an inspirational touchstone through the stories of courageous individuals like Vera Triplett, Mark Klein, Carolyn Lukensmeyer, and Frances Moore Lappé, all of whom made the decision to stop leading "divided lives." Stepping into a place of uncertainty, they each pursued that which they felt deeply called to contribute.

Allowing that impulse to flourish across our society is what both the idea of open source and the practice of democracy are all about. As my friend Joel Rogers once told me, "the beauty of democracy is that you never know who the messenger will be." The historic opportunity now before us is to marry that eloquent ideal with the unique potential unleashed by the open-source movement.

If we are able to do this, the next chapter of democracy and human progress can be authored collectively, by a generation of messengers whose combined wisdom and will we are just beginning to appreciate.

AFTERWORD

Enthusiastic partisans of the idea of progress are in danger of failing to recognize—because they set so little store by them—the immense riches accumulated by the human race on either side of the narrow furrow on which they keep their eyes fixed: by underrating the achievements of the past, they devalue all those which still remain to be accomplished. If men have always been concerned with only one task—how to create a society fit to live in—the forces which inspired our distant ancestors are also present in us. Nothing is settled; everything can still be altered. What was done, but turned out wrong, can be done again. The Golden Age, which blind superstition had placed behind [or ahead of] us, is in us.

—CLAUDE LÉVI-STRAUSS

And the end of all our exploring
Will be to arrive where we began
And to know the place for the first time.

—T. S. ELIOT

UPON THE close of the Constitutional Convention in Philadelphia in 1787, a departing Benjamin Franklin was approached by an anxious Mrs. Powel. According to legend, she asked, "Well Doctor, what have we got, a republic or a monarchy?" Franklin responded with a line that has since resonated throughout American history: "A republic . . . *if you can keep it.*" With that news, America announced to the world that we would attempt to fulfill the unmet promise of the democratic experiment begun by the ancient Greeks so long ago.

As a people, Americans have, in many ways, kept and expanded the promise at the heart of the republic and our larger democratic experiment in the intervening years. Somewhat ironically, this has most often meant revisiting and changing the very conflicted documents that the founders of the country signed that day in Philadelphia—amending the Constitution to grant the right to vote to women in the 1920s, then to young people over the age of eighteen in the 1970s. Indeed, it wasn't until the 1960s—less than fifty years ago—that major legislation was passed extending equal rights to people of color.

True, democracy has an imperfect history and has often failed to live up to its own ideal. As much as Athenian democracy was direct, it also directly excluded slaves and women, as America did for much of its own history. Even the movements listed above were efforts simply to *get* the vote, not to explore the many different ideas of how we might make democracy work better than its "1.0" form. Relatively speaking, then, we are really still in the beginning stages when it comes to fulfilling democracy's potential.

Yet there is a self-renewing power to democracy that makes that potential almost inexhaustible. Based on the idea that power should come from us, together, not from divinely appointed rulers (unless we consider everyone as such), the only limits to what democracy can accomplish are whatever limits there may be to what humanity itself can accomplish.

Remember that "democracy" comes from the Greek words *demos* and *kratia*, meaning "the people" and "power" or "rule," respectively. Democracy is about the power of the people. The word "power," in turn, has roots that mean "to be able." Literally, then, democracy is about the "ability of the people."

Robert Kennedy invoked the "ability of the people" in Indiana in 1968, on no less an occasion than announcing to the city of Indianapolis the assassination of Rev. Dr. Martin Luther King Jr. He harked back to the Greek democratic experiment and quoted the playwright Aeschylus. Our fragile experiment, however faltering and uneven in attempt, he said, has ever since been "to tame the savageness of man and make gentle the life of this world."

When he wrote that, Aeschylus may have been striving to find words that could describe the Greek concept of *eudaimonia*, which translates roughly to "human flourishing" and which Aristotle later described as the highest, most inclusive good at which "every art and every scientific inquiry, and similarly every action and purpose, may be said to aim."[1]

Regardless of Aeschylus's intent then, it is clear that we must aspire greatly when we ponder our ability as a people in the present day. Indeed, the circumstances in our world today are far less innocent than at any other period in our history. Rather than affecting the fate of one nation or one race in one nation, climate destabilization has changed the stakes for the planet, posing the question of whether human *civilization* and our experiment in democracy will be able to persevere to see the dawn of the second half of the twenty-first century.

For instance, before the climate crisis emerged, our actions, or inactions, never had the power to determine the type of world that future generations would inhabit. By "type of world," I do not mean merely culture or politics but literally the climate and makeup of the physical space of this planet. And with nearly seven billion people now inhabiting our planet, never before have we been in danger of excluding such a sheer number of humans from the opportunity to meet their full potential if we get it wrong. For good or ill, how this generation responds to the interconnected social, political, and environmental circumstances of our time will have the greatest consequence—in years and lives—yet seen in the history of human existence.

Let us remember that modern civilization began only about ten thousand years ago, when some of our ancestors could worry about more than mere survival in a rapidly changing environment and began building complex social structures aided by the advent of agriculture.

In the millennia since, we have set about exploring the myriad mysteries of our world and expressing the inexhaustible potential of the human mind and heart. When I was in college, I would walk through the stacks of our library while working on my thesis. Row upon row of books on subjects I had never even heard of stretched beyond my sight, and I tried to imagine how many lifetimes it would take to learn everything stored between each set of covers. The sheer volume and complexity of the knowledge we have discovered, developed, and, in some cases, deployed over those ten thousand years is pretty near unfathomable.

Now our contribution threatens to be something far less welcome. With the climate, our actions over the next few years could very well determine the world that people will live in tens of thousands of years from now. As world-renowned climate scientist James Hansen, director of NASA's Goddard Institute and the first to testify to the U.S. Congress on climate destabilization, all the way back in 1988, recently warned, in order for humanity to merely "preserve a planet similar to that on which civilization developed," we must stay below 350 parts per million of carbon dioxide in our atmosphere, far below our current level of pollution. If we fail to do this, we will lock in an amount of climate disruption and warming that will swamp our ability to do anything but scramble to adapt to an ever-unstable world, for centuries.

More specifically, Hansen predicts, "If we follow business as usual I can't see how west Antarctica could survive a century. We are talking about a sea-level rise of at least a couple of meters this century."[2] It's worth pausing here for some context. A mere one-and-a-half-meter rise in sea level would displace seventeen million people in Bangladesh. Two meters would create, in Hansen's estimate, "hundreds of millions of refugees" around the world.

A third of the world's population, and at least that much of our civilization's infrastructure, is located in coastal areas.[3] Go ahead: Name a major international city not on a coast. I tried; it's not easy. Of the ten most populated cities in the world, only one—Mexico City—is not coastal.[4] Yet unless we take immediate, sweeping action to abandon fossil fuels and move to clean energy, "no stable shoreline [will] be reestablished in any time frame that humanity can conceive."[5]

How can we allow this to happen? Unfortunately, there is no reset button. Nor do I expect that there will be some divine intervention or breakthrough technology that will automatically reverse two hundred years of fossil-fueled history. As Bill McKibben has written, "the world apart from man is gone; the solution to the planet's problems is going to have to come from the species that caused them."[6] Or as President John Kennedy once said, "here on earth, God's work must truly be our own."

I am reminded of Dr. King, who once wrote, "The arc of the moral universe is long, but it bends toward justice." The continuation of that moral arc of progress, as inspiring as it is, is not a foregone conclusion. It has bent toward justice because *we* have bent it. Now, the preconditions that have allowed civilization to flourish— enough resources to thrive and not merely survive, a predictable climate, and relative societal stability—could be stolen from us if we don't act to bend the circumstances of our world to our will yet again.

The great danger in trying to do so with a challenge of such overwhelming magnitude is that we are tempted to do so in overly centralized ways, forgetting the great lesson that the open-source movement has revealed to us. Frances Moore Lappé puts it this way:

> Top-down strategies are efficient, we still hear, even though they got us into this mess to begin with and suppress precisely the networks of creativity and commitment on which real solutions depend. We have no time for democracy, we're still told, even though it's inconceivable that we can make right our relation- ship to the earth without making right our relationship with one another.[7]

As Frankie suggests, an even greater mess may come to pass if we fail to engage more problem solvers in the process of changing the trajectory we are on. But it should also be said that even if it is too late to forestall some of the worst eventualities predicted by climate scientists, fostering more open-source models of participa- tion is still our best bet going forward. As the aftermath of Hurri- cane Katrina showed us, empowered communities of local problem solvers will be more resilient and durable, should such a future come to pass.

Yet even with the specter of climate destabilization, I still believe that this time of ours *can* be the most creative and gentle era we have ever seen. To make it so, we need to stop seeing one another as the cause of the problem and instead see in one another potential solutions. Building on our democratic inheritance, let us combine all of that knowledge stored in and outside of our libraries with the wisdom and will of people the world over to realize a future more worthy of our promise.

Indeed, while many environmentalists lament the enormity of our human population, actually solving an issue as complex as climate destabilization will probably necessitate *nothing less* than the problem-solving energy and ability of our nearly seven billion brains and pairs of hands. *We* are the greatest untapped reserve of energy on this planet.

As author Jeff Howe has written, "crowdsourcing is rooted in a fundamentally egalitarian principle: every individual possesses some knowledge or talent that some other individual will find valuable."[8] When we see one another in this way, it becomes clear that we *do* have all the time in the world, or at least the two billion to six billion spare hours that a billion people in advanced economies are estimated to have between them each day.

So while we undoubtedly need, in the words of Energy Secretary Steven Chu, some "Nobel-level" breakthroughs on carbon-neutral energy sources, even more than that we need to unleash and connect the diverse, innumerable talents across our society for the greatest possible benefit. With an all-hands-on-deck moment, we need a ship of state that allows for all hands on deck.

Democracy is not meant to be a static thing, nor is there any reason it has to be. Consider that only a hundred years ago, many observers thought that the bulk of questions that science could answer were over and dealt with. They thought that, as a discipline, science was closing in on the end point of its work, with "only a few turrets and pinnacles to be added, a few roof bosses to be carved." The author Bill Bryson sets the record straight:

> In fact, of course, the world was about to enter a century of science where many people wouldn't understand anything and none would understand everything. Scientists would soon find themselves adrift in a bewildering realm of particles and antiparticles, where things pop in and out of existence in spans of time that make nano-seconds look plodding and uneventful, where everything is strange. Science was moving from a world of macro physics, where events transpire with unimaginable swiftness on scales far below the limits of imagining. We were about to enter the quantum age.[9]

The recent history of politics and economics is similar but in reverse. We have figured out the realm of individualism. We have every product imaginable on our store shelves and every conceivable individual interest group knocking on the doors of Congress in Washington. What is waiting for us is a whole new field—figuring out how to harness our collective wisdom and power to advance the common good in a century of unprecedented challenge and opportunity.

What the open-source revolution offers our model of democracy is not some totally new direction, but rather a realization of its fullest potential. My hope and prediction is that accomplishing this will be the great project and legacy of our generation. If that is to happen, our responsibility—whether as writer or reader—is not merely to reflect on the state of the world but to try, however clumsily in attempt, or seemingly foolhardy for that attempt, to improve our human condition.

Doing so will take a dynamic balance of both authentic passion and committed open-mindedness. For if we have too much passion, the danger is that reason and inconvenient facts will be too easily discarded, leading us down the dangerous road of belligerence and dogmatic ideology. Yet if we are so open-minded that we would wait for perfect clarity and consensus before daring to work for a better world, such a wait would doubtless be endless and unfulfilling.

I believe that it is only when we are willing to take a leap—while also admitting that we don't have all the answers—that we can hope to find the truths for which we search. Maybe then, with deliberate thought and action, we will help to shape a better world by joining in common cause with those willing to do likewise. That brave impulse was present in ancient Greece when the idea of democracy was born, in America during the revolution that resuscitated it, and it lives in us still today.

ACKNOWLEDGMENTS

Those who don't imitate anything create nothing.

—SALVADOR DALÍ

Good work finds the way between pride and despair.
It graces with health. It heals with grace.
It preserves the given so that it remains a gift.
By it, we lose loneliness:
we clasp the hands of those who go before us, and the hands of those who
come after us;
we enter the little circle of each other's arms,
and the larger circle of lovers whose hands are joined in a dance, and the
larger circle of all creatures, passing in and out of life, who move also in
a dance, to a music so subtle and vast that no ear hears it except in
fragments.

—WENDELL BERRY

LET ME be the first to acknowledge that the ideas in this book are not necessarily new. Rather, my primary purpose in writing has been to connect intriguing people and their stories with some of the best ideas I've gleaned from *other* writers and thinkers (who, in turn, would likely say the same about "their" ideas and writing) to try to craft a coherent narrative of some of the important shifts I see happening in our society. In this sense, this book is part of a rich commons that, traced to its roots, would go back farther than I can comprehend and would also include far more people than I could ever list.

Thankfully, though, there are many whom I can name and include here (I ask for understanding and offer apologies to any I may accidentally omit). First, all of the people I interviewed who entrusted me with their stories. From Vera Triplett and Lamar Roberts in the New Orleans chapter to Ben Berkowitz and Mark Klein later on, I was humbled and honored by the honesty and courage of all the leaders I got to know, either over the phone or in person.

In terms of the writing and research I relied on, the following authors were instrumental in developing my understanding of some of the core themes of this book. For their writing on open source, free software, wikis, and Web 2.0 efforts in general, I am deeply appreciative of the work of authors Richard Stallman, Linus Torvalds, Eric Raymond, Steven Weber, James Surowiecki, Clay Shirky, Jeff Howe, and Andrew Lih, in particular. In addition to those authors, leading thinkers such as Tim O'Reilly, Yochai Benkler, and Micah Sifry have also written at length about the promise of Government 2.0, open-source economics, and open-source politics, respectively.

For pioneering work related to the Millennial generation, I relied heavily on Neil Howe and William Strauss, Morley Winograd and Michael D. Hais, Don Tapscott, John Zogby, and Michael Connery, among yet more.

My work in the final chapters was inspired by and dependent upon the many leaders in the growing field of deliberative democracy. Ever since I first heard Carolyn Lukensmeyer speak in 2003, I have been awed by her vision and commitment to improving our democracy. If President Obama would let me pick him a new chief of staff, she would be far and away my top recommendation. Beyond Carolyn, the entire team at America*Speaks* deserves great thanks, especially Joe Goldman, Evan Paul, Wendy Jacobson, and Susanna Haas Lyons. Outside of America*Speaks*, author and connector (and pretty much everything else) Matt Leighninger provided initial encouragement, as did the great team at the Orton Family Foundation.

I was first inspired to write this book while with the Sierra Student Coalition, particularly after hearing scores of "green fire stories" that mentioned the transformative power of books during summer program (Sprog) trainings across the country, from Vermont to Washington. Thanks most especially to wonderful friends and organizers Dave Karpf, Nathan Wyeth, Rachel Ackoff, Juan Martinez, Christina Billingsley, Juliana Williams, Timothy Den Herder-Thomas, Andrew Nazdin, Rachel Guillory, Zo Tobi, Seth Wade, and David Bronstein, all of whom provided encouragement for this book.

Similarly, I am deeply appreciative for all the amazing leaders and friends across the Energy Action Coalition, specifically Billy Parish, Josh Lynch, Liz Veazey, Julian Keniry, Meg Boyle, and Jessy Tolkan. From Middlebury, which is its own piece of the climate movement altogether, sincere thanks to May Boeve, Jon Warnow, and all the rest of the marchers, StepItUppers, and 350.orgers who model open-source organizing better than anyone else.

When I initially made the tough decision to leave my job as a climate and youth organizer to write this book, two of the very first people to offer their support were Bob Perkowitz and Lisa Renstrom. I am forever grateful for their incredible confidence and friendship. Likewise, I owe a debt of gratitude to Lee Bodner and the team that comprised ecoAmerica while I did the early research for this book there, as a fellow.

Astute and dedicated research assistance was provided by Imran Battla and Nate Maton. For their service as critical readers of my book proposal and, in some cases, subsequent chapters, I am also very grateful for the time and thoughtfulness of friends Bethany Robertson, Rafael Reyes, Marc Sorel, Richard Rowe, Michael Silberman, Kara Davidson, Teryn Norris, Lucas Merrill Brown, Sarah Cowan Johnson, Alex Dewar, Thomas Hand, Andrew Savage, Clare Sierawski, Dena Simmons, J. R. Wallace, Tristan Brown, Rachel Barge, Peter Murray, Joshua Gorman, and Carolyn Wills April (as well as others who are listed elsewhere in these acknowledgments for additional reasons). Thanks also to David Stern and MixedInk for allowing all the feedback from these readers to be collected in one place, in a collaborative format in keeping with the Web 2.0 theme of the book.

At Demos, my home throughout the writing of this book, thanks is due first and foremost to Lew Daly, who believed in this project from the very beginning and has ever since served as a true mentor and friend. Miles Rapoport and Tamara Draut deserve immense thanks as well, for their support of this project, certainly, but even more for leading and stewarding such an amazingly dynamic and supportive community for all the authors and fellows who are lucky enough to call Demos home. Special thanks at Demos also goes to David Callahan, who was instrumental in helping me figure out how to craft the proposal for this book and who then introduced me to my wonderful agent, Andrew Stuart, who made sure I landed with exactly the right publisher.

At Bloomsbury, thanks to publishing legend George Gibson for taking a chance on a first-time, twenty-five-year-old author, as well as to Nick Trautwein for crucial early support. And, of course, to Benjamin Adams, senior editor extraordinaire, whose wisdom and keen eyes are evidenced in numerous places throughout this work. As soon as I saw the Jon Lester bobblehead sitting among the manuscripts he was editing, I had a sense that Ben was the right editor for this project. That has turned out to be incredibly true and I hope there will be more projects that we work on together, TK.

For their generous investment in this project in more ways than one, it would be impossible for me to ever give enough thanks to Jessica Bailey and the Rockefeller Brothers Fund and Diane Ives and the Kendeda Fund. For additional grants that provided crucial support for this book, special thanks to Daniel Katz and the Over-brook Foundation, Renstrom Perkowitz Social Investments, John Esterle at the Whitman Institute, Jee Kim and the Surdna Foundation, and David Grant.

In the course of writing this book, I was twice given the great gift of a week away for pause and reflection. For that and much more, thanks to my wonderful friend Michael Cox, as well as to Peter Forbes, Helen Whybrow, and the whole team at the Center for Whole Communities, in Vermont.

While some writers need total silence, I prefer to have a soundtrack for my work. Many artists graced my playlists while I wrote, but I had some favorites: Garett Brennan, Brett Dennen, Mat Kearney, Feist, and Keb' Mo'. Thanks to all for their amazing music and to Garett additionally for his friendship and leadership for the climate.

Almost all of my writing was done in the comfy confines of Yale Divinity School's Day Missions Library. To the friendly students and staff there, and especially to Dean Dale Peterson, thank you. Before my move to New Haven, early motivation for this work was also found at All Souls Church, in Washington, D.C. In particular, special thanks to the Reverends Rob Hardies, Shana Lynngood, and Louise Green for their amazing sermons and community leadership.

For their role in fostering my appreciation for some of the subjects in this book and helping me develop as a writer, sincere gratitude is, of course, also due to a number of my teachers and professors. From Lebanon High School, Mary Maxfield, William Tift, Deb Springhorn, and Denise Labrie were especially important to me. At Wheaton, I will always be grateful for classes with and mentorship from Professors Jay Goodman, Russell Williams, Gerry Huiskamp, John Miller, Stephen Mathis, Barry Shelley, and Darlene Boroviak.

For investing in me and the vibrant communities of shared passion they nurture, thanks to Sharon Smith and the Earth Island Institute, Melissa Millage and the Morris K. Udall and Stewart L. Udall Foundation, and Fred Slabach and the Harry S. Truman Scholarship Foundation. And for, in turn, helping make most of these awards possible, cheers to my great mentor and friend, the incomparable Dean Alex Trayford.

Other friends who provided crucial support were Mike Lieberman and Terri Lodge, who generously let me live with them for four months at the very beginning of this journey. My dear friend Emilie Kapp went out of her way to host me in New York on many of my early Bolt Bus trips up from D.C. when I was meeting with various editors and publishing houses. And I could thank my great New Haven friends Barton and Jaime Creeth for many things, but will stop at their introducing me to hurling (the Gaelic sport, not the drinking one), which helped ensure that I didn't spend *all* my time in front of my computer, and also for a celebratory Indian buffet after I turned in my manuscript.

I am overwhelmingly humbled to be able to say that some of my personal heroes have also become my close friends over the past few years. For their wisdom and encouragement, I am deeply grateful to Frances Moore Lappé, Bill McKibben, Van Jones, Joel Rogers, and Jon Isham. Each of these leaders has inspired me not only with their thoughts, words, and deeds, but also by modeling how to live a good and balanced life, with compassion for all around them. Each has taken me under their wing at different times throughout this process, generously hosted me in their home, and given me an example to aspire to as I try to, in the words of Thoreau, "live the life I've imagined."

Underlying that possibility, of course, is the love and support of my family. While my dad, William Duval, had his own unique form of encouragement—"Get that book finished so you can go to grad school!"—I appreciated it greatly. Likewise, my sister Juliet, who was incredulous when she heard about my fellowship ("Let me get this right: Someone is going to pay you just to think and write?!"), provided the kind of love only a sister can.

My mom, Alice Blackmer, has probably done more than anyone else to make this book possible. From the time I was young she helped expose me to the fascinating world of writing, ideas, authors, and books. Indeed, the two most influential books I read while in high school and college were not assigned to me by teachers or professors but rather were gifts from her. *Believing Cassandra*, by Alan AtKisson, and *The Vermont Papers*, by Frank Bryan and John McClaughry. Thanks to advice and encouragement from her and my stepfather, Sam Dorrance, this whole book-writing thing seemed a lot more doable than it otherwise would have.

Lastly, I couldn't have done this without Joan, the person who has been with me from the time I first made the decision to write this book (in her old backyard on Irving Street) to when I finished it (in our new backyard on Nicoll Street). Joan, your love and friendship underlie this book and so much else in my life: Thank you for everything.

NOTES

Introduction

1. Here I should note that nearly all of my organizing experiences, from the Dean campaign to Tanzania, were enabled by the amazing support of the advising and career programs at my college. Due to Wheaton's generosity, I twice received fellowships that allowed me to devote a summer to volunteer work, not to mention the help and guidance I got in applying for scholarships that made the tuition bill easier to manage. If you or someone you know is looking at colleges, I cannot recommend any more highly than Wheaton, in Massachusetts.

2. While the terms most popularly used to describe this trend are "climate change" and "global warming," I prefer to use the term "climate destabilization" because it is a more accurate description of what scientists are telling us is actually happening. Yes the climate is "changing," but it is always and has always been changing. The difference now is the pace and magnitude of that change—which is on a scale that is *destabilizing* to natural processes. Similarly, "global warming" does not really convey the full reality of what might happen, as a destabilized climate does far more than warm temperatures. It also leads to more intense hurricanes, floods, droughts, etc.

3. Mbendi Information Services, "An MBendi Profile: An MBendi Industry (Sector) Profile for Tanzania," May 5, 2006, http://www.mbendi.co.za/indy/powr/af/ta/p0005.htm.

4. International Federation of Red Cross and Red Crescent Societies, "Tanzania Food Insecurity," April 7, 2004, http://www.ifrc.org/docs/appeals/rpts04/TZ040407.pdf.

5. Jared Duval, "Climate of Negligence: Climate Destabilization and the US Political Agenda," 72.

6. Ibid., 74.

Chapter 1: Katrina Revisited

1. Personal communication, Michael Tippett, April 28, 2009.

2. Lev Grossman, "Time's Person of the Year: You," *Time*, December 13, 2006.

3. NowPublic, "Katrina Missing Persons Board," http://www.nowpublic.com/katrina_missing_persons_board_0.

4. Tippett prefers the term "participatory media" to the more frequently used "citizen journalism." He sees the reporting that NowPublic hosts as the raw material that provides leads for professional journalists, not as a substitution for their work. Personal communication.

5. Open Source: Christopher Lydon in Conversation on Arts, Ideas and Politics, "Participatory Media Coverage of Hurricane Katrina," http://www.radioopensource.org/participatory-media-coverage-of-hurricane-katrina/.

6. NowPublic, "Katrina Missing Persons Board," http://www.nowpublic.com/katrina_missing_persons_board_0?page=1, accessed May 2009.

7. Ibid., 3.

8. Ibid., 6.

9. Ibid.

10. While looking into NowPublic.com, I registered with a user name and was then given a phone number I could call to record voice reports. I now have that number saved in my phone. Hopefully, I won't ever have to use it, but it's comforting to know that in the case of an emergency I can just call from my cell phone and instantly report what is happening, from anywhere.

11. Mark Glaser, "NOLA.com Blogs and Forums Help Save Lives After Katrina," Online Journalism Review, September 13, 2005.

12. Ibid.

13. Personal communication, Lamar Roberts, November 2009.

14. Farhad Manjoo, "Why FEMA Failed," Salon.com, September 7, 2005, http://dir.salon.com/story/news/feature/2005/09/07/fema/index.html.

15. Stephen Barr, "Coast Guard's Response to Katrina a Silver Lining in the Storm," *Washington Post*, September 6, 2005.

16. Amanda Ripley, "Hurricane Katrina: How the Coast Guard Gets It Right," *Time*, October 23, 2005.

17. Gina Pace, "Katrina Makes Coast Guard Heroes," CBS News, September 19, 2005.

18. Today, the Coast Guard is part of the Department of Homeland Security and, in times of war, can be directed to operate with the Navy. Interestingly, that makes the Coast Guard the only branch of the armed services allowed to act both as a military service and as domestic law enforcement. Unlike other members of the armed services, Coastguardsmen are allowed to carry firearms, execute warrants, and make arrests on U.S. soil.

19. Donald T. Phillips and Admiral James M. Loy, *Character in Action* (Annapolis, MD: Naval Institute Press, 2003), 6.

20. Barr, "Coast Guard's Response."

21. Personal communication, Brian Thomas, May 2009.

22. Government Accountability Office, *COAST GUARD: Observations on the Preparation, Response, and Recovery Missions Related to Hurricane Katrina*, July 2006, www.gao.gov/cgi-bin/getrpt?GAO-06-903.

23. Phillips and Loy, *Character in Action*, 94.

24. Gerald R. Hoover, *Brotherhood of the Fin* (Tucson, Arizona: Wheatmark, 2007), 128.

25. Government Accountability Office, *COAST GUARD: Observations*, 11.

26. Ibid.

27. Government Accountability Office, *COAST GUARD: Observations*, 23.

28. Hoover, *Brotherhood of the Fin*, 156–57.

29. Phillips and Loy, *Character in Action*, 62.

30. Ibid.

31. Manjoo, "Why FEMA Failed."

32. In a hopeful sign that FEMA is learning from its past failures, President Obama's FEMA administrator, Craig Fugate, stated in 2009 that "he will devote considerable efforts to boosting citizen participation in disaster preparedness" and will view "the public as a resource, not as a liability." See Ed O'Keefe, "FEMA Encourages Public Participation," *Washington Post*, June 4, 2009.

33. Italics mine. CNN, "'Can I Quit Now?' FEMA Chief Wrote as Katrina Raged," November 4, 2005, http://www.cnn.com/2005/US/11/03/brown .fema.emails.

34. Allen has since been promoted to the rank of admiral and is now serving as the commandant of the U.S. Coast Guard

35. James Kitfield, "Coast Guard Official Fills Leadership Void in Katrina Relief Effort," GovernmentExecutive.com, September 23, 2005, http:// www.govexec.com/dailyfed/0905/092305nj1.htm.

36. GCR and Associates Inc., *Population Estimates for Orleans Parish, July 2007*, http://www.gcr1.com/resettlement_trends_july07.htm.

37. Robert B. Olshansky, Laurie A. Johnson, Jedidiah Horne, and Brendan Nee, "Planning for the Rebuilding of New Orleans," *Journal of the American Planning Association* 74, no. 3 (Summer 2008): 273.

38. Richard D. Knabb, Jamie R. Rhome, and Daniel P. Brown, "Tropical Cyclone Report: Hurricane Katrina: 23–30 August 2005," National Hurricane Center, December 20, 2005; updated August 10, 2006, http://www .nhc.noaa.gov/pdf/TCR-AL122005_Katrina.pdf.

39. Bruce Katz, Matt Fellowes, and Nigel Holmes, "How Will We Know When New Orleans Is Rebuilt?," Brookings, December 7, 2005, http:// www.brookings.edu/opinions/2005/1207cities_katz.aspx.

40. Abigail Williamson, "The Role of Citizen Participation in the Unified New Orleans Plan," Association for Public Policy and Management annual meeting, Washington, D.C., November 8, 2007, 28.

41. Olshansky et al., "Planning for the Rebuilding," 275.

42. Williamson, "Role of Citizen Participation," 7.

43. Ibid.

44. Personal communication, Dr. Vera Triplett, June 24, 2009.

45. Ibid.

46. Olshansky et al., "Planning for the Rebuilding," 277.

47. Steven Bingler, "Unified New Orleans Plan Approved: Citizens Demand Clustering of Neighborhood Facilities," *The Planning Report*, August 2008, http://www.planningreport.com/tpr/?module=displaystory&story_ id=1357&format=html.

48. James Surowiecki, *The Wisdom of Crowds* (New York: Anchor Books, 2005), 158–63.
49. David Brooks, "Globalism Goes Viral," *New York Times*, April 27, 2009, http://www.nytimes.com/2009/04/28/opinion/28brooks.html.
50. Frances Westley, Brenda Zimmerman, and Michael Quinn Patton, *Getting to Maybe: How the World Is Changed* (Toronto: Vintage Canada, 2006), 9.
51. Bingler, "Unified New Orleans Plan."

Chapter 2: The Rise of the Open-Source Movement

1. Richard M. Stallman, "Free Software: Freedom and Cooperation," transcript of speech given at New York University, May 29, 2001, http://www.gnu.org/events/rms-nyu-2001-transcript.txt, 3.
2. Unlike the corrupted popular-media usage that refers to computer criminals, "hacker" as originally used by programmers and coders is a term of merit used to describe someone, in the words of Eric Raymond, who is "an enthusiast, an artist, a tinkerer, a problem solver, an expert." See Eric Raymond, *The Cathedral and the Bazaar* (Sebastopol, CA: O'Reilly & Associates Inc., 1999), 2.
3. Stallman, "Free Software."
4. Ibid., 6.
5. If "GNU's Not Unix" doesn't make clear what a recursive acronym is, try "NIAGARA Is A Great, Archetypal Recursive Acronym"—get it?
6. Reuven M. Lerner, "Stallman Wins $240,000 in MacArthur Award," *Tech* 110, no. 30, July 18, 1990, http://tech.mit.edu/V110/N30/rms.30n.html.
7. For a description of how Stallman came to use the term "copyleft," see Richard Stallman, "The GNU Project," GNU.org, http://www.gnu.org/gnu/thegnuproject.html.
8. Stallman, "Free Software."
9. Steven Weber, *The Success of Open Source* (Cambridge, MA: Harvard University Press, 2004), 84. In a way, this is the same ideal that underlies the sustainability movement, which in turn is inspired by an idea expressed in the Great Law of the Iroquois, which reads in part, "In every deliberation, we must consider the impact on the seventh generation."

10. Aside from Torvalds's own book, *Just for Fun*, co-authored with David Diamond, the two sources that I found to be the most helpful profiles of Torvalds were Gary Rivlin, "Leader of the Free World," *Wired*, November 2003, http://www.wired.com/wired/archive/11.11/linus.html, and Marjorie Richardson, "Interview: Linus Torvalds," *Linux Journal*, November 1999, http://www.linuxjournal.com/article/3655.

11. The circumstances surrounding Torvalds's start with computers supports the argument that Malcolm Gladwell lays out in his book *Outliers: The Story of Success*. Yes, Torvalds is an exceptionally talented coder. However, there were also singular factors in play during his early life that gave him access to the right tools at the right time, enabling him to accomplish what he has. In this way, he is similar to the leaders Gladwell profiles in *Outliers*, from Bill Gates (who also at a young age got an amount of computer access rare for his time) to Mozart. See Malcolm Gladwell, *Outliers: The Story of Success* (New York: Little, Brown, 2008).

12. Linus Torvalds and David Diamond, *Just for Fun* (New York: HarperBusiness, 2001), 71.

13. Ibid., 104.

14. Ibid., 70.

15. Ibid., 88.

16. Kernel.org, "Notes for Linux Release 0.01," http://www.kernel.org/pub/linux/kernel/Historic/old-versions/RELNOTES-0.01.

17. Torvalds and Diamond, *Just for Fun*, 94.

18. For an exhaustive case as to why the full operating system (but not the Linux kernel) should be referred to as "GNU/Linux," see Richard Stallman, "GNU/Linux FAQ by Richard Stallman," GNU.org, http://www.gnu.org/gnu/gnu-linux-faq.html.

19. Rivlin, "Leader of the Free World."

20. "The Halloween Documents," catb.org, http://catb.org/~esr/halloween.

21. Weber, *Success of Open Source*, 55.

22. Rivlin, "Leader of the Free World."

23. One can only imagine that Torvalds's grandfather, the statistics profes-

sor who first started using computers to run equations, would be immensely proud of what his grandson has helped enable.

24. Raymond, *Cathedral and the Bazaar*, 62.

25. Richardson, "Interview: Linus Torvalds."

26. Personal correspondence, Richard Stallman, November, 2009.

27. Torvalds and Diamond, *Just for Fun*, 96, 194.

28. Jun Auza, "20 Great Quotes from Richard M. Stallman," *TechSource*, http://www.junauza.com/2008/06/20-great-quotes-from-richard-m<->stallman.html.

29. Although you have probably heard more about the spread of "open source" over the past decade, the free software movement, pursuing a purer and stricter approach, is also flourishing. Stallman now travels the world working with governments to design "free-software only" policies and laws, which have been adopted from Norway to South Africa and from India to Brazil. Commenting on his government's free-software policy, Ecuadoran president Rafael Correa has said that "it is necessary that we all adopt, on a public and private level, the use of free software. In that manner, we will guarantee the sovereignty of our states. We will depend on our own efforts, and not on the external forces on the region. We will be producers of technology, and not simple consumers." See Eduardo Avila, "Ecuador: The President Pushes Free Software," *GlobalVoices*, http://globalvoicesonline.org/2007/05/24/ecuador-the-president-pushes-free-software.

30. Wikipedia.com, accessed December 7, 2009.

31. For a much more in-depth overview of the story of Wikipedia, I recommend *The Wikipedia Revolution*, by Andrew Lih, a key source for much of the information about Wikipedia that appears in this section. Andrew Lih, *The Wikipedia Revolution* (New York: Hyperion, 2009), foreword and chapter 4. The ranking is according to ComScore and Alexa. See Lih, *Wikipedia Revolution*, 231.

32. Respectively, these refer to the following: "If a cat always lands on its feet and toast always lands buttered-side-down, would a buttered cat simply levitate above the ground?" and "A satirical term for any legal strategy

that seeks to overwhelm its audience with nonsensical arguments." Ibid., 117–18. For the accuracy claim, see Daniel Terdiman, "Study: Wikipedia as Accurate as Britannica," CNET News, December 15, 2005, http://news.cnet.com/Study-Wikipedia-as-accurate-as-Britannica/2100-1038_3-5997332.html.

33. Lih, *Wikipedia Revolution*, 114.

34. The top-ten languages represented on Wikipedia are, in declining order, English, German, French, Polish, Chinese, Italian, Dutch, Spanish, Portuguese, and Russian. Note: These statistics are based on figures from http://www.wikipedia.org, accessed December 7, 2009.

35. Of the naturally occurring variety, consider the text of this book itself: If you were to tally up the frequency at which I have used assorted words, you would probably find the same thing, with a handful of words appearing far more frequently than the rest (though I beg you to just take my word for it and continue on).

36. Lih, *Wikipedia Revolution*, 137.

37. Less obvious examples that also help to make this point include Kellogg, from "killer of hogs," Day, for "dairy worker," and Leach, which was once (no kidding) an interchangeable name for "Doctor."

38. For a wonderful talk on changes in how people are able to use their free time, or "cognitive surplus," see Clay Shirky, "Where Do People Find the Time?," Web 2.0 Expo, http://www.youtube.com/watch?v=AyoNHIl-QLQ. Perhaps more than anyone else, Shirky is the great social and technological philosopher for this unique moment in our history. As the increasingly widespread desire to shape public events intersects with our increasingly technology-enabled capabilities to do so, he has become a faithful guide whom I and many others return to again and again for help in making sense of the mind-boggling array of possibilities now before us.·

39. Weber, *Success of Open Source*, 264.

40. Jeff Howe, "The Rise of Crowdsourcing," June 2006 Wired.com http://www.wired.com/wired/orchive/14.06/crowds.html

41. If you must know, the winner was a glazed sour cream doughnut with

bits of toffee on top. See "Create Dunkin's Next Donut Contest," https://www.dunkindonuts.com/donut/#/home.

42. Jeff Howe, *Crowdsourcing: Why the Power of the Crowd Is Driving the Future of Business* (New York: Crown Business, 2008), 4.

43. "Our Philosophy," Slow Food, http://www.slowfood.com/about_us/eng/philosophy.lasso.

44. Thanks to Ben Towne, a Ph.D. student at Carnegie Mellon, for helping to develop this articulation.

45. To his credit, while Howe's book mainly focuses on the trend of crowdsourcing in product development and business, it does include the hopeful line "What if the solutions to our greatest problems weren't waiting to be conceived, but already existed somewhere, just waiting to be found, in the warp and weave of this vibrant human network?"—presumably hinting that he believes that "crowdsourcing" should also be applied to more publicly beneficial forms of problem solving.

Chapter 3: Millennials: The Open-Source Generation

1. The six organizations that made up the Climate Campaign were the Sierra Student Coalition (SSC), the Student Environmental Action Coalition (SEAC), the Student PIRGS, ECO-Northeast, Envirocitizen, and Free the Planet. The groups they worked with outside of the Northeast were mainly Greenpeace, the California Student Sustainability Coalition, and Religious Witness for the Earth.

2. Josh Lynch, "A History of Energy Action," It's Getting Hot in Here, http://itsgettinghotinhere.org/2010/02/07/climate-generation-a<->history-of-energy-action-2005.

3. Brian Byrnes, "Conference Students Rally to Free the Planet," http://www.uvm.edu/~envprog/news/bittersweetvine/bit-stu.htm.

4. In the year before I took over the directorship of the SSC, for instance, the full list of our national priority campaigns included the Arctic National Wildlife Refuge, fair trade, the World Bank bonds boycott, forest protection, clean energy, and clean buses, not to mention our political and trainings work. Soon after I became director, we consolidated our

efforts around only one priority campaign: the Campus Climate Challenge.

5. Mentioning some leaders by name while omitting others is always a difficult balancing act. Suffice it to say that many others were vital to the coalition's being where it was by June of 2005, including Meg Boyle and Adi Nochur in the Northeast, Maureen Cane, Arthur Coulston, and Marcia Winslade in California, Nick Algee in the Southeast, and Lindsay Telfer and Jeca Glor-Bell in Canada. I mention the three I do in the text for their roles as leaders among leaders.

6. Actually, the SSC had two directors in attendance at that meeting: myself as the incoming director and Derek Brockbank as the outgoing director. Our employment overlapped by a month.

7. http://www.youtube.com/watch?v=HJn/DW;5L1K

8. Weber, *Success of Open Source*, 164.

9. Personal communication, Josh Lynch, April, 2009.

10. Juliana Williams, "Climate Generation: From Humble Beginnings to a Global Movement," It's Getting Hot in Here, January 5, 2010, http://itsgettinghotinhere.org/2010/01/05/climate-generation-from-humble-beginnings-to-a<->global-movement.

11. Josh Lynch, "Rising to the Challenge Final Report," It's Getting Hot in Here, February 13, 2007, http://itsgettinghotinhere.org/2007/02/13/week-of-action-final-report.

12. The number of countries represented was 181, to be exact. The only countries that did not see 350 events were North Korea, Monaco, Angola, Lesotho, Djibouti, Equatorial Guinea, Eritrea, Guinea-Bissau, Mauritania, Namibia, Liechtenstein, and San Marino. Personal communication, Jon Warnow, 350.org, February 2010.

13. Bill McKibben, "No Time for Tears in Copenhagen," Grist, December 13, 2009, http://www.grist.org/article/2009-12-13-no-time-for-tears-in-copenhagen.

14. Sarah Kuck, "Worldchanging Interview: Bill McKibben," Worldchanging.org, June 11, 2009, http://www.worldchanging.com/archives/009974.html.

15. To view the slide show of images of those calling for 350 around the world, see http://www.350.org.

16. I mean this literally: See the book written by Bill McKibben and Step It Up and 350.org's organizers, *Fight Global Warming Now: The Handbook for Taking Action in Your Community* (New York: Holt Paperbacks, 2007).

17. "MTV/CBS News Poll: Environment and Diversity," May 30–June 9, 2006. CBS News conducted the poll of thirteen- to twenty-four-year-olds on behalf of MTV. The margin of error is plus or minus four percentage points. See http://www.icpsr.umich.edu/icpsrweb/ICPSR/studies/04618.

18. Scott Keeter and Paul Taylor, "The Millennials," Pew Research Center Publications, December 11, 2009, http://pewresearch.org/pubs/1437/millennials-profile?src=prc-latest&proj=peoplepress.

19. Personal correspondence, Carl Pope, Sierra Club, January 12, 2010. In Pope's case, I happen to think this is mostly a matter of emphasis. I know for a fact that he believes in the importance of a growing climate movement; it's just that he also believes that a strong and vibrant Sierra Club is the biggest contribution he can make toward that end.

20. Personal communication, Diane Ives, Kendeda Fund, January 12, 2010.

21. Ibid.

22. Ibid.

23. Personal communication, Julian Keniry, National Wildlife Federation, January 11, 2010.

24. Personal communication, Ted Glick, Chesapeake Climate Action Network, May 8, 2009.

25. Personal communication, Erin Mazursky, April 24, 2009.

26. Today, the official name is STAND: The Student Division of the Genocide Intervention Network.

27. Personal communication, Mark Hanis, Genocide Intervention Network, February 10, 2009.

28. Jina Moore, "Anatomy of a Start-Up Charity," *Christian Science Monitor*, September 11, 2007, http://www.echoinggreen.org/files/christian-science.pdf.

29. The bill was designed to officially designate the conflict in Darfur as genocide and to thus increase funding of peacekeeping operations in Sudan.

30. Morley Winograd and Michael D. Hais, *Millennial Makeover: MySpace, YouTube & the Future of American Politics* (New Brunswick, NJ: Rutgers University Press, 2008), 265.

31. Sam Graham-Felsen, "Divestment and Sudan," *Nation*, April 20, 2006, http://www.thenation.com/doc/20060508/grahamfelsen.

32. Katie Becker, "In the Face of Genocide," *Swarthmore College Bulletin*, October 2009, http://media.swarthmore.edu/bulletin/?p=308.

33. Nicholas D. Kristof, "The Age of Ambition," *New York Times*, January 27, 2008, http://www.nytimes.com/2008/01/27/opinion/27kristof.html?ref=opinion.

34. Jane Wei-Skillern and Sonia Marciano, "The Networked Nonprofit," *Stanford Social Innovation Review*, Spring 2008, www.socialinnovation exchange.org/files/event/attachments/Networked%20nonprofit%20SSIR %20article.pdf.

35. Indeed, among all the authors, think tanks, and pollsters to use the Millennial term, only the relatively short eleven-year span of 1985 to 1996 is agreed upon by all.

36. However, the Center for American Progress has the generation end with those born in 2000, while the New Politics Institute stops at 1996.

37. In terms of descriptive value, I think the terms offered by Zogby (First Globals) and Tapscott (Net Generation) are particularly apt, because each highlights a unique outlook or experience of our generation, rather than an arbitrary calendar event. However, since Millennial is most commonly used and, more important, because the generation itself selected the term, it is the default name that I will use to refer to the generation for the rest of the book.

38. Keeter and Taylor, "The Millennials."

39. Scott Keeter, Juliana Horowitz, and Alec Tyson, "Young Voters in the 2008 Election," Pew Research Center, November 12, 2008.

40. Ibid.

41. "Massachusetts Senate Election: Youth Turnout Was Just 15%, Compared to 57% for Older Citizens; Young Voters Favored Coakley," Center for Information and Research on Civic Learning and Engagement (CIRCLE), http://www.civicyouth.org/?p=369.

42. Corporation for National and Community Service, 2006.

43. "Fall 2008 Survey," Harvard Institute of Politics, October 22, 2008, http://www.iop.harvard.edu/Research-Publications/Polling/Fall-2008-Survey.

44. Michelle Conlin, "Youthquake," *BusinessWeek*, January 9, 2008, http://www.businessweek.com/magazine/content/08_03/b4067000290367.htm.

45. I ran the search in the early summer of 2008. To finish off the top five, the number two and three results then were "Alps Glaciers Gone by 2050, Expert Says" and "U.S. Hispanic Population to Triple by 2050."

46. John Zogby, *The Way We'll Be: The Zogby Report on the Transformation of the American Dream* (New York: Random House, 2008), 193.

47. Specifically, the polls I refer to include those of Pew, Harvard's Institute of Politics, CIRCLE, the Center for American Progress, and Zogby International, among others. Books where these traits appear (many of which cite yet more polls specifically commissioned for their writing) include Neil Howe and William Strauss's *Millennials Rising: The Next Great Generation* (New York: Vintage, 2000), Don Tapscott's *Grown Up Digital: How the Net Generation Is Changing Your World* (New York: McGraw-Hill, 2009), Winograd and Hais's *Millennial Makeover*, and Zogby's *The Way We'll Be*.

48. Author Don Tapscott compiled a similar list for his book, *Grown Up Digital*: "The eight Net Gen norms: 1) freedom; 2) customization; 3) scrutiny; 4) integrity; 5) collaboration; 6) entertainment; 7) speed; and 8) innovation." See Tapscott, *Grown Up Digital*, 74.

49. Tapscott, *Grown Up Digital*, 308. "As the Net Generation grows in influence, the trend will be toward networks, not hierarchies, toward open collaboration rather than command, toward consensus rather than arbitrary rule, and toward enablement rather than control."

50. Six out of ten Millennial adults (those aged eighteen to thirty-two in 2010) are white, while four in ten are racial minorities. More specifically, 18 percent of Millennial adults are Hispanic, 14 percent are black, 5 percent are Asian, and 3 percent are other or multiracial. Compare this to the next two older generations, in which only one in four adults hails from any racial minority group. See Winograd and Hais, *Millennial Makeover*, 66.

51. On this point specifically, see Zogby's *The Way We'll Be*, 119. "While First Globals poll 'liberal' on many issues, they're more devoted than any other age group to finding common ground on tough social issues."

52. David Madland and Ruy Teixeira, "New Progressive America: The Millennial Generation," Center for American Progress, May 13, 2009, 14.

53. For instance, "'Women should return to their traditional roles in society.' Completely disagree—GI's & Silent Generation: 40%, Baby Boomers & Gen X: 50%, Millennials: 60%." See "Trends in Attitudes Toward Religion and Social Issues: 1987–2007," Pew Research Center Publications, March 22, 2007, http://pewresearch.org/pubs/614/religion-social-issues. Also see Tapscott, *Grown Up Digital*, 33, which reveals that "91 percent of Net Gen respondents agree that interracial dating is acceptable, compared with 50 percent of the G.I. Generation."

54. Keeter and Taylor, "The Millennials."

55. "American Students Studying Abroad at Record Levels: Up 8.5%," Institute of International Education, November 12, 2007, http://opendoors.iienetwork.org/?p=113744.

56. Larry Gordon, "Students' Options Changing by Degrees," *Los Angeles Times*, June 3, 2008, http://articles.latimes.com/2008/jun/03/local/me-major3.

57. "Spring 2007 Survey," *Harvard Institute of Politics*, http://www.iop.harvard.edu/Research-Publications/Polling/Spring-2007-Survey.

58. Zogby, *The Way We'll Be*, 94.

59. Richard C. Levin, "Globalization and the University," Poder Conference, Washington, D.C., November 8, 2006, http://opa.yale.edu/president/message.aspx?id=9.

60. James Glanz, "Web Archive Opens a New Realm of Research," *New York Times*, May 1, 2001, http://www.nytimes.com/2001/05/01/science/01ARCH.html?pagewanted=1.

61. Zogby, *The Way We'll Be*, 110.

62. Curtis Gans, "African-Americans, Anger, Fear and Youth Propel Turnout to Highest Level Since 1964: Possible Pro-Democratic Realignment, GOP Disaster," American University, December 2008.

63. Michael Connery, "CIRCLE Increases Youth Turnout Estimates; The Youth Vote Impact in Pictures," FutureMajority.com, http://futuremajority.com/node/3969.

64. Keeter and Taylor, "The Millennials."

65. The Iowa Democratic Party does not release official vote counts, so this assertion is based on a bit of a "back-of-the-envelope calculation." Here are the figures and assumptions I used: (a) *Newsweek* reported that 250,000 people attended the Democratic caucuses. (b) Obama received 34.91 percent support in the caucuses, representing a total of 87,275 caucus-goers (here I assume that the percentages of "votes" in the caucuses—which, it should be said, are not the same as votes in the traditional sense—are roughly equal to the corresponding percentages of people who caucused for a candidate). (c) CIRCLE reported that 46,640 under-thirty youth attended the Democratic caucuses and that 57 percent of them went for Obama, or approximately 26,584. (d) Meanwhile, a total of 31.20 percent supported Clinton and Edwards, representing about 78,000 caucus-goers each, based on *Newsweek*'s report of the total. Thus, although it is nearly impossible to know how caucus dynamics would have played out without certain people in attendance, especially with the multiple candidates available as a second choice, I will simply say that the 26,854 youth who are estimated to have caucused for Obama are nearly three times the margin (9,275) of overall caucus-goers he is estimated to have held over Clinton and Edwards together.

66. "Young Voters in the 2008 Presidential Election," CIRCLE, November 24, 2008, updated December 19, 2008. http://www.civicyouth.org/PopUps/FactSheets/FS_08_exit_polls.pdf.

67. David Von Drehle, "The Year of the Youth Vote," *Time*, January 31, 2008, http://www.time.com/time/politics/article/0,8599,1708570,00.html.

68. Conlin, "Youthquake."

69. Winograd and Hais, *Millennial Makeover*, 66, and Madland and Teixeira, "New Progressive America."

70. Tapscott, *Grown Up Digital*, 33.

71. John Halpin and Karl Agne, "The Political Ideology of the Millennial Generation," Center for American Progress, May 13, 2009, http://www.americanprogress.org/issues/2009/05/political_ideology_youth.html.

72. Tapscott, *Grown Up Digital*, 210.

Chapter 4: Dispatches from the Front Lines of a Next Generation Democracy

1. "Frequently Asked Questions," FixMyStreet, http://www.fixmystreet.com/faq.

2. Note here that the default neighborhood settings are determined by "shapefiles" based on Census data that SeeClickFix has loaded to the site. However, anyone can create a set of boundaries that conforms to their own experience/definition of their neighborhood.

3. "Yale Shuttle Ran Red Light," SeeClickFix, http://seeclickfix.com/issues/1696.

4. "Speeding First Student Buses," SeeClickFix, http://www.seeclickfix.com/issues/4646.

5. Ben Berkowitz, "The End of Apathy. The Beginning of Giving a Shit," SeeClickFix, September 25, 2009, http://www.seeclickfix.blogspot.com/2009/09/reporting-potholes-gateway-drug-to.html.

6. "See, Click, Fix," WBTV.com, http://www.wbtv.com/global/Category.asp?c=181037.

7. Full translations are in Spanish, Greek, Russian, French, German, and Bulgarian. Partial translations thus far include Italian, traditional Chinese, and Japanese.

8. See Life in the Model City: Stories of Urban Renewal in New Haven, http://www.yale.edu/nhohp/modelcity.

9. Less world-changing but still notable firsts supposedly include the lolli-pop, the Frisbee, and A. C. Gilbert's Erector Set.

10. Douglas W. Rae, *City: Urbanism and Its End* (New Haven, CT: Yale University Press, 2003), 324.

11. "Cities: No Haven," *Time*, September 1, 1967, http://www.time.com/time/magazine/article/0,9171,837213,00.html.

12. "Hunk of Boat Discarded," SeeClickFix, http://www.seeclickfix.com/issues/1638.

13. The elevation is significant for being in what biologists refer to as an "ecologically fragile zone."

14. Note: I have served on the Orton Family Foundation's Board of Trustees since 2007.

15. Personal communication, Lyman Orton, February 2010.

16. Italics mine. Ibid.

17. "Birth of a Heart & Soul Planning Movement," Orton Family Foundation, October 26, 2007, http://www.orton.org/who/heart_soul/birth_planning_move.

18. It's often surprising and very interesting to find out what kinds of things really mean a lot to a place. Here in New Haven, an issue that has been blowing up on SeeClickFix of late is a plan to remove the "clicky" sign at Union train station. See "Save the Clicky Mechanical Sign at Union Station!," SeeClickFix, http://www.seeclickfix.com/issues/10494, and Paul Bass, "Tune Changed on Solari," *New Haven Independent*, December 30, 2009, http://www.newhavenindependent.org/archives/2009/12/two_years_two_v.php.

19. "Durbin Invites Participation in Nightly Broadband Policy Discussions," July 20, 2007, http://www.durbin.senate.gov/record.cfm?id=279504.

20. See "Senator Durbin Live Thread," OpenLeft, July 24, 2007, http://www.openleft.com/diary/375, and https://spreadsheets.google.com/ccc?key=0AicOiRAlPqhddFBjZ2ZfSHlnLTFnaoFFcHgtSUdtbEE&hl=en.

21. Personal communication, Russell Newman, November 2009.

22. Dick Durbin, "Thank You," OpenLeft, August 1, 2007, http://www.openleft.com/diary/526.

23. See Chris Wallace, "Coming Up on 'FOX News Sunday': Rick Davis and Sen. Dick Durbin," Fox News, August 8, 2008, http://www.foxnews.com/story/0,2933,399585,00.html.

24. Since the initial effort of Senator Durbin's office, OpenLeft, and RedState, the idea of Legislation 2.0 has taken hold with a number of other groups, most notably the Sunlight Foundation. See its Web sites http://www.publicmarkup.org and http://www.opencongress.org.

25. See "Create Real-World Issue Reporting System," Project 10^{100}, http://www.project10tothe100.com/ideas.html.

26. To the administration's credit, starting an organic garden was, in fact, one of the first things done After the Obamas moved into the White House.

27. Mark Klein, "Open for Questions—A Critique of Idea Sharing Sites," http://markklein.wordpress.com/2009/01/06/a<->critique-of-idea-sharing.

28. Personal communication, Mark Klein, MIT, October 2009.

29. Personal communication, Beaudry Kock, MIT, November 2009.

30. See Climate Collaboratorium, http://www.climatecollaboratorium.org.

Chapter 5: A Systems Approach to Change

1. Italics mine. Barack Obama, *The Audacity of Hope* (New York: Crown, 2006), 41.

2. Barack Obama, "Remarks for Senator Barack Obama: AFL-CIO," Philadelphia, April 2, 2008, http://www.barackobama.com/2008/04/02/remarks_for_senator_barack_oba_3.php.

3. Barack Obama, "Obama Says Special Interests Are Blocking Energy Reform, Proposes Short-Term Steps to Relieve the Pressure of Rising Prices," Indianapolis, April 25, 2008, http://www.barackobama.com/2008/04/25/obama_says_special_interests_a.php.

4. Politifact.com, http://www.politifact.com/truth-o<->meter/promises/promise/517/health-care-reform-public-sessions-C<->SPAN.

5. Peter Orszag, "Promoting Transparency in Government," Whitehouse. gov, December 8, 2009, http://www.whitehouse.gov/blog/2009/12/08/promoting-transparency-government.

6. "Illinois Sen. Barack Obama's Announcement Speech," *Washington Post*, February 10, 2007, http://www.washingtonpost.com/wp-dyn/content/article/2007/02/10/AR2007021000879.html.

7. Vivek Kundra, "Opening Doors: Finding Keys to Open Government," panel discussion, Center for American Progress, Washington, D.C., March 20, 2009.

8. Orszag, "Promoting Transparency in Government."

9. As an aside, isn't it patronizing, bordering on arrogant, to assume that the most citizens can contribute to policy-making efforts is some question at a staged White House press conference?

10. For another cautionary tale of what can happen when you fail to provide a structure for meaningful participation, see "Release Godzilla on an Unsuspecting Public," White House 2 http://whitehouse2.org/priorities/22-release-godzilla-on-an-unsuspecting-public.

11. See "Open for Questions," Whitehouse.gov, http://www.whitehouse.gov/open/innovations/OpenforQuestions.

12. If you are curious, it was May 10, 1775.

13. Andrew LaVallee, "Only 13% of Wikipedia Contributors Are Women, Study Says," *Wall Street Journal*, August 31, 2009, http://blogs.wsj.com/digits/2009/08/31/only-13-of-wikipedia-contributors-are-women-study-says.

14. Sam duPont, "Open Government Coming to a Government Near You," NDN.org, December 10, 2009, http://ndn.org/blog/2009/12/open-government-coming-government-near-you.

15. Politifact.com.

16. Hank De Zutter, "The First Profile: What Makes Obama Run?," *Chicago Reader*, January 15, 2009, http://www1.chicagoreader.com/obama_reader/what_makes_obama_run/?q=012009K.

17. Ryan Lizza, "Making It: How Chicago Shaped Obama," *New Yorker*, http://www.newyorker.com/reporting/2008/07/21/080721fa_fact_lizza?currentPage=11.

18. Ibid.

19. "Barack Obama's Announcement Speech," *Washington Post.*

20. For an interesting argument that Obama's very own team may be the reason that the vision behind this rhetoric remains elusive, see Tim Dickinson, "No We Can't," *Rolling Stone,* February 2, 2010, http://www.rollingstone.com/politics/story/31961846/no_we_cant.

21. Tapscott, *Grown Up Digital,* 260.

22. If you're ever driving along Route 25 through Waits River, Vermont, and want some free-range, organic eggs for only $2.50 a dozen, feel free to stop in (look for the egg sign by the mailbox). If Dad's not around—his name is Bill—just leave the money in the cooler.

23. For a wonderful introduction, see Donella H. Meadows, *Thinking in Systems: A Primer* (White River Junction, VT: Chelsea Green, 2008).

24. "Sisyphean task" refers to the Greek myth of Sisyphus, a king who was condemned to roll a boulder up a hill for eternity. Every time he managed to get it to the top, the boulder would roll back down, and Sisyphus would have to start all over again. Also, thanks to Juliana Williams for helping me brainstorm this set of sayings.

Chapter 6: Realizing Democracy's Promise

1. See PublicCampaign, http://www.publicampaign.org/where.

2. "The 25 People Who Changed Food in America," *Gourmet,* http://www.gourmet.com/food/2008/05/25people?slide=25#slide=25.

3. David Bornstein, *How to Change the World: Social Entrepreneurs and the Power of New Ideas* (New York: Oxford University Press, 2007).

4. Frances Moore Lappé, "The Real Crisis," speech at Xavier University, Cincinnati, July 10, 2005, http://www.youtube.com/watch?v=4jasiJfZMeY&feature=related.

5. Katy J. Harriger and Jill J. McMillan, *Speaking of Politics: Preparing College Students for Democratic Citizenship Through Deliberative Dialogue* (Kettering Foundation Press, 2007).

6. Center for Responsive Politics, OpenSecrets.org, http://www.open secrets.org/lobby.

7. Frances Moore Lappé, *Getting a Grip: Clarity, Creativity and Courage in a World Gone Mad* (Cambridge, MA: Small Planet Media, 2007), 14, 23.

8. Fareed Zakaria, *The Post-American World* (New York: W. W. Norton, 2009).

9. William Greider, *Who Will Tell the People* (New York: Touchstone, 1992).

10. James Fallows, "How America Can Rise Again," *Atlantic*, January/February, 2010.

11. Natasha Singer, "Harry and Louise Return, with a New Message," *New York Times*, July 16, 2009, http://www.nytimes.com/2009/07/17/business/media/17adco.html?_r=1.

12. Center for Public Integrity, http://www.buyingofthepresident.org/index.php/the_hanna_project/election_year/1992_clinton_vs_bush.

13. Jonathan Rauch, *Government's End:* (New York: Public Affairs, 1999), 65.

14. Cass R. Sunstein, *Infotopia: How Many Minds Produce Knowledge* (New York: Oxford University Press, 2006), 12.

15. See http://www.agree.org.

16. "Strengthening Our Nation's Democracy," America *Speaks*, http://www.americaspeaks.org/_data/n_0001/resources/live/strengthening_democracy.pdf.

17. Thanks to Susanna Haas Lyons, who served as a project associate for the British Columbia citizens' assembly, for helpful conversations about the effort and the context in which it occurred.

18. See http://www.citizensassembly.bc.ca/public.

19. For a comprehensive overview of the history and future prospects of citizens' assemblies, see http://www.isolon.org.

20. http://www.midwestdemocracynetwork.org/templates/media/Five%20State%20Report.pdf.

21. For more information, see Campaign Legal Center, Me Policy Program, http://www.campaignlegalcenter.org/FCC-198.html.

22. Transcript of *State of the Union with Candy Crowley*, CNN, February 10, 2010, http://transcripts.cnn.com/TRANSCRIPTS/1002/21/sotu.01.html.

23. Paul Wellstone, "Winning Politics," *Nation*, February 2, 2001.

Afterword

1. Daniel N. Robinson, *Aristotle's Psychology* (New York: Columbia University Press, 1999).

2. Ed Pilkington, "Climate Target Is Not Radical Enough—Study: Nasa Scientist Warns the World Must Urgently Make Huge CO_2 Reductions," *Guardian*, April 7, 2008.

3. Alyssa Fetini, "What the World Will Look Like by 2050," *Time*, April 13, 2009, http://www.time.com/time/arts/article/0,8599,1890927,00.htm.

4. "Largest Cities in World by Population," *Times Atlas of the World*, 10th ed., http://www.worldatlas.com/citypops.htm.

5. James Hansen, "Global Warming Twenty Years Later: Tipping Points Near," testimony to Congress, Washington, D.C., June 23, 2008, http://www.columbia.edu/~jeh1/2008/TwentyYearsLater_20080623.pdf.

6. Rebecca Tuhus-Dubrow, "Bill McKibben: The Making of an Environmentalist," *Nation*, July 1, 2008, http://www.thenation.com/doc/20080721/tuhus-dubrow.

7. Lappé, *Getting a Grip*, 131

8. Howe, *Crowdsourcing*, 134.

9. Bill Bryson, *A Short History of Nearly Everything* (New York: Broadway, 2003), 119.

INDEX

A NOTE ON THE AUTHOR

Jared Duval is a fellow at Demos, a New York think tank. Previously, he directed the Sierra Student Coalition, the national student chapter of the Sierra Club and the largest student environmental organization in America. A recipient of the David Brower Youth Award and the Morris K. Udall and Harry S. Truman scholarships, he graduated summa cum laude from Wheaton College in Massachusetts in 2005. Originally from the Upper Connecticut River Valley of Vermont and New Hampshire, he currently lives in New Haven, Connecticut.

CALLING YOUNG THOUGHT-LEADERS!

Next Generation Democracy was written by Jared Duval while a fellow at Dēmos, a research and advocacy organization based in New York City. Dēmos works for a revitalized American democracy, shared economic prosperity, restored public faith in government, and responsible U.S. leadership in an interdependent world.

Jared is part of Dēmos' "Emerging Voices" initiative for young thought-leaders, which was launched within their Fellows Program in 2009 to support the vital contributions of young writers and thinkers in the marketplace of ideas.

The program provides financial support, comprehensive assistance with important writing projects, mentoring by Dēmos senior staff and fellows, and a full package of media tools and communications supports to promote fellows' work and ideas in the public square.

With a strong commitment to promoting greater diversity in the marketplace of ideas, Demos is especially interested in supporting young writers and thinkers of color.

To learn more about Dēmos' support for young thought-leaders, or if you wish to apply for a fellowship, visit Dēmos' website, demos.org/fellowsapp.cfm, and follow the instructions.

To learn more about Dēmos' overall vision, programs, and current activities, please visit www.demos.org.

Dēmos